The Colour Encyclopedia of
KNOWLEDGE

by David C. Lambert

Illustrated by Philippe Degrave
Robert Dallet
Jean Giannini

Collins Glasgow and London

First published in this edition 1973
Published by William Collins Sons and Company Limited, Glasgow and London

© 1971 Éditions Lito, Paris
© 1973 English language edition William Collins Sons and Company Limited

Printed in Spain

ISBN 0 00 106118 6

CONTENTS

THE WORLD OF NATURE

The Universe	7	Life in Cretaceous Times	25
Star Islands in Space	8	Life in Tertiary Times	26
How Stars Are Born	9	Life in Recent Times	27
The Star we Call the Sun	10	The Age of Ice	28
How the Earth Began	12	Man's Family Tree	29
Earth and Moon	13	The Men-apes of Africa	30
Shaping the Earth's		Javanese Upright Man	31
Surface	14	Life in the Early Old	
Earth History in Rocks	15	Stone Age	32
The Dawn of Life	16	More Clues to Man's	
Life in Cambrian Times	18	Fossil Past	33
Life in Ordovician Times	19	Neanderthal Man	34
Life in Silurian Times	19	How Neanderthal Man	
Life in Devonian Times	20	Lived	35
Life in Carboniferous Times	22	How Neanderthal Man	
Life in Permian Times	23	Died	36
Life in Triassic Times	23	How Stone-Age Tools	
Life in Jurassic Times	24	Were Made	37

War and Cannibalism 38
Cro-Magnon Man 38
The Golden Age of
    Hunting 40
The Dawn of Art 41
Strange Sculptures from
    the Late Stone Age 42
Design and Decoration in
    the Old Stone Age 43
Art Galleries Under the
    Ground 44
The Middle Stone Age 45
The New Stone Age 46
Oceans that Girdle the
    Earth 47
The Ocean Bed 48
Life in the Oceans 49
The Restless Ocean 50
The Waves and Tides 51
Unweaving the Web of Life 52
Lowly Creatures of the
    Waters 53
The Fishes 55
Sea Mammals 56
The Amphibians 59

The Reptiles 60
The Birds 63
The Insects 66
Three Kinds of Mammal 68
Mammals that Eat Meat 70
Mammals that Eat Plants 73
Mammals which Chew
    the Cud 75
Two Kinds of Horns 76
More Mammals that Eat
    Plants 79
Mammals with Nails or
    Claws 81
The Primates 82
Three Varieties of Man 85
When Races Mingle 86
The Peoples of Europe 87
Peoples of North Africa 88
Peoples of South-West
    Asia 89
Peoples of Southern Africa 90
Peoples of India 91
Peoples of the Far East 92
Peoples of the Pacific 93
Amerindians and Eskimos 94

MAN MASTERS THE EARTH

Man at the Dawn of
    History 95
The World's First Cities 96

The Bronze Age 96
Inventing the
    Wheel 98

Making Mud as Hard as Rock	98
Temples, Tombs and Palaces	99
The Backward Europeans	100
The Age of Iron	101
City States of South-East Europe	101
Engineers of Alexandria	104
The Age of Rome	106
Europe's Dark and Middle Ages	110
Medieval Art and Architecture	112
Harnessing the Winds and Waters	113
Cannons and Caravels	114
Paper and Printing	116
Mechanical Clocks	117
The Age of Discovery	118
Birth of the Industrial Age	122
Iron and Industry	123
Harnessing the Power of Steam	125
Steam Power Comes of Age	126
Man Takes to the Air	127
From Alchemy to Chemistry	128
The Horseless Carriage	131
Steamships Span the Seas	132
Steam, Rails, and Speed	134
Sending Instant Messages	135
Telephone and Phonograph	136
Steel and Aluminium	136
Speeding the Presses	138
A Fire Inside the Engine	138
Airship and Aeroplane	140
Putting Electricity to Work	142
'Windmill Sails' Spun by Steam	143
Power without Smoke	144
Unlocking Nature's Secrets	145
Drawing Pictures with Light	145
Making Images Appear to Move	146
Sending Messages on Waves	148
The Story of Television	149
From Magic to Medicine	151
Building Artificial Brains	155
Liquid 'Gold' from Underground	159
Towers that Scrape the Sky	162
Ships Beneath the Sea	164
Exploring the Ocean Depths	166
Unleashing the Energy in Atoms	169
Cushioned by Air	173
Highways in the Sky	175
The Challenge of Space	177
Putting Man in Space	180
Exploring the Solar System	182
Living in Space	184
Man on the Moon	186
Worlds of Tomorrow	188

The vault of heaven as an artist imagined it about 500 years ago.

The Dawn of Life

THE UNIVERSE

Peering up into the sky from their fields and towns, unaided by telescopes, our ancestors saw the stars as mere spots of light set in a great curved dome forming a kind of shell around the earth.

They believed that the sun, moon, and planets were all placed below this shell and that they all circled the earth. Until about three centuries ago most of them also saw the heavenly bodies as mysterious signs in the sky, the sources of astrological influences on men's lives.

Thanks to modern knowledge of astronomy we now know that the lights in the sky are in fact great balls or clusters of solid or gaseous matter, and that many millions of them scattered and clustered through space make up the universe.

Few of us can truly comprehend the vast distances of space. From the earth to the moon – the earth's nearest neighbour – is 384,400 kilometres (over 200,000 miles); from the earth to the sun is 150 million kilometres (93 million miles); from the earth to the next nearest star (Proxima Centauri) is 40,000 million kilometres (25,000 million miles) – a gulf so great that no earth-based standard of measurement can properly convey it. To assess the huge interstellar distances astronomers use special units called *light years*, each based on the distance a ray of light moves in a year. Since light travels at 300,000 kilometres per second (186,000 miles per second), we can say that Proxima Centauri is 4·3 light years away. When we know that radio telescopes have detected stellar objects 13,000 million light years distant we can see how unlikely is the old unscientific notion that our earth was the centre of the universe. In fact, compared with the great mass of stars, it is no more than a sand grain on an immense seashore.

The great disc of the Milky Way; the arrow shows the position of our own solar system.

The Milky Way seen edge on.

STAR ISLANDS IN SPACE

If you gaze at the clear night sky, you will see one area which seems brighter than the rest. Astronomers using powerful telescopes have proved that this hazy lane of light, popularly called the Milky Way, consists of an immense mass of stars making up a *galaxy*, or island of stars.

Seen from the earth, the Milky Way galaxy looks like a fuzzy band. But astronomers believe that we are only viewing the galaxy edge on; that its true shape is that of a gigantic catherine wheel with fiery spiral arms. The total number of stars in the Milky Way is probably as many as 100,000 million stars.

They calculate that our solar system (the sun with the earth and other planets) lies on the inside of one great stellar arm. The whole galaxy is as much as 100,000 light years across and over 20,000 light years thick, and it spins through space at 2,160,000 kilometres (1,350,000 miles) an hour.

Our galaxy is by no means unique; once every 225 million years it revolves round 2,500 other galaxies forming a stellar super cluster. All told, astronomers compute that there are about one million galaxies in the universe. By studying the light which galaxies emit, astronomers have also proved that they are rushing apart from one another at fantastic speeds.

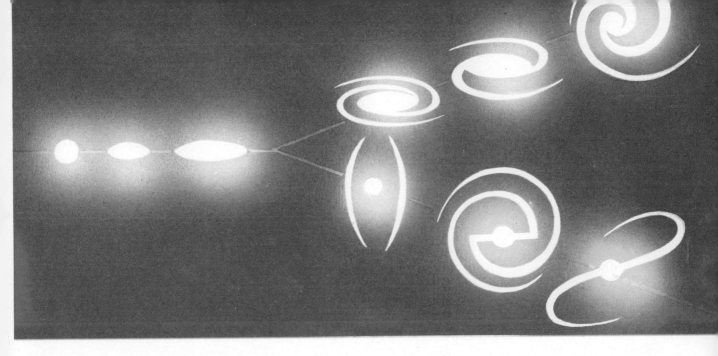

Different kinds of galaxy: from left to right, *one spherical, two elliptical, three spiral (above right), and three barred spiral (below right).*

HOW STARS ARE BORN

While the galaxies move through space, their stars undergo dramatic, if often imperceptibly slow, alterations. In fact stars — like people — are born, mature, grow old and die.

Many people believe that these cosmic processes start in giant clouds of condensing gas. As a mass of lightweight hydrogen gas contracts, intensely high pressures and temperatures build up inside it, producing a relatively 'light' but huge type of star. As the compression continues the star becomes so hot that thermonuclear reactions occur inside it which start to change the hydrogen to the heavier substance helium. When one-tenth of the hydrogen has been converted into helium the star becomes a so-called red giant. Its thermonuclear process speeds up, and the star becomes hotter and shrinks. Eventually all the hydrogen is consumed, leaving behind a small, dim, but immensely 'heavy' burnt-out star called a white dwarf. From start to finish the whole process can take many thousand million years.

Astronomers using powerful telescopes have detected stars at all stages of growth and decay. Largest of all known stars is the red giant Epsilon Aurigae B which is 4,000 million kilometres (2,500 million miles) in diameter, or so large that if its centre were in the same position as our sun, the star would envelope Mercury, Venus, the earth, Mars, Jupiter and Saturn — the sun's six nearest planets. At the other end of the size scale is the white dwarf known as LP 327-186, only half the diameter of our moon. Stars have also been found which differ vastly in weight: from supergiants containing only one-millionth of a gram of matter per cubic centimetre to white dwarfs like Sirius B in which one thimbleful of matter weighs thousands of kilograms, or several tons. Stars vary enormously in brightness, too; Rigel, one of the brightest, shines as brilliantly as 20,000 suns. But the brightest star in the sky is Sirius, also known as the Dog Star.

In one respect the sun once seemed a unique star: no other was known to have planets circling it. Now it seems that millions possess planets.

As it ages, a star goes through the size and colour changes shown below. It starts as a large blue star like those on the left; glows brightly in shrinking and growing hotter; and ends as a dim dwarf star.

THE STAR WE CALL THE SUN

In astronomer's terms our sun is no more than a yellow dwarf, a rather elderly average-sized star. Yet it profoundly affects our earth and the eight other planets, various moons, and thousands of tiny asteroids whirling round it. The very fact that these objects stay circling the sun instead of flying off into space is due to the gravitational pull exerted by the great mass of matter making up the sun — a glowing ball of gases occupying an area into which more than a million earths would easily fit, and containing 99 per cent of all the matter in our solar system.

The sun's second great influence stems from the heat it produces. Consuming 4,000 million kilograms of hydrogen a second (rather like a continuously exploding hydrogen bomb), it produces internal temperatures reaching an unbelievable 35 million degrees Centigrade. Its surface, however, is relatively cool at a mere 5,000,000 degrees Centigrade. But even this temperature is high enough to raise the sun-facing sides of Mercury and Venus (the sun's nearest planets) to about 450 degrees Centigrade — far too hot for life as we know it. On the other hand Pluto (the planet farthest from the sun) receives so little heat that no known plant or animal could live there. Only the earth (the third planet out from the sun) receives the right amount of heat to support advanced life forms over most of its surface, and this is largely due to the earth's protective blanket of air which filters out rays that would otherwise harm living things. Astronomers believe that the sun is gradually cooling down. But, fortunately for the world's plants and animals, they think that its heat will continue to support life on earth for several thousand million years.

A section through the sun, showing its white-hot core and molten flares spurting from its outer surface.

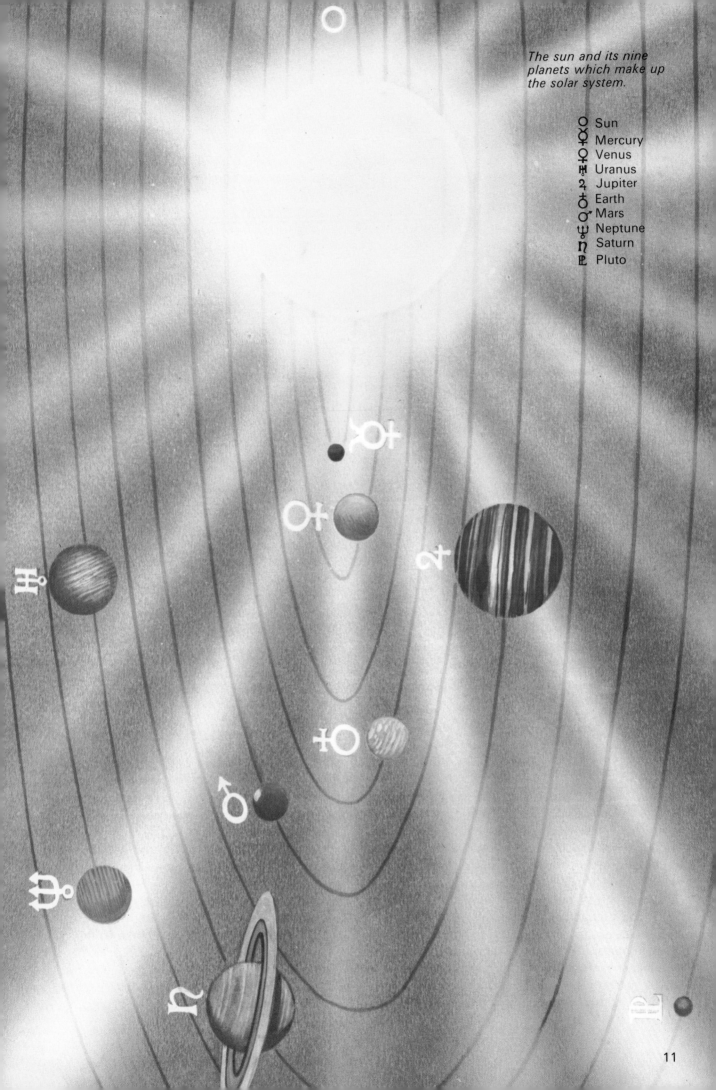

The sun and its nine planets which make up the solar system.

○ Sun
☿ Mercury
♀ Venus
♅ Uranus
♃ Jupiter
♁ Earth
♂ Mars
♆ Neptune
♄ Saturn
♇ Pluto

11

An artist's impression shows how the planets may have begun as clouds of gas spiralling round the sun (the hazy red shape in the top right-hand part of the picture).

HOW THE EARTH BEGAN

No one knows just how the earth and other planets came into being, but astronomers have suggested that most of the solar system is the product of a huge cloud of gas and dust which once circled the sun. According to this theory, parts of the cloud collected together and began to spin like water eddies in a river; particles of gas and dust collected in the centre of each eddy, attracting other particles, and in this way each eddy eventually contracted to produce a planet.

Astronomers by no means agree about just what the planet earth looked like in its early days, perhaps 6,000 million years ago. Possibly it was just a solid lump of barren, waterless rock. However it seems likely that inside the earth, the great heat produced by intense pressures and by radioactive substances eventually melted the interior. Heavy substances like iron would have sunk down and collected in the central core, while relatively light ones — such as oxygen, hydrogen and silicon — would have floated up to the surface. These substances combined in different ways. Some produced silicates which cooled and solidified, giving the earth a hard outer crust. Others, lighter still, rose above the surface as steam and other gases. Probably the earth's atmosphere consisted largely of poisonous methane and ammonia, or of suffocating carbon dioxide. Only gradually did life-supporting oxygen seep up through the melted rocks.

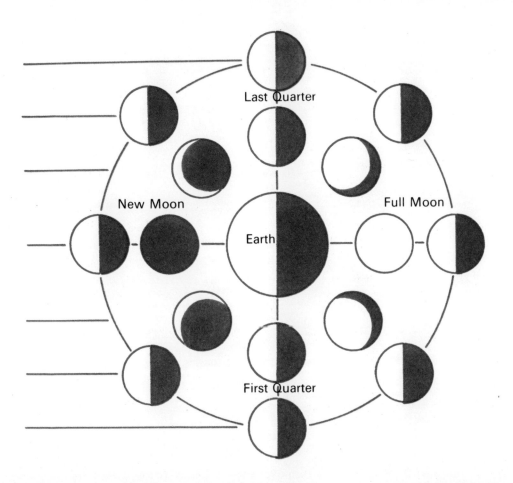

The outer ring of spheres shows the positions of the moon as it circles the earth. Always one side of the moon (white) faces the sun's rays (horizontal lines). But as seen from the earth, the moon's appearance varies (inner ring of spheres), producing the effects which we call the moon's phases.

Last Quarter

New Moon

Earth

Full Moon

First Quarter

EARTH AND MOON

Colossal changes like those described helped to produce the earth as we now know it: an almost ball-shaped planet some 12,756 kilometres (7,900 miles) in diameter, with a circumference of roughly 40,000 kilometres (24,900 miles). Scientists believe that its heart consists of a hot but solid iron and nickel core. Around this lies an outer core of molten iron and nickel; outside the outer core is the mantle, a layer of hot and semi-plastic rocks about 2,900 kilometres (1,800 miles) thick; above the mantle lies the crust, a thin 'skin' from 8 to 30 kilometres (5 to 20 miles) thick, cradling the oceans which occupy nearly three-quarters of the earth's surface. Above this surface floats the atmosphere, a mixture of gases, more than three-quarters nitrogen, over one-fifth oxygen. These gases are prevented from floating off into space by the earth's gravitational pull. The crustal surface, the oceans, and the atmosphere make up the *biosphere*, the thin film where living things are found.

The earth has over a dozen separate motions through space, but the two that concern us here are, firstly, its spin, roughly every 23 hours 56 minutes, on an imaginary axis drawn through the North and South poles. This is the motion which makes the sun seem to move across the sky, and creates on earth day and night as, alternately, we turn towards the sun and then away from it. Secondly, the earth travels round the sun in a great 950 million-kilometre (595 million-mile) elliptical orbit once every 365 days, 6 hours and 9 minutes, moving at about 106,000 kilometres (66,000 miles) an hour. Because the earth spins as it whirls round the sun the earth's northern half tilts towards the sun from March to September (producing summer), and away from September to March (producing winter). In the Southern Hemisphere the opposite happens, and the seasons are accordingly reversed.

As it orbits the sun, the earth is itself orbited (once every 29 days, 12 hours and 44 minutes) by the moon — a ball of airless, waterless rock whose life-less, crater-pitted surface has probably changed little over many million years. As it orbits, the moon turns on its axis so that the same side always faces the earth. Its circling motion means that the part of its sunlit surface visible from earth changes from full moon to new moon to full moon roughly every twenty-eight days.

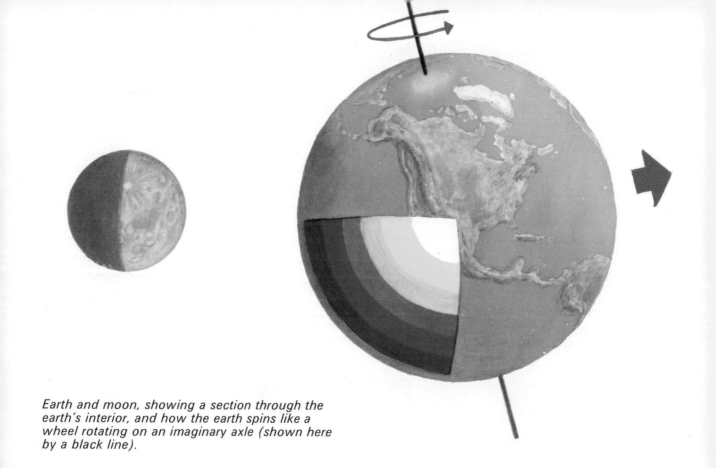

Earth and moon, showing a section through the earth's interior, and how the earth spins like a wheel rotating on an imaginary axle (shown here by a black line).

SHAPING THE EARTH'S SURFACE

Although the earth's ball-like shape was formed several thousand million years ago, long ages passed before its areas of land and sea took on the outlines familiar on today's world map. We must imagine the earth's ancient surface fissured by colossal earthquakes, and torn by shattering volcanic explosions as molten rock forced its way up through the thin crust. The atmosphere was filled with steam and other gases and a lurid light lay across the earth's seething crust.

Gradually, though, rocks cooled and hardened, and steam condensed to rain. The rain ran down and across the rocks and gathered in low lying areas to form lakes and oceans. The sun's heat drew evaporating water back up from the surface of the oceans, thus starting the ceaseless rain cycle. Rain and rivers washed broken rock into the oceans, and immensely thick layers of sediments were built up which pressed down upon the seabed forcing it deep into the hot inner layer of the earth's crust. Heat and pressure hardened the sediments into rock and under the weight the crust buckled to form the first great mountains. The cycle began of rain, breaking down, building up, and breaking down.

Many geophysicists think that, meanwhile, under the crust, gigantic rivers of hot semi-liquid rock began to shift great tracts of land about upon plate-like layers of sub-crustal rock. Imperceptibly the continents drifted – and indeed still drift – across the world like scum on water.

When the moon gets between earth and sun the moon's shadow produces a solar eclipse on earth; when the earth gets between moon and sun the earth's shadow produces a lunar eclipse on the moon.

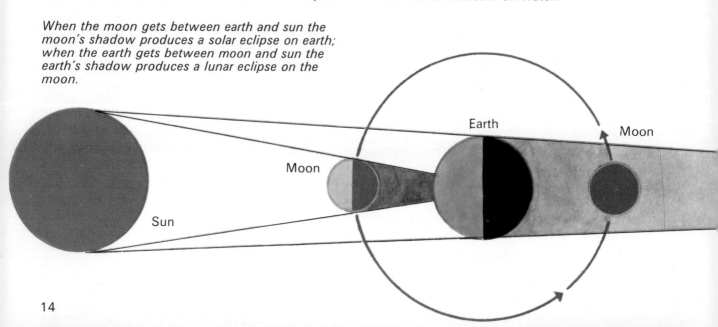

Sun · Moon · Earth · Moon

EARTH HISTORY IN ROCKS

Centuries ago many people believed that all living things were created in their present forms at a single stroke. In the 18th century such beliefs were challenged by the discoveries of two men. Reconstructing long-dead animals from their fossil bones preserved in rocks, the French anatomist Baron Cuvier showed that many had no living counterparts. And in the 1790s the English land surveyor William Smith found that some fossil shells occurred in certain rock layers but not others. Together, their discoveries laid the foundations of *geology*, the study of the development and history of the earth. This science is based on the idea that different layers of rock contain the fossils of different plants and animals, thus preserving stone records of the immense changes which the earth's surface and its life forms have undergone over an almost immeasurable time span. Thanks largely to geology, and enlightened by Charles Darwin's belief in the evolution of life forms through the struggle for survival, we have a panoramic view of how life began and living things evolved, diversified, and spread across the globe.

Many geologists divide the history of life on earth into four great time blocks called *eras*, beginning perhaps 4,000 million years ago with the Pre-Cambrian era, continuing through the Palaeozoic and Mesozoic eras and ending with the present Cenozoic era which began some 65,000,000 years ago. Each era is divided into *periods* and the periods into *epochs*. The following pages describe some of the great landmarks in earth history: how tiny germ-like blobs gave rise to the million kinds of animals and 335,000 kinds of plants now inhabiting the earth, and how many life forms were mysteriously snuffed out.

Red hot lava, pumice, and steam spurt from a volcano fed by molten rock from deep in the earth.

THE DAWN OF LIFE

Biologists usually define living things as those which can absorb particles from their surroundings and use them as materials from which to build copies of themselves. In other words, living things are those that reproduce themselves. Traces of tiny organisms found in ancient rocks suggest that life began on earth in Pre-Cambrian times, at least 3,000 million years ago. The first fragile life forms may have appeared even earlier.

These were probably no more than microscopic self-duplicating molecules formed by the chance meeting of certain chemicals in the mineral-rich 'soup' of shallow Pre-Cambrian seas. Warmed by the often intense heat from the sun, fretted by frequent shafts of lightning, and shrouded in methane or carbon dioxide gas, the seas were like huge tepid cauldrons where myriads of chemicals interacted. Under these special conditions, large self-repeating molecules could have coalesced to form tiny cells that were alive yet neither distinctly plant nor animal, rather like a modern virus.

Some of these cells eventually acquired the ability to trap energy from sunlight and use it to produce chemical reactions between sea water and dissolved carbon dioxide, creating carbohydrates and releasing oxygen as waste. In other words, these tiny organisms had begun the food-making process called photosynthesis which distinguishes green plants from all other living things. After the first plants became established, another kind of organism could evolve — one which obtained its food at second hand simply by eating plants. When this had happened, animals had also emerged.

The first known life forms were tiny algae and bacteria. Only after millions of years did such simple living cells begin combining in colonies to produce larger organisms like seaweeds, sponges, worms, corals, jellyfish — some equipped with special groups of cells designed for feeding, moving, reproducing and so on. When this had happened, the great tree of evolution depicted on the facing page began to grow and throw out branches.

All the sea plants and creatures named above had appeared by the time the Pre-Cambrian era ended some 600 million years ago; meanwhile the earth's land masses remained as lifeless as the moon.

One-celled life forms   Flatworm   Seaweed   Sponges

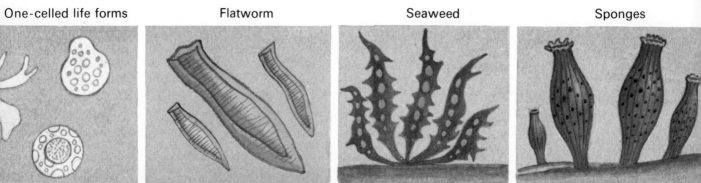

Different kinds of invertebrate which flourished in the Pre-Cambrian or Palaeozoic eras.

Corals

Sea lilies

Ammonite

Nautiloid

Anemone

Cyclotropis   Trilobites

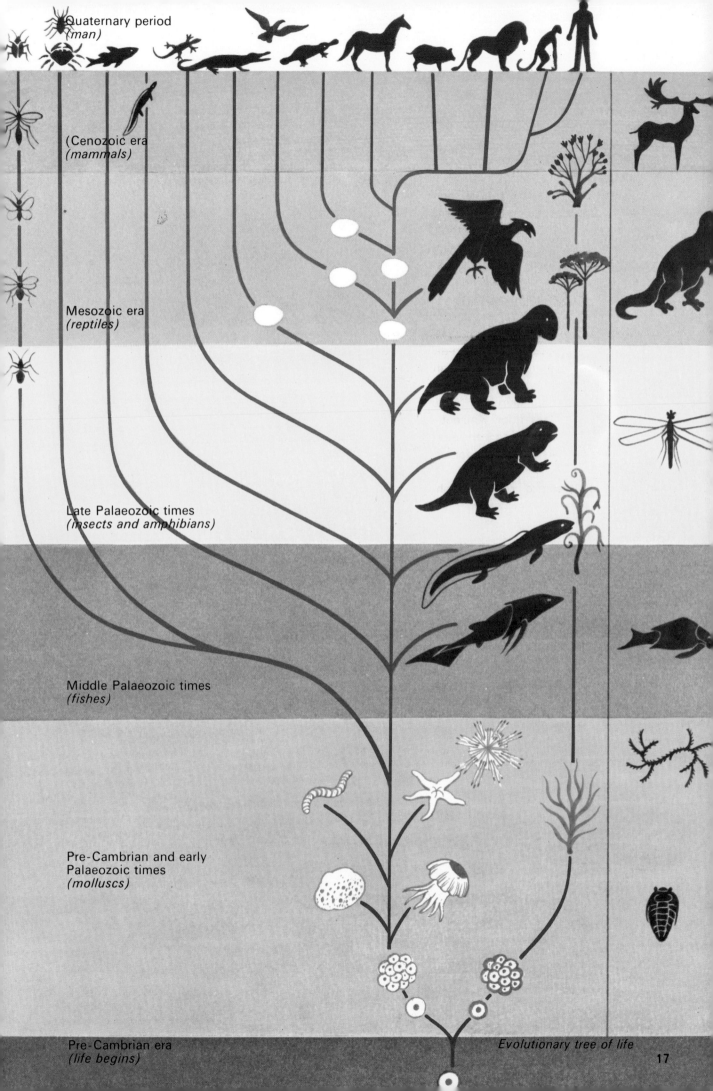

Quaternary period
(man)

(Cenozoic era
(mammals)

Mesozoic era
(reptiles)

Late Palaeozoic times
(insects and amphibians)

Middle Palaeozoic times
(fishes)

Pre-Cambrian and early
Palaeozoic times
(molluscs)

Pre-Cambrian era
(life begins)

Evolutionary tree of life

17

LIFE IN CAMBRIAN TIMES

About 600 million years ago the 375 million-year Palaeozoic era, or Age of Ancient Life, began. Its earliest period was the Cambrian, named from its fossils, which were first identified in *Cambria* (the Latin name for Wales).

These fossils show that 600 million years ago the seas teemed with life forms, though there were as yet no fishes — this was the great age of marine invertebrates or sea-dwelling creatures without backbones.

Much of the warm, shallow, sea bottom was dotted with rooted seaweeds and with sponges, soft-bodied animals — some vase-shaped, some round, some tree-like. Fixed to one spot, they depended on the movement of the water passing food particles through tiny openings in their bodies. Marine worms, some of them brilliantly coloured and decorated with fantastic 'plumes', burrowed in the sand round the sponges or moved slowly across the sea bed. Larger, leathery-skinned, slug-like sea cucumbers also crawled about the sea floor. Ancient ancestors of our modern starfish, brittle stars and sea urchins, also scavenged or waited motionless for passing scraps of food.

The sea bed teemed with shellfish, and slow-moving snails browsed on the sea plants rooted in rocky seashore pools, much as winkles browse today. By Cambrian times many such creatures had developed hard protective outer shells; some as defences against both predators and the threat of drying up in the intertidal zones.

Above these creatures of the sea floor the delicate flimsy bodies of translucent jellyfish were wafted to and fro by ocean currents, capturing shrimps and other tiny creatures with their stinging tentacles.

Many of these animals were ancestral to modern forms of ocean life. But Cambrian animals also included some with no modern counterparts, among them the trilobites, nicknamed 'masters of the Cambrian seas' from the fact that their fossils are the commonest of all from Cambrian times. These distant relatives of modern crabs were insect-like seabed dwellers with flattened bodies divided into segments. Ranging from less than a centimetre to over 60 centimetres (two feet) long, trilobites must have looked like small oval-shaped venetian blinds with legs as they crawled over seabed mud feeding on dead or dying creatures. If attacked by a predator, they simply doubled up their flexibly armoured bodies, curling into a defensive ball. These curious creatures lived only during Palaeozoic times.

Three kinds of arthropod which lived in ancient Palaeozoic seas.

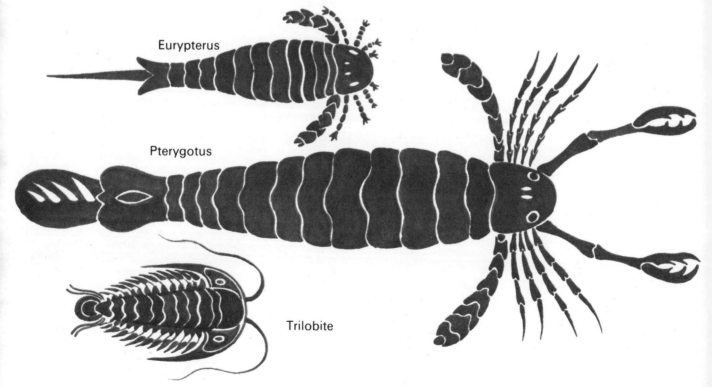

Eurypterus

Pterygotus

Trilobite

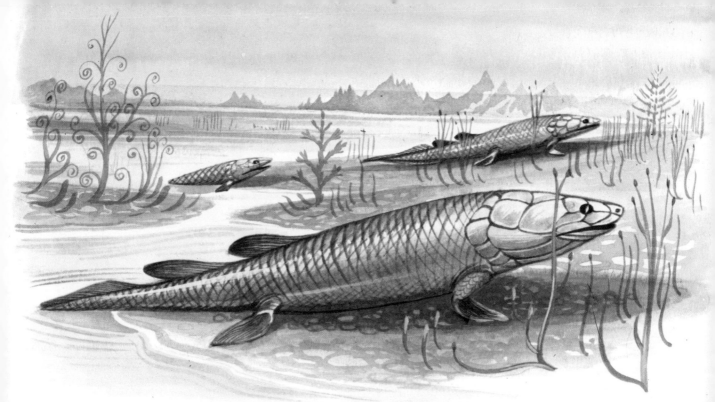

Lobe-finned fishes invading the land.

LIFE IN ORDOVICIAN TIMES

The Ordovician period takes its name from the Ordovices, an ancient tribe inhabiting West Wales, the area where the rocks were first studied. The Ordovician began about 480 million years ago and lasted some 45 million years. During this time the pattern of sea and land had probably changed little from that of Cambrian times. A great land mass which geographers call Gondwanaland straddled much of the Southern Hemisphere, embracing what are now South America, and Africa, and sprawling east across the Indian Ocean to Australia. Most of the Northern Hemisphere was ocean, and life was still restricted to the sea.

During Ordovician times many Cambrian life forms continued to flourish. But molluscs began challenging the trilobites as the most numerous of living creatures. Among them were bivalve animals like clams and oysters, and animals in a single protective shell, like whelks and limpets. One of the most successful groups of mollusc were the cephalopods, or 'animals with feet on their heads'. This group included the now extinct straight-shelled nautiloid shown on page 16, and the ancestors of the modern, coiled-shell pearly nautilus and shell-less octopus.

But by far the most important animals to appear in Ordovician times were the jawless fishes — the first known animals with backbones. Their strong, yet flexible, lightweight structure made these fishes more manoeuvrable than the invertebrates and they became the groundplan for later, higher forms of life.

LIFE IN SILURIAN TIMES

Silurian limestones, shales, and sandstones were laid down between about 440 million and 400 million years ago in much of Europe and North America. Like rocks from the two previous periods they were first studied in Wales and named from a Welsh tribe, the Silures. Seemingly, mild, constant temperatures persisted in this period and only violent mountain-building at its close shattered the prevailing calm conditions.

Life went on much as before in the ocean. In estuaries and rivers, however, big changes were afoot. Here, tiny, jawless, bony-headed, scale-protected fishes called ostracoderms scavenged in the mud successfully enough to multiply dramatically. Later came placoderms — fishes with jaws and fins. But invertebrates still dominated the seas, and the first fishes must have gone in fear of voracious arthropods, like those shown on the facing page, which included eurypterids or sea scorpions up to 3 metres (9 feet) long.

Meanwhile startling changes were taking place on the once barren land. Heat, frost, rain, and wind had begun to break down its surface rock into soil capable of growing plants. Now, at last, plants began to colonise the land, in particular the branched-stem, small-leaved psilopsids. Land plants provided food for air-breathing animals; perhaps millipedes were among the first land animals. More time was to pass before vertebrates, like those above, left the water.

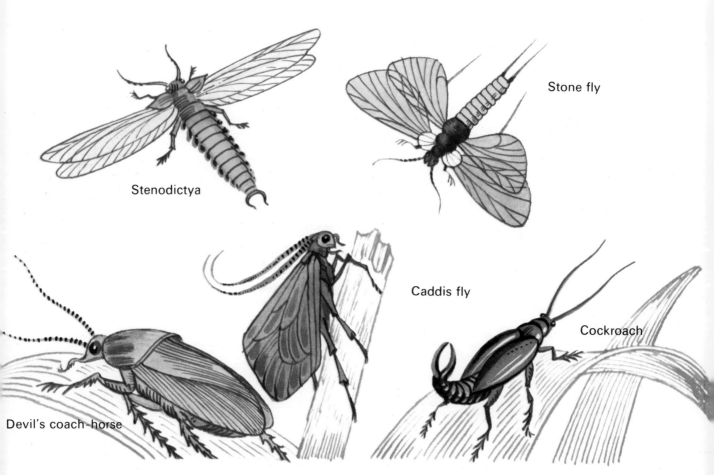

Stone fly

Stenodictya

Caddis fly

Cockroach

Devil's coach-horse

Many of the winged insects that lived in the Palaeozoic era were little different from modern kinds.

LIFE IN DEVONIAN TIMES

The Devonian period which began about 400 million years ago and lasted 50 million years was a restless age of mountain building, fierce rains, and great droughts, and is best known as the age of fishes. It was at this time that the seas and rivers began to teem with many kinds of fish. There were 'old-fashioned' bony-plated ostracoderms like the one shown opposite. There was also an increasing range of armoured placoderms including Bothriolepis, Pterichtys, Acanthodians or spiny sharks, and Coccosteus (all depicted on the facing page), and ranging in size from the tiny Climatius (a freshwater fish of 8 centimetres — 3 inches — long) to the marine giant Dinichthys, 9 metres (30 feet) long.

Gradually, over thousands of years, other kinds of fish evolved. One group included Cladoselache, 60 centimetres (2 feet) long, a sharp-toothed, torpedo-shaped relative of the modern sharks — predatory fishes with hard cartilage in place of bone.

But from the historical point of view, by far the most important fishes in existence at that time were the small-scaled bony fishes. They were an offshoot of the placoderms, and ancestral to most fishes alive today. One group of Devonian bony fishes were the ray fins, so called from the stiff rods which supported the fins. Another group (related to the modern lungfish) were known as lobe-fins from the muscular lobes attaching their fins to their bodies. These fishes eventually included the curious deep-sea coelacanth, believed extinct until fishermen caught one off South Africa in 1938. But most Devonian lobe-fins lived in rivers, among them Osteolepis and Eusthenopteron, both shown here.

When droughts dried up rivers, many fishes died of suffocation. But the gill-breathing lobe-fins survived by using their air bladders as a lung, and by dragging their bodies to the nearest water on their sturdy fins. By the time the Devonian period had ended, lobe-fins had given rise to clumsy four-legged, tailed amphibians — the world's first vertebrates able to spend much time on land. There, they would have crawled along the water's muddy edge eating the wingless ancestors of the insects pictured here.

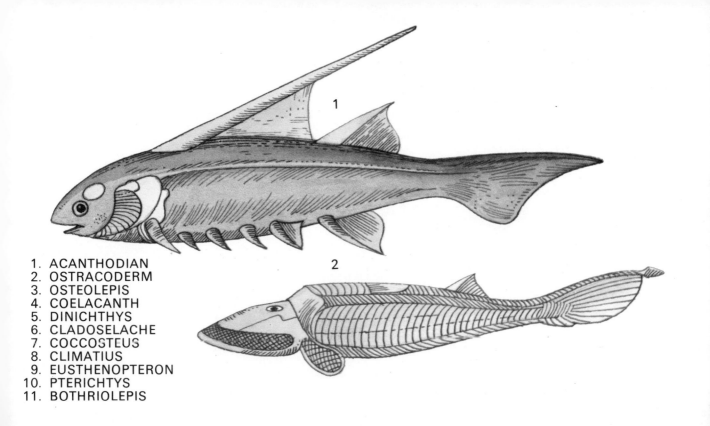

1. ACANTHODIAN
2. OSTRACODERM
3. OSTEOLEPIS
4. COELACANTH
5. DINICHTHYS
6. CLADOSELACHE
7. COCCOSTEUS
8. CLIMATIUS
9. EUSTHENOPTERON
10. PTERICHTYS
11. BOTHRIOLEPIS

Different kinds of fishes which evolved in Palaeozoic seas and rivers

Meganeura dragonfly
(75-cm wingspan)

Lepidodendron

Horsetail

Sigillaria

Ferns

LIFE IN CARBONIFEROUS TIMES

About 350 million years ago, the Palaeozoic era entered its fifth period. In its early stages, the remains of myriads of sea molluscs, corals and other animals piled up on the beds of shallow seas to form limy muds which later hardened into great beds of limestone rock. But this so-called Carboniferous period takes its name from the coal-rich rocks (coal is a form of carbon) laid down in its later stages, which ended around 270 million years ago. These rocks were the remains of vast forests that covered the then hot, swampy lands where North America and Europe now stand. As the land slowly sank and rose old forests drowned and new ones sprouted. Eventually the buried layers of dead vegetation were compacted into peat, then soft brown coal, later into hard seams of streaky black coal, and finally into anthracite, the oldest of all.

Most trees of coal forest times were different from almost any plants today. Ancient relatives of modern horsetails soared up 21 metres (70 feet), while so-called scale trees, related to our tiny club mosses, towered 30 metres (100 feet) above the lush undergrowth of ferns, two of the commonest being the slim-trunked Lepidodendron and the fuzzy-topped Sigillaria. None of these plants had flowers.

Filtering dimly through the forest canopy the hot sun glinted on the insects like Meganeura, a dragonfly with a 75-centimetre (30-inch) wingspan, one of the world's first and largest-ever flying insects. On the forest floor giant cockroaches lurked under rotting logs with snails, scorpions, centipedes, spiders and other small invertebrates, seeking protection from the creatures that gave late Carboniferous times the nickname 'Age of Amphibians'. Just as in Devonian times a few kinds of fish gave rise to a bewildering variety, so all kinds of amphibians now appeared, from tiny newt-like creatures to some as big as crocodiles; most crawling on four stubby limbs, but others limbless and slithering or swimming snake-like through the swamps in search of living prey. We shall see that both the forests and their creatures were to face a major threat to their survival.

LIFE IN PERMIAN TIMES

The Permian period (named after Perm in Russia), marked the last phase of the great Palaeozoic era and lasted about 50 million years, starting about 270 million years ago. In Permian times, a huge ice cap smothered the great southern continent of Gondwanaland; in the Northern Hemisphere volcanic eruptions tore the land and great mountain ranges arose, isolating areas of sea and swamp which began to dry out.

Only plants and animals able to withstand a drying world could survive such conditions. The spores of the great trees and the soft-skinned eggs of the soft-bodied amphibians depended on a damp atmosphere, so that these kinds of living thing began dying out as swamps dried up. But some amphibians developed tough drought-resistant skins and eggs, which were protected from drying up by their harder, outer shell. In fact, they had become reptiles. Meanwhile fern-like seed-bearing plants appeared: plants in which male pollen grains fertilized a female 'spore' encased in a damp, protective housing called a seed. When the Permian period ended, seed-bearing conifers had replaced ancient trees, and reptiles were masters of the land.

LIFE IN TRIASSIC TIMES

The Mesozoic era or Middle Age of Life opened with the Triassic period (about 225 million to 180 million years ago), named from the word *Trias* (three) after three kinds of rock layer laid down in this phase of earth's history.

During Triassic times, a great northern continent stretched from North America to Russia, while Gondwanaland still straddled much of the world south of the equator. Hot deserts covered huge areas and many land plants dried out under their harsh conditions, although drought-resistant conifers and cycads (stumpy trees crowned by palm-like fronds), and ferns persisted outside deserts.

Among animals, reptiles tightened their hold upon the land. These scaly, often long-limbed and mobile creatures included thecodonts (ancestors of both modern crocodiles and birds), which ranged from small lizard-like beasts to others over 6 metres (20 feet) long. There was also Trilyton, a dog-sized reptile whose fossil bones suggest that it had warm blood, and fur. Meanwhile, some reptiles had adapted themselves to the sea — among them a prehistoric turtle, and the big fish-like ichthyosaurs.

Several kinds of prehistoric amphibian distantly related to modern newts and salamanders.

Urocordylus scalaris

Microbrachis pelikani

Branchiosaurus salamandroides

Dolichosoma longissimum

Archaeopteryx
(pigeon sized)

Pterodactyl
*(up to 8 metres
wingspan)*

Diplodocus
(27 metres long)

Brachiosaurus
(22 metres long)

Animals of Jurassic and Cretaceous times

LIFE IN JURASSIC TIMES

Rocks laid down in France and Switzerland, between about 180 million and 130 million years ago, were later raised up as the Jura Mountains which gave their name to the Jurassic period of earth's history. During the Jurassic, myriads of minute marine organisms laid down tiny egg-like structures made from lime; these eventually piled up into thick layers of oolitic limestone rock, named from the Greek word *oon*, 'egg'. Jurassic rocks are also rich in fossil ammonites: cephalopods with beautifully coiled and rippled shells.

A variety of large aquatic reptiles scoured shallow Jurassic seas for fish and molluscs, among them turtles, marine crocodiles, ichthyosaurs, and long-necked, sharp-toothed plesiosaurs propelled by paddle-shaped limbs.

Great changes now occurred on land. The great southern continent of Gondwanaland began breaking up, and the northern continent was split in two.

Everywhere, millions of years of weathering had worn down mountains, and rains now turned old deserts into warm, humid swamps — homes for many of the reptiles called dinosaurs, from the Greek for 'terrible lizards'. Dinosaurs ranged in size from small lizard-like beasts to the biggest land animals that ever lived. Among these were huge-bodied, small-brained monsters like Diplodocus which grew up to 27 metres (87 feet), and Brachiosaurus which weighed as much as 50,000 kilograms (50 tons). Such monsters' peaceful habits belied their terrifying bulk, for they were vegetarians which largely spent their time quietly cropping swamp plants and relying on water to buoy up their massive bodies.

Above the giant dinosaurs flew small reptiles called pterosaurs whose forelimbs had evolved, bat-like, into skin-membrane wings. Although their leathery wings and tapered jaws recall the giant dragons of mythology, many pterosaurs, known as pterodactyls, were the size of a crow; however, Pteranodon, one of their descendants, had a 7·5-metre (25-feet) wing-

Tyrannosaurus
(14 metres long)

Styracosaurus
(10 metres long)

Triceratops
(6 metres long)

Elasmosaurus
(13 metres long)

span and was the largest flying creature ever. By mid-Jurassic times reptiles had produced another kind of flying creature: Archaeopteryx had developed warm blood and scales modified as feathers. It was the first known bird.

These were by no means the only major changes in the Jurassic world of animals. Palaeontologists (scientists who study fossils) have also detected rare fossil remains of small shrew-like ancestors of modern mammals – creatures which produce their young alive instead of laying eggs, and nourish them with milk from special glands.

LIFE IN CRETACEOUS TIMES

The Cretaceous period (about 135 million–70 million years ago) is aptly named from the Latin *creta* (*chalk*), for vast belts of chalk were laid down in the Cretaceous seas covering great areas that are now dry land.

At first, plesiosaurs like the enormous Elasmosaurus shown here still swam about the seas, and huge dinosaurs still roamed the land, many of them specially adapted for aggression or defence. Perhaps the fiercest predator was the 14-metre (45-feet) long Tyrannosaurus (the largest-ever flesh eater). On its powerful hind legs Tyrannosaurus chased vegetarian dinosaurs and tore their bodies with its colossal jaws. However, horned dinosaurs like Triceratops and Styracosaurus could offer some resistance to attack, while other dinosaurs evolved a body cover of bony plates.

No such protection saved plant-eating dinosaurs from the climatic changes that set in, drying up the swamps and favouring deciduous *flowering* plants (including trees like oaks and maples) at the expense of the old perennially-leaved cycads, whose seeds were less well protected. Large vegetarian reptiles, which had lost much of their food supply, simply starved, indirectly killing off the beasts that preyed upon them.

25

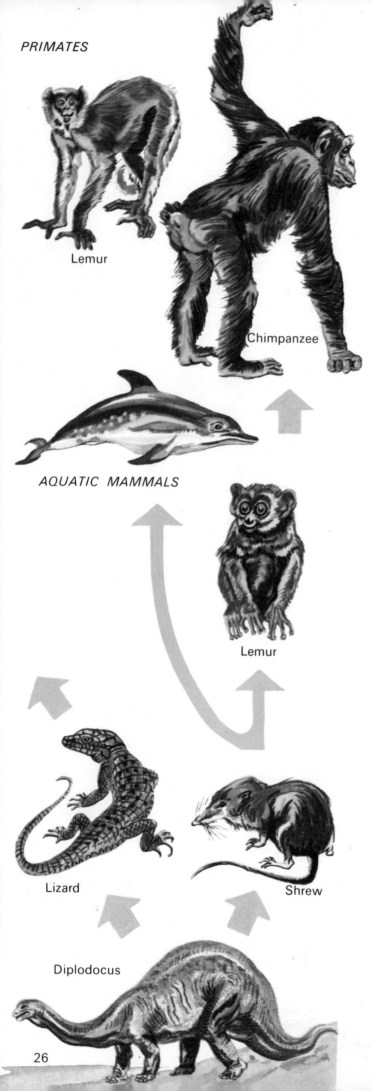

PRIMATES

Lemur

Chimpanzee

AQUATIC MAMMALS

Lemur

Lizard

Shrew

Diplodocus

Gorilla

The evolution of mammals from reptilian stock (not Diplodocus itself) to modern primates.

LIFE IN TERTIARY TIMES

As the Middle Age of Life ended, so began the Age of Recent Life – the Cenozoic Era in which we live today. Palaeontologists divide it into two great periods, starting with the Tertiary period which took up all but the last 3 million of the Cenozoic's 70 million years. This was the time when the earth's great mountain chains – Alps, Himalayas, Rockies, Andes – were thrust upwards. Meanwhile the continents were taking on their present shapes.

During this period the world's climate became cooler, and this condition proved unfavourable for the cold blooded reptiles, which needed the sun's lifegiving heat. However, many relatively small reptiles survived, including ancestors of our modern lizards, turtles, snakes, and crocodiles.

Now it was the turn of the mammals to dominate the land. Adapted to maintain the level of their body temperature independently of the sun's heat, and able to protect their unborn young inside their bodies and feed them through a special structure called a placenta, the so-called placental mammals proved better able to withstand climatic changes than the egg-laying reptiles. Cut off from the mainstream of mammal development by seas, Australia's mammals remained more primitive. Some were furry and warm-blooded but laid eggs like their present-day descendants, the platypus and echidna. Others produced

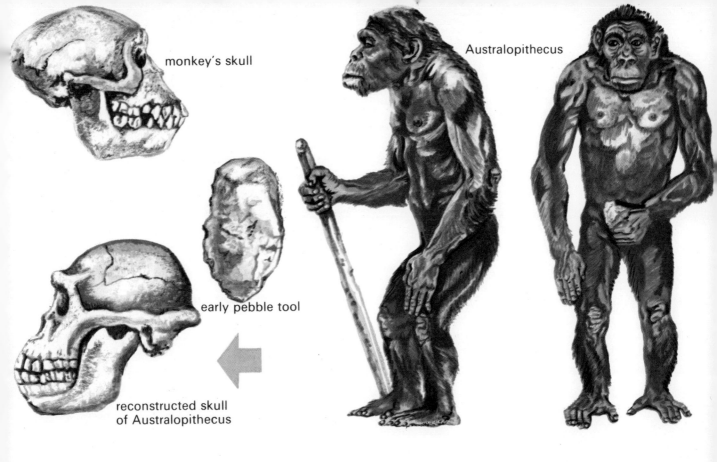

monkey's skull

Australopithecus

early pebble tool

reconstructed skull
of Australopithecus

tiny, underdeveloped babies and reared them in pouches as kangaroos do today.

As the Tertiary Period wore on, all kinds of mammal species appeared, adapted to life in different surroundings. Some returned to the sea and evolved into whales; some took to the air as bats; some gave rise to the modern horse, rhinoceros, and camel, all of them grazers of the grasses which had now also appeared; yet others gave rise to flesh-eating carnivores like dogs and cats.

From the human viewpoint easily the most important mammals were the so-called primates, which had earlier emerged with ancestors of today's tiny, sharp-nosed, clawed shrews: creatures with indifferent eyesight but a keen sense of smell. From creatures like tree-shrews sprang larger primates, with bigger brains, smaller, less sensitive noses, but larger, forward-looking eyes able to judge distances accurately. They had nails instead of claws, borne upon five grasping digits including a thumb. When the Tertiary period ended, primates had come to include tree-shrews, lemurs, tarsiers, monkeys, apes, and now-extinct, ape-like creatures.

These last animals were weak and slow compared with big carnivores; and unlike the rhinoceros and elephant they lacked the protection of a tough outer hide. Yet their large brains and adaptable hands were to give them immense advantages in the constant struggle to survive.

LIFE IN RECENT TIMES

Among living creatures the evolution of man was the great feature of the Quaternary, the second period of the Cenozoic era. It began some 3,500,000 years ago and is the one we live in today.

Exactly when the first recognisably human animal evolved remains unclear. To some extent its dating depends upon what we mean by 'man'. Most scientists consider that the first man was the first primate capable of purposefully making tools. Certain undoubtedly non-human animals will pick up twigs or stones and use them for special purposes: for instances chimpanzees will raid ants' nests with the help of twigs, and some Egyptian vultures drop stones on ostrich eggs to break them. But only a more complex brain than that of monkeys, chimpanzees or birds seems capable of enough foresight to chip a formless lump of stone into a crude yet effective tool.

Pebble tools found with fossil bones about 2 million years old convince some scientists that the first true toolmakers were the Australopithecines or Southern Apes — hairy creatures like the ones pictured above, half-ape, half-man in appearance. Scientists believe, too, that such creatures probably lived in East Africa as much as 6 million years ago. Much was to happen to their descendants and those of other prehistoric men-like creatures before people like ourselves eventually appeared on earth.

THE AGE OF ICE

Early man and other mammals faced harsh climatic changes during the first or Pleistocene epoch of the Quaternary period, an epoch which lasted for about one million years and ended only 20,000 years or so ago. Great waves of cold, each lasting roughly 60,000 years, brought huge ice sheets down from the Arctic, gouging out valleys and blanketing Canada and much of Europe.

Animals in the bitterly cold lands at the ice's rim died out, moved out, or became adapted to life in Arctic climates. Among the most successful survivors were those which grew thick coats to trap body warmth; creatures like the great, tusked mammoth and woolly rhinoceros, which grubbed in the snow for grasses and lichens. Between glaciations, previously frozen areas warmed up enough for such tropical creatures as lions and hippopotamuses to range north as far as England.

Eventually the last ice sheets melted, dumping huge tracts of rock and soil upon the land that they had covered. Perhaps they have gone forever; or perhaps we are simply living in yet another warm phase which will end within a few thousand years. Of one thing we can be certain: when the ice receded it left the world peopled by creatures much the same as those alive today. The huge mammoths and the woolly rhinoceroses had all died out, but men like ourselves — once rare, vulnerable creatures — were mastering the land.

Mammals whose warm thick coats protected them from the bitter Ice Age cold.

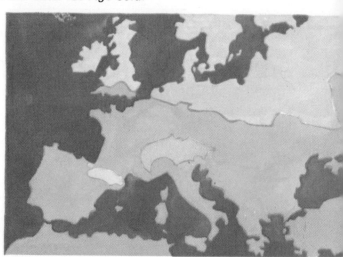

Map showing the extent of the great ice sheets that covered much of Europe in the recent prehistoric past.

Mammoths

Woolly rhinoceros

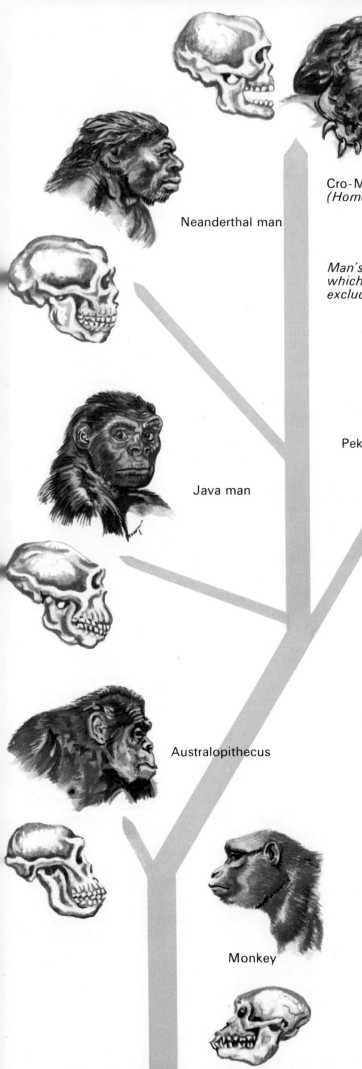

Cro-Magnon man
(Homo sapiens)

Neanderthal man

Man's family tree (from which the monkeys are excluded)

Java man

Peking man

Australopithecus

Monkey

Upright man (above) evolved from four-legged primates (below)

MAN'S FAMILY TREE

While the great ice sheets ground and rumbled over northern lands, different kinds of prehistoric man were evolving to the south. Man's family tree, shown on this page, depicts some of the types whose fossil bones have been discovered.

To be more accurate, the tree represents the hominid branch and twigs of the great tree of primates. If we could trace this branch from lower down we should see where other branches have diverged from the main primate stem — first, the lemurs, then the tarsoids, New World monkeys, Old World monkeys and, lastly, the modern apes.

The great feature which separates the hominid branch from the ape and monkey branches is the fact that hominids gave up their four-legged stance and began walking upright. Apart from Peking and Java man, who were almost identical, by far the most important differences between the pictured hominids above are the skulls. These show the development of the skull from a small brain cavity to the larger brain cavity of Cro-Magnon man. In the next pages we shall look more closely at these creatures and the ways in which they lived and died.

Prehistoric men-apes hunting an ibex with stick, stone, and bone weapons.

THE MEN-APES OF AFRICA

For our first close look at near-human and human life in prehistoric times, we must turn back to the oldest-known man-like creatures: the Australopithecines of South and East Africa who flourished a million and more years ago.

In many ways they were utterly different from modern man. They were tiny — no more than four feet tall; they also had massively projecting jaws like those of a chimpanzee, and a brain half as large as that of most modern men.

In other ways however they looked much more like men than apes. Their brow ridges were less pronounced than those of the big modern apes; their foreheads also looked much more human; and the backs of their skulls were rounded instead of ridged. Moreover their teeth were more like the teeth of modern man than ape-shaped and, just like us, they evidently wore them down by side-to-side jaw movements, rather than the forwards and backwards movements used by the apes. They also walked on their hind legs in a semi-upright posture.

From these details and from the places where their fossil bones have been found, we can be sure that they lived in fairly open country, and many experts believe that their upright stance was indirectly due to this fact. Some time previously, in the Tertiary period, their prehistoric forest-dwelling ape ancestors had lived in a drying climate which slowly killed off forests. These tree-climbing primates were forced out into more open country where, gradually, their descendants began to use their hind limbs for walking. Thus their fore limbs were freed for grasping the sticks, stones, and bones with which they protected themselves from sharp-fanged carnivores, and for attacking and killing small animals for food.

Without the protection of the trees which their agile ancestors had enjoyed, the Australopithecines must have been specially vulnerable when they slept. Perhaps they sought the natural refuge of caves. Certainly numbers of their bones have been found in such places, together with the skulls of baboons showing signs of crushing such as the Australopithecines could have inflicted with the help of a piece of wood, bone, or stone. This might suggest that the Australopithecines were agile hunters, for baboons are clumsy but fast runners. However some experts question the meaning of such finds, and think that the bones found in the caves were dragged there by hyaenas or other carnivores.

In any event we can be almost certain that many thousand years passed before the Australopithecines learned to make purposeful tools — if indeed they ever did so, for we are by no means certain. At least some of the ancient pebble tools found near their fossil bones have proved to have been shaped by the battering action of waterfalls.

Without doubt the first purposefully shaped stone tools were found beside the remains of two kinds of early man or near-man. The first type was, unquestionably, an Australopithecine; the second, nicknamed Handy man, was perhaps a different kind of hominid who actually used these tools to kill the first. Whether this is indeed what happened we may never know; almost certainly, however, as different kinds of near-men competed for survival in one area they must have met and fought. The ones who survived would have been those with the brains capable of devising the more effective weapons. This may explain why the Australopithecines mysteriously died out long, long ago.

JAVANESE UPRIGHT MAN

Discoveries of early kinds of prehistoric men have followed no smooth pattern, but occurred in widely scattered places and at different times throughout a century and more. Curiously, perhaps, discoveries of some of the oldest near-men (the Australopithecines) have been among the most recent, occurring largely in the middle 20th century, while many discoveries of later kinds of fossil men came earlier.

One of the first important finds came in the early 1890s in the Indonesian island of Java. A Dutch army surgeon, Marie Eugene Dubois, was digging in a river bank and unearthed bits of fossil skull, jaw, and thighbone, which were clearly man-like yet unlike those of any living race of man. For one thing the skull and jawbone had belonged to a creature with beetling brows, a low forehead, and a forward thrusting jaw with a receding chin. The creature had a much bigger brain than the Australopithecines (although rather smaller than that of most modern men) and had been capable of shaping distinctive, if crude, chipped stone tools. He had grown to about five feet high and had walked upright.

Later, many more fossils of this creature were unearthed in Java and elsewhere, and it became plain that they were of men or near-men of a kind which had flourished as much as 1,500,000 years ago.

Dubois gave his discovery the scientific Latin name of *Pithecanthropus erectus* (Upright Apeman), but there can be no doubt that Java man, as he is also known, was far more man than ape.

For this reason, experts have generally agreed to change his scientific name to *Homo erectus javanensis*, or Javanese Upright Man, so making him a close relative of modern man. Indeed some authorities believe he is so close a relative that Java man represents one of our direct, if remote and uncouth looking, ancestors.

But we can only guess the answers to some of the most intriguing questions about Java man. For instance, was he capable of speech? By studying the shape of those parts of the skull and jaw which we use in talking, anatomists decided that Java man could have made sounds to express the ideas which his relatively powerful brain was capable of forming. But further studies have shown that bone shapes are by no means a sure indication of the ability to speak. Instead, archaeologists suggest that the spread of similar tools over a wide area would be a truer indication, since their makers would have needed words to tell each other how and why to shape the tools. By this yardstick, Java man almost certainly had speech of some kind, for the chipped stone toolkit of *Homo erectus* has been found in places many thousands of miles apart.

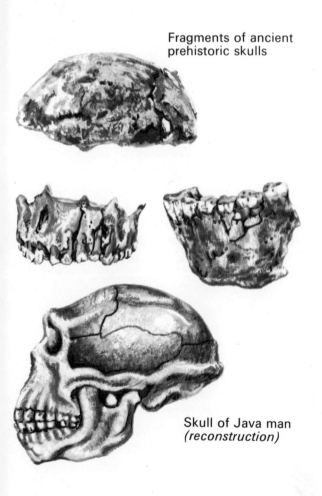

Fragments of ancient prehistoric skulls

Skull of Java man
(reconstruction)

Java man

backed point   burin   scraper

burin   scraper   burin

scraper   scraper

backed point   burin   scraper

Part of a toolkit from the Old Stone Age

LIFE IN THE EARLY OLD STONE AGE

From fossil bones, bits of stone, and fragments of charcoal we can form some kind of picture of life in early Palaeolithic (Old Stone Age) times, named from the simple kinds of stone tool made by Java man and others.

Wandering in small family groups, these early peoples would have led a hunting, food-gathering way of life, roaming the untamed countryside in constant search of food and fear of starvation, killing small animals and collecting edible berries, bulbs, and roots.

With practice, they would have become skilled at making simple tools to help them: mainly sharp-edged stone, wood, and bone tools for piercing, cutting, and scraping. Asian men of the *Homo erectus* type made distinctive 'chopper' tools by bashing one stone with another to produce a sharp, roughly chipped cutting edge. Some toolmakers became skilful enough to trim this edge more delicately, producing crude knives for cutting up animals they had

killed, and perhaps for whittling wood to produce sharply pointed spears. In Africa and much of Europe, Old Stone Age peoples eventually learned how to chip big stones into small, sharp-edged flakes and flat-sided, pear-shaped, hand-axes — multipurpose tools which they could use for daggers, scrapers, and even trowels.

Even these useful tools and weapons would have left early man no match for some of the huge sharp-toothed, sharp-clawed carnivores that shared his world. Fortunately for Old Stone Age man, the once-widespread sabre-toothed tigers, perhaps the most fearsome animals of all, survived into Palaeolithic times only in North and South America — continents which were still uninhabited by man in the early Old Stone Age.

Perhaps man's best defence against not only hostile beasts but the penetrating cold of northern climates, was fire. From charred bits of fossil bone and other substances we know that at least some early Old Stone Age men had learnt to produce flames by rubbing sticks or striking stones together.

1. SABRE-TOOTHED TIGER
2. AUROCHS
3. WILD HORSE
4. CAVE BEAR
5. IRISH ELK
6. EUROPEAN BISON

Six kinds of large mammal that flourished in the Old Stone Age.

MORE CLUES TO MAN'S FOSSIL PAST

We have seen that some of the first men and men-like creatures inhabited warm lands in Africa and Indonesia. Once man had mastered fire, however, he could warm himself artificially. This allowed people to spread farther north, closer to the chilly fringes of the shifting ice sheets. The first known fire-maker — Peking man — was a close relative of Java man and flourished in northern China about one million years ago. Fossil finds from caves near Peking show that many generations of Peking man had lived there, making fires, and cooking venison and also human flesh by charring it in the flames. Big bones were cracked open to suck out the juicy marrow.

Meanwhile, far to the west, people like Peking man were spreading into Europe where the oldest-known human fossil is that of Heidelberg man, represented simply by a lower jaw 600,000 years old found in a German sand pit in 1907.

Java man, Peking man, and Heidelberg man all belonged to our own biological sub-family, the genus *Homo*. But *erectus* (erect), the second part of their scientific name, shows that they belonged to a different species from modern man, whose second scientific name is *sapiens* (wise).

Some of the oldest relics of *Homo sapiens* are three broken bits of skull found with flint hand-axes 6 metres (20 feet) deep in the gravel banks of the River Thames at Swanscombe, near London. Experts think that Swanscombe man lived about 250,000 years ago, and they are sure that he was a big-brained but ancient type of modern man.

Fossils found near such ancient people show that they still inhabited a world that would have been strange to us. Now-extinct kinds of bear, elephant, rhinoceros, and the Irish elk (whose massive antlers spanned up to 3 metres – 11 feet – and over), roamed the Thames Valley 250,000 years ago. But not all the big mammals of those days would have seemed strange to our much more recent ancestors: the wild ox or aurochs, for instance, died out less than four centuries ago. Indeed, wild horses and European bison (both of them familiar to Palaeolithic man), still flourish in the protection of special zoos and nature reserves.

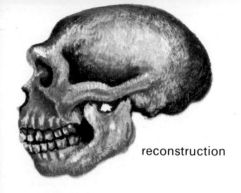
reconstruction

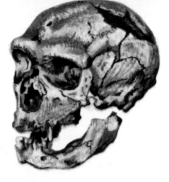
Neanderthal skull
found in France

scraper

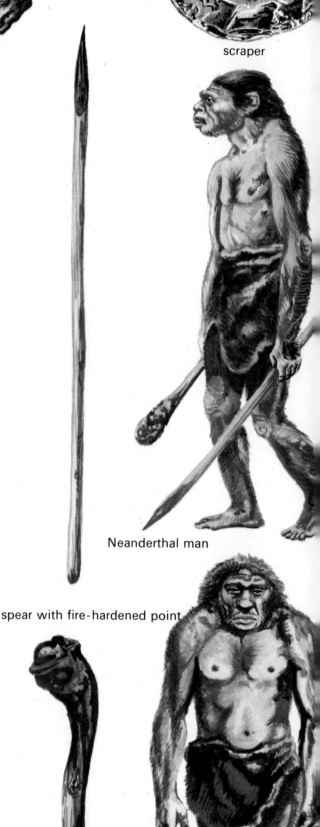

NEANDERTHAL MAN

So far we have described kinds of prehistoric men known only from rare discoveries of their bones, suggesting that these men were far from numerous. As the great Ice Age drew towards its close, however, a more abundant variety of man appeared — one whose bones have been unearthed from places as far apart as France, Uzbekistan in central Asia, North Africa, and Palestine, while others closely resembling them have been found in southern Africa and south-east Asia.

The first of their bones to be recognised came in 1856 from the Neander Gorge near Düsseldorf in Germany, hence the name Neanderthal man used to describe this variety of prehistoric man who flourished from 110,000 to 30,000 years ago.

Neanderthal man looked enough like modern man for many scientists to place him in the same species, *Homo sapiens*; but he was also different enough for them to add the sub-specific name *neanderthalensis* to distinguish him from *Homo sapiens sapiens*, to give modern man his full scientific title.

At around 152 centimetres (five feet) high, Neanderthal man was evidently shorter than the average modern male. They were, nonetheless, strongly built, deep-chested people, with powerful muscles and large, capable hands. Study of their backbones and leg bones suggests that they must have walked as uprightly as we do. Perhaps the clearest evidence of how they must have differed in appearance from ourselves comes from the shaping of their thick, flat-roofed skulls, sloping foreheads, bony brow ridges, and massively jutting, yet chinless, jaws armed with big teeth.

Though their faces may often have resembled those of brutes, their brains had at least the same capacity as ours. It was their large brains that made the Neanderthalers intelligent enough to flourish in so many places, adapting their way of life in some areas to sub-Arctic cold, in others to the heat of tropical jungles.

Neanderthal man

spear with fire-hardened point

wooden club

Neanderthal men hurling rocks to kill cave bears as they emerge from their rocky lair.

HOW NEANDERTHAL MEN LIVED

Life for Neanderthal man was in many ways little different from life in the much earlier times of Peking man. Neither had any certain food supply, and were obliged to spend their days hunting and food-gathering. Probably the Neanderthalers lived in small, widely scattered family groups, for several square miles of land are often needed to support one family of hunters.

Their whole lives must have revolved round the act of hunting, which was probably undertaken by the men using wooden clubs and fire-hardened spears, pit-traps, and stone balls. These were most likely linked by thongs and hurled to trip up long-legged animals, in much the same way as the South American cowboy hurls his *bolas*.

The bones of huge mammoths and woolly rhinoceroses found at Neanderthal camp sites hint at the bravery with which these ancient hunters tackled beasts much larger and more powerful than themselves. Perhaps driven to desperation by hunger, they sometimes even attacked the fierce cave bears. Probably they hid near the bear dens, then as the animals emerged, hurled rocks at them to wound, or crush, before finishing them off with clubs and spears.

The Neanderthalers could then not only eat the bears but move inside their caves which — with fire and the skins and furs that served for clothing — gave them at least some protection against the bitter cold which gripped much of Europe during the late Ice Age.

While the men went off on hunting expeditions, their womenfolk would doubtless have tended the children, fed the camp fire, gathered roots and berries, or perhaps used stone scrapers to clean fat from the animal skins which were to serve for clothing.

A Neanderthal family band trudges across a snowbound landscape seeking new and richer hunting grounds.

HOW NEANDERTHAL MEN DIED

Sometimes Europe's Neanderthal people found they were losing the struggle for survival. When snow covered the ground, driving away the beasts they depended upon for food, hunters must have returned to their waiting womenfolk empty-handed day after day. At such times their famine-stricken families would have gathered up the few skins, tools and weapons which made up their entire belongings, and trudged off hungrily in search of new and more fruitful hunting grounds.

Hunger was a constant threat to life, but there were others equally serious, for these brawny people found that their physical strength gave no protection against injury or illness. From their skeletal remains we learn that some must have suffered cruelly from rheumatism, perhaps contracted by sleeping in damp and draughty caves, while others showed signs of bone deformities and fractures caused by falls or fights with other men or powerful animals. Superficial wounds would probably have healed of their own accord; but deep and infected injuries must have caused lingering and often fatal illnesses.

However, because Neanderthal men lived in small scattered groups he was at least reasonably free from infectious killing diseases like smallpox, plague, and cholera which swept through the densely peopled cities of later times.

But there can be no doubt that hunger, injury, and illness took a heavy toll of life, and that few if any Neanderthalers could expect to survive to middle age as we know it. By studying the fossil remains of 187 Neanderthal people who lived in Europe, one scientist has found that more than one in every three had died before his or her twentieth birthday, most of the rest before the age of 40, and of the 16 left, very few had reached 50.

Early death had been a commonplace of life throughout the hundreds of thousands of years of the Old Stone Age. But Neanderthal men evidently treated death differently from all earlier kinds of man. Instead of simply abandoning a dead relative or eating him (as Peking man would probably have done), he often scraped out a grave, laid the corpse inside it, then covered it with soil or rock to protect it from birds and beasts of prey.

One such grave in France contained the skeleton of a teenage Neanderthaler placed in a sleeping position and surrounded by stone tools and the remains of pieces of roasted meat. Carefully arranged ibex skulls and bear skulls have been found with other burials. Such discoveries strongly suggest that, unlike his less imaginative predecessors, Neanderthal man believed that life continued after death, and he accordingly made sure that when the dead awoke from their unnatural sleep they were well provided for with essentials.

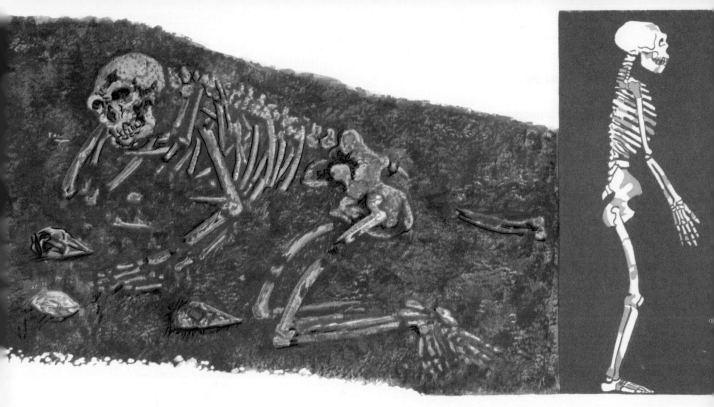

A Neanderthal skeleton and stone tools found in a prehistoric grave.

This map shows places which gave their names to the prehistoric cultures whose relics were discovered there: for instance Abbevillian, Acheulian, Chellean (Early Old Stone Age), Mousterian (Middle Old Stone Age), Aurignacian, Gravettian, Magdalenian, Solutrean (Late Old Stone Age).

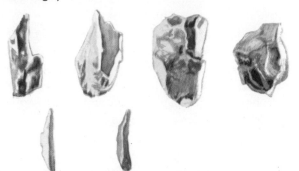

Burins and blades made from flint flakes.

HOW STONE-AGE TOOLS WERE MADE

Like the prehistoric peoples before them, Neanderthal men knew of no substance which could make harder, sharper tools than stone. But the stone tools which they made were sufficiently different from those of earlier times to earn their part of the Old Stone Age the special name of Middle Old Stone Age.

Like many men of the preceding Early Old Stone Age, Neanderthalers simply blocked out their tools by taking large pebbles or flint nodules and striking them with hammer stones so as to break off suitable flakes. But they went on to trim these flakes into their final shapes by the much more precise method of pressing on one side of the edge of the flake with a sharp piece of bone. With this pressure-flaking technique they could prise off a row of tiny regular chips. In this way the Neanderthalers produced their characteristic large D-shaped scrapers, and tri-angular points – tools with much more carefully controlled shapes than those made by most men of the Early Old Stone Age.

We shall see that pressure-flaking later helped men like ourselves to create the far more varied toolkits of the Late Old Stone Age.

All told, over a 250,000-year period, dozens of different Stone Age toolkits developed in Western Europe; the map on this page shows where some of the most important were found.

37

WAR AND CANNIBALISM

Archaeologists exploring a cave near the little Yugoslav village of Krapina discovered 500 bits of fossilised human bone, mixed with ashes and charcoal, prehistoric stone tools and animal bones. Prehistorians who studied the bones were intrigued to find that the big human leg bones had been cooked in a fire and split open lengthwise in order to reveal the tasty marrow.

However, it seems that cannibalism was by no means the only reason why Neanderthal peoples killed one another. A further discovery which throws light on this gruesome subject was made on the far side of the world, on the Indonesian island of Java.

There, near the modern village of Ngandong, archaeologists dug up the remains of a camp of Neanderthal headhunters. As they probed deep in the soil they laid bare ancient skulls, nine of which had been broken open at the base and had their jawbones removed. This and other evidence led people to think that the skulls belonged to the headhunters' victims. Possibly the heads were impaled on stakes driven into the ground round the camp and exhibited there as battle trophies.

Such discoveries suggest that rival bands of Neanderthal men were sometimes driven to fight to keep outsiders out of their precious hunting grounds; or in the outsiders' case to enter lands already occupied. Warfare, it seems, is as old as the Old Stone Age.

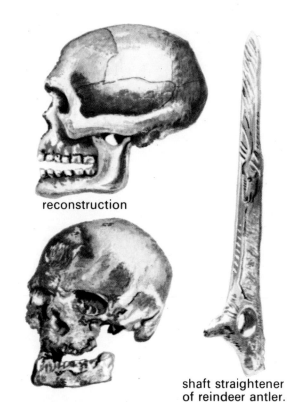

reconstruction

skull of an old Cro-Magnon man from south-west France

shaft straightener of reindeer antler.

CRO-MAGNON MAN

In 1868 at a remote place called Cro-Magnon in south-western France, workmen building a railway discovered a group of ancient skeletons in a rock shelter. They had accidentally stumbled upon the first of a series of proofs that a new kind of man had appeared in the world some 30,000 years ago, just as the great Ice Age was drawing to its close.

Cro-Magnon man, as he came to be called, had larger jaws, teeth, and a bigger face than most modern men, but, like the Eskimos, he may have enlarged these parts of his head by heavy chewing. More significantly, he was rather slightly built, walked perfectly upright, had a large brain, steep, rounded forehead, and small teeth set in a jaw with a prominent chin. In all these respects Cro-Magnon man — perhaps a remote descendant of Swanscombe man — was probably no different from many present-day Europeans; indeed he may well be among their ancestors. Since only his bones remain we cannot be sure of his skin colour, but it seems likely that he or his close relatives gave rise to all the races which now people the earth.

What is more certain is the new high level of skill and invention which Cro-Magnon and similar men brought to bear on Old Stone Age technology. With the help of the pressure-flaking technique already described, men of the Cro-Magnon type punched out a variety of stone blades for use as knives, saws, scrapers, and burins — blades with the sides obliquely sliced at one end to produce a chisel-like edge. The burin was a tool used for working with softer substances like bone, wood, and ivory from which these people made pins, awls, needles, harpoons, and hafted spears.

We might expect that Cro-Magnon man's powerful armoury would have helped him to crush Europe's less inventive Neanderthal inhabitants. But in fact these earlier men seem to have vanished from Western Europe before Cro-Magnon man appeared, perhaps killed off by a last onset of Ice Age cold.

flint blade delicately
chipped into the shape
of a laurel leaf

oil lamp made of
hollowed stone

harpoon-head made
of reindeer antler

hunter of the Late Old Stone Age

reindeer-bone needle

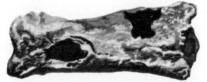

whistle made of reindeer bone

reindeer-antler linkshaft
for a socketed spear

How Solutrean hunters drove wild horses to their deaths in eastern France

THE GOLDEN AGE OF HUNTING

Cro-Magnon man and his close relatives of the Late Old Stone Age roamed the great grassy plains which once covered Russia and Europe south of the ice sheets. These pastures supported huge herds of mammoths, bison, reindeer, and wild horses. Each autumn, the great herds moved south, for instance from Russia to the Danube Valley; each spring they returned. Farther west the same kinds of big, meaty mammal browsed on the limestone hills of central France. Once a year, Europe's rivers also teemed with spawning salmon.

Perhaps never before had men seen such an abundance of food animals; certainly, never before were there men so well equipped to hunt them. For, besides spears, clubs, and stones, many hunters were now armed with spear throwers (levers which extend the distance over which a spear can be thrown), bows and arrows, fishhooks and harpoons.

We have reason to believe that many Late Old Stone Age hunters were skilled trappers, locating animal trails and capturing the beasts in dugout pits concealed with brushwood.

What was most important of all, hunters learned to pool their efforts, and so make hunting more effective than ever before. For instance, in parts of Austria, Czechoslovakia, and Russia they evidently learned to hide in narrow passes through which they knew the mammoths must pass on their spring and autumn migrations. Waiting until the mammoths were deep inside the mountains they would spring out upon the startled beasts, drive them into a gully, and rain down a hail of spears before the great hairy elephants could escape or skewer their attackers on their gleaming tusks. How successful the ancient mammoth hunters were can be judged from the bones of over 1,000 mammoths found at one Czechoslovakian camp site alone. Making clever use of natural barriers, other hunters learned how to trap a herd of horses and terrify them so that dozens leaped off a high cliff to their deaths.

By following the moving herds, Late Old Stone Age men found that there was always plenty to eat. This meant that they were able to live together in larger numbers than Neanderthal man — sometimes in caves, sometimes in temporary villages of sunken pit dwellings which they scooped from soft earth and roofed with skins and turfs. Crouching inside their dark low huts, they stitched fur skins for clothes and warmed themselves by burning bones, for wood was very scarce.

human figure carved from reindeer antler

engravings on a knife-shaped object made of reindeer antler

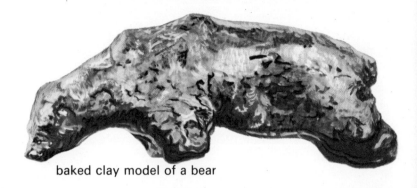

baked clay model of a bear

cow and bull aurochs engraved on a cave wall

THE DAWN OF ART

In the Late Old Stone Age a successful big-game hunt would have provided enough food to supply several families for many days, which must have meant that Cro-Magnon man and his relatives had more leisure time than hunters had ever previously enjoyed. Some people no doubt spent much of this time making weapons for the future; others, however, seem to have used their leisure hours to create the world's first works of art. Primitive man drew, painted and sculptured (both in the round and in relief) – and, in fact, he pioneered what have since become the major art forms.

Instead of canvases or cartridge paper, early man had only such unpromising drawing materials as cave walls, lumps of rock, stone slabs, bits of bone, reindeer antlers, mammoth tusks, and pebbles; for modelling clay he improvised a kind of dough by kneading animal fat into a mixture of mud and powdered bone; for paints he used charcoal and brightly coloured kinds of earth mixed with animal grease and applied with a moss brush from a palette consisting of a flat stone or a deer's shoulder blade. To engrave his drawings he used flint flakes with chisel-shaped edges.

An artist's workshop typically included a sort of hearth scooped out inside a cave, smeared with mud, and crudely roofed to produce a primitive oven where he could bake his sculptured models. Around it lay the bits of bone, tusk, horn, and antler on which he worked, and the flint toolkit required for carving or engraving. Artists carried out much of their work deep in remote caves, where they laboured by the dim light of stone lamps filled with animal fat, which burnt with a black stinking smoke. The only light from such lamps would be a lurid, flickering glow upon the rocky walls.

In these almost secret places, artists painted hunting scenes alive with such beasts as cattle, bison, mammoths, horses; they also made realistic statuettes of beasts and stylised ones of people; and they drew animals in outline on stone, bone, ivory, and antlers. Some art historians consider that the ways in which they depicted the proportions and movements of living creatures have never been surpassed.

Let us look more closely at this first great period in the history of art, which appeared some 30,000 years ago, reached its peak some 15,000 years ago, then degenerated into stereotyped pattern-making before dying out in the last phases of the Old Stone Age.

STRANGE SCULPTURES FROM THE LATE STONE AGE

Bison, cave bears, lions, reindeer, snowy owls, wild horses, and mammoths beautifully shaped in clay and other substances show the skill with which ancient sculptors made realistic copies of the mammals and birds inhabiting their world.

These lifelike models are the more remarkable when we consider that they were made without the help of binoculars or photographic records – in fact solely from remembered glimpses of beasts that would have been far too shy knowingly to let any man approach them closely.

It must therefore seem particularly strange that the creature which the sculptors knew best of all – man himself – was modelled less realistically than any other. What is more he, or rather she, was always depicted in the same curious fashion. The illustrations on this page show grotesque female figurines of the kind that were typical of Old Stone Age sculptures.

The so-called Venus of Willendorf, found in Austria, and one of the best known of all such ancient works of art, is a carved stone figurine less than six inches high, showing a stumpy, thickset woman with big breasts, belly, and buttocks, stumpy limbs, and a faceless head surmounted by a shock of curly hair.

The Lady of Lespugue, an ancient French 'Venus', was carved from a mammoth tusk. Little larger than the Venus of Willendorf, she has a tiny featureless head and relatively slim chest but a large abdomen, big buttocks, and fat thighs below which are tiny tapering legs.

A third famous Venus figurine from Vestonice in Czechoslovakia was made from a paste of bone ash, soil, and animal fat and baked in an oven. She, too, has thighs out of all proportion to her body as a whole, yet only a blank for a face.

Found scattered across Europe from Russia to France, such figurines of carved ivory and stone and baked, modelled clay, all show naked or near naked and often pregnant women, and exaggerate those parts of their bodies connected with bearing and suckling babies. This makes it certain that they represent an ancient veneration of motherhood, in an age when the father's part in producing children was dimly understood if grasped at all. Woman alone, it was clear, had the ability to produce new life inside her body. The prehistoric Venuses, then, were recognition of this great biological fact, and served as symbols of that female fruitfulness upon which the survival of all human life depends.

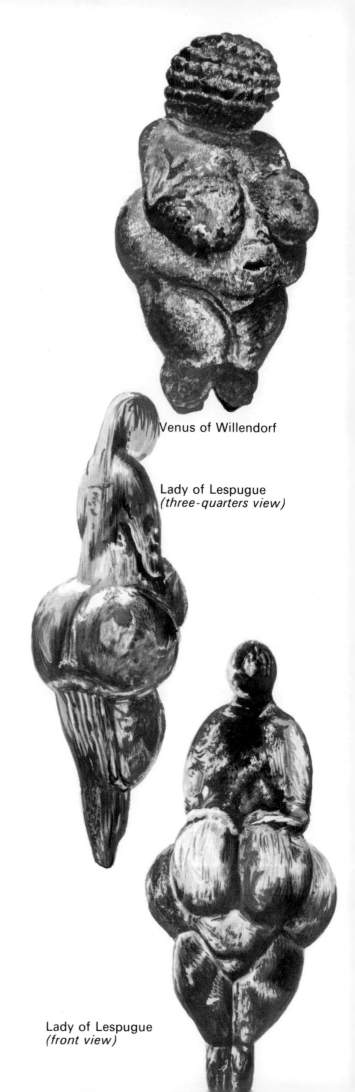

Venus of Willendorf

Lady of Lespugue
(three-quarters view)

Lady of Lespugue
(front view)

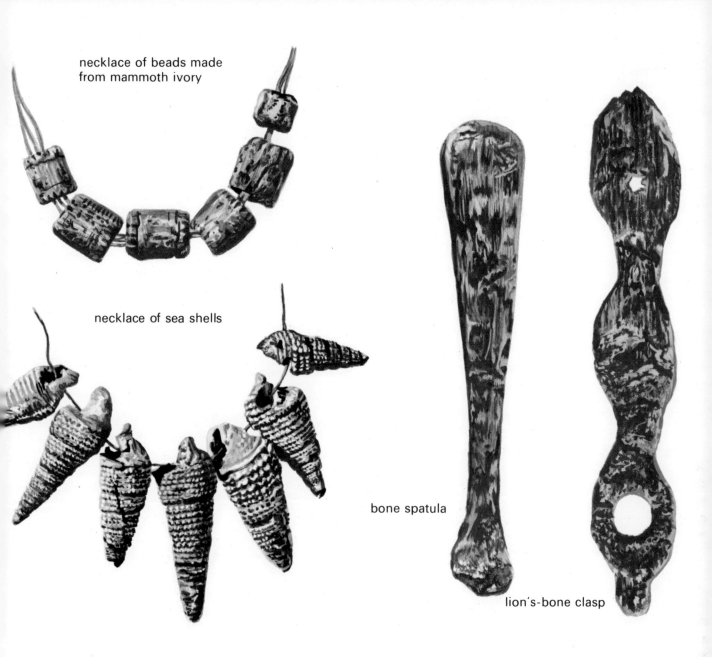

necklace of beads made
from mammoth ivory

necklace of sea shells

bone spatula

lion's-bone clasp

DESIGN AND DECORATION IN THE OLD STONE AGE

In the great flowering of art which distinguishes the Late Old Stone Age, men began seeing new ways of using the substances and shapes around them. At the very root of their technology was this new awareness of how to transform the shapes of naturally occurring objects into tools specially designed to serve different purposes – ranging from spear throwers and spear straighteners to bone forks, whistles made of reindeer bone, cups improvised from reindeer skulls, hooks for fastening fur clothes, body-hugging trousered suits, and strange objects which we know as staffs of office.

At the same time their interest in shapes for purely decorative purposes spilled over into the embellishment of the tools they made, and even of pieces of bone, tusk, and antler which lacked any specifically useful shape. Such decorations, scratched lovingly with sharp-edged flint burins or gravers, showed an awareness of perspective and they ranged from semi-abstract outlines to sophisticated animal shapes. A whole zoo of animals was created in this way, including mammoths, aurochs, bison, reindeer, horses, woolly rhinoceroses, chamois, ibexes, hares, bears, and boars; and more rarely, wolves, otters, foxes, reptiles, birds and fishes.

Just as they began ornamenting their tools, so men now began to decorate their own bodies, evidently painting them with coloured clay, and adorning them with necklaces and bracelets made from sea shells, small cylindrical bits of mammoth ivory, and the sharply pointed canine teeth of bears, wolves, and foxes. Very likely these body ornaments also served a magical purpose, for instance as talismans protecting their wearers against disease or injury of any kind.

Part of a group of bison painted by prehistoric artists in the French cave of Niaux.

ART GALLERIES UNDER THE GROUND

Prehistoric artists proved themselves master sculptors and engravers; yet, unquestionably, it is their paintings for which we remember them. Most of these faded deep inside forgotten caves, and vanished long ago, but some were protected from the erosive action of wind and rain and have survived remarkably preserved. Of the many caves where prehistoric artists worked, two in particular are world famous as treasure houses of prehistoric painting. Curiously, their pictures were discovered largely by the chance wandering of children.

In 1879, a Spanish archaeologist was probing a cave near Altamira in northern Spain when his small daughter cried out *'Toros! Toros!'* (Bulls! Bulls!) and excitedly pointed to bull-like figures of bison painted in red ochre and black manganese shading on the cave roof. Further search by her father soon revealed a whole herd of bison bulls and cows each of them up to 180 centimetres (6 feet) long. These rough sketches had been engraved in the limestone then painted over, some 15,000 years ago by artists of the Magdalenian period.

In 1940 at Lascaux in southwest France, another remarkable discovery was made because a rabbit-hunting dog fell down a hole left by an uprooted tree and a boy went in search of his dog. The boy found himself in a cave whose walls glowed with engraved and brightly painted oxen, horses, red deer, ibexes, and bison — a subterranean art gallery created by Gravettian painters who had laboured deep underground some 18,000 years before.

Experts studying the ancient animal paintings of Altamira, Lascaux, Niaux, and other caves, soon realised that many were not merely portraits: they showed beasts caught in traps or with spears projecting from their bodies. Some paintings even bore marks where real spears had been hurled against them. It became almost certain that the artists had painted these animals from no simple love of art but because they believed that by making a picture of an animal caught or killed by hunters they could actually bring about such an event. Painting (and sculpting), then, was often an act of magic; probably one of many performed in secret caves under the supervision of a sorcerer (perhaps the painter himself). One such person was vividly depicted in the French cave of Trois Frères wearing a stag's antlers, a horse's tail, a bear's paws, and an animal skin. Perhaps such sorcerers took the rôles of wild beasts and acted out a successful hunt in much the same way as some Australian aborigines do at the present time.

THE MIDDLE STONE AGE

Cave paintings, sculptures, and ancient burials like the Italian one illustrated here, show that for more than 15,000 years men of the Late Old Stone Age lived and hunted over Europe south of the great ice sheet. But by 15,000 years ago a great climatic change had set in which was to have enormous consequences for the ancient Europeans and other peoples.

Bit by bit summers became warmer, winters less cold. Year by year, the ice sheet shrank back towards the Arctic, shedding huge quantities of water into the existing oceans, raising the level of the seas, and drowning low-lying coasts. Australia was cut off from New Guinea, Spain from Africa, North America from Siberia, and Great Britain from mainland Europe.

The warmer climate had an effect on the plants and animals of the Northern Hemisphere. Trees now flourished in lands which had been too cold to support any plant life except for small, shallow-rooted mosses, lichens, grasses, and shrubs. As forests swallowed up their pastures, the big animal herds were faced with starvation or emigration; reindeer drifted northwards to the Arctic edge of Europe; horses moved east into the great plains of Russia.

Europe's Stone Age hunters, robbed of their great walking larders, were forced to find new ways of feeding themselves from the swamps and forests which now covered what had once been open country. The large, strong spears which were once so useful for killing huge beasts like bison and mammoths were of little use for hunting fish, shellfish and wildfowl. Accordingly, men had to develop a new toolkit of finer, smaller weapons.

Now, for the first time, bows and arrows became widely used. At the same time men learned to produce *composite* weapons such as fish harpoons; their barbed heads were slotted with tiny stone blades, or microliths, into a shaft of wood or bone.

With the help of the world's first true axes, which had heads crudely shaped from lumps of flint, forest dwellers began to fell trees, clearing the ground to make travel easier and perhaps, incidentally, finding out that the felled trees would be useful for travel on water. Logs then became dugout canoes — perhaps the world's first boats. Men also learned to make use of trees for building shelters.

At the same time he now sought help from dogs — probably the first animals to be domesticated. Originally camp scavengers, wild dogs learned that by sniffing out quarry in the tangled vegetation of swamp and forest, they would gain food rewards from human hunters. Eventually, in association with

Skeletons of an old woman and child buried in a cave in northern Italy in Late Old Stone Age times.

man, dogs became tame enough to retrieve ducks shot down by arrows over water.

As we have just described men changed their way of life and in doing so they left behind the Palaeolithic (Old Stone) Age and moved into the Mesolithic (Middle Stone) Age. By no means all peoples reached this stage at the same time; for example the new microlithic toolkits probably originated in Africa and spread to Europe. Nor did the Mesolithic Age end simultaneously everywhere; Kalahari Bushmen and some Australian aborigines still live Mesolithic lives.

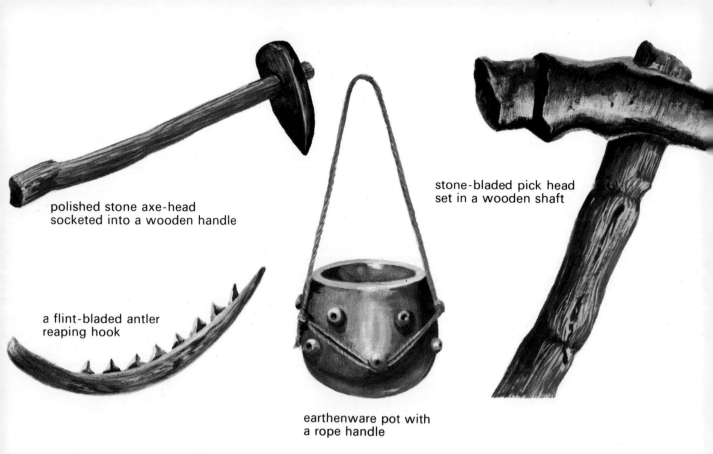

polished stone axe-head
socketed into a wooden handle

a flint-bladed antler
reaping hook

earthenware pot with
a rope handle

stone-bladed pick head
set in a wooden shaft

THE NEW STONE AGE

About 10,000 years ago, Stone Age peoples living somewhere between Turkey and India made what has been called the greatest discovery of all: how to control their food supply.

Instead of relying on chance encounters with meaty animals like wild sheep, goats, and cattle, some hunters learned to trap wild flocks and herds in natural ravines and keep them alive until they needed fresh supplies of meat. By breeding from the most docile creatures they produced the world's first flocks and herds of farm animals. Hunters who took this step had turned herdsmen, devoting their lives to tending animals in return for a reliable supply of meat, milk, hair and hides.

Meanwhile south-west Asian peoples were also learning to reap wild wheat and barley with sickles made of flint microliths slotted into a stick, like teeth in a jawbone. Eventually they found that they could produce more of such edible grain if they cleared wild plants from plots of land, replaced them with wheat or barley seeds, and protected the seedlings from weeds and pests until they produced ripe ears of grain. The cultivators could then harvest more than enough for their immediate needs and store the surplus in special pits, or pots made from clay hardened in a furnace. Such people were the first farmers – men and women forced by their crops to abandon the old wandering life of their hunter ancestors, and to settle down in what became the first villages.

The assured food supply which came from raising crops and animals freed some people from the constant search for food, and gave them more spare time to devise useful objects such as digging sticks, quern stones for grinding grain into flour, ovens for baking bread and pottery, and clothing made from woven plant fibres. Moreover men now found time to give their stone tools the finely ground finish which earns this last and shortest period of the great Stone Age the name of Neolithic (New Stone) Age, which took place about 2,500 years before the birth of Christ.

With a relatively reliable food supply and tools for gathering, storing and cooking it, more Neolithic peoples could live off a given patch of land than almost any of the Mesolithic or Palaeolithic peoples before them. Where farming and herding took root, then, man's numbers began multiplying rapidly. This first happened in south-west Asia. But the idea of farming spread to Europe, Africa, and eastern Asia; and in the Americas it evidently sprang up independently.

After a million years of wresting an uncertain living from a hostile world, man had at last learned how to work *with* nature to his own advantage. When this happened, prehistoric times drew towards their close, and the way of life which we call civilisation was about to begin. Starting on page 95 we shall trace civilisation from its birth to its maturity.

OCEANS THAT GIRDLE THE EARTH

Step by step we have so far traced the slow changes which gave rise to the kinds of men and animals which now inhabit the earth. Before we follow the fascinating path of invention and discovery which was to make men like ourselves masters of all other living things, let us look more closely at the natural world which formed the setting for their achievements. Let us start with the sea: the cradle of life, controller of climates, and sculptor of coasts.

Although all the great bodies of sea are connected, geographers divide them for convenience into four great oceans: the Pacific Ocean, Indian Ocean, Atlantic Ocean, and Arctic Ocean. Besides these oceans and their deep inlets, there are smaller, landlocked seas such as the Caspian Sea and Aral Sea of Central Asia. Altogether, seas cover over seven-tenths of the earth.

Anyone who has tasted a drop of sea water knows that the oceans consist of more than just water. Their briny taste shows that they contain a large proportion of salt; but chemists have also proved that they contain other substances; in fact all the minerals found on the earth's surface, including magnesium, sulphur, and gold. Such substances gradually accumulated in the seas as they were washed out of the earth's rocks by rivers. Over millions of years the substances have steadily built up their concentrations until in some places (for instance the Dead Sea of Israel and Jordan, which is 400 metres below sea level), they have made the sea water so dense that even non-swimmers are buoyed up and drowning is almost impossible.

Minerals dissolved in sea water play an immensely important part in building the bodies of sea plants and animals as do the gases dissolved in the seas; plants depend on carbon dioxide dissolved in sea water. But the pure water itself is also vital for life, for plants break it down chemically into the gases hydrogen and oxygen as part of their food-making processes.

47

THE OCEAN BED

Just by looking at the ocean's surface we can gain little idea of the depth of water beneath the waves. But scientists using special echo-sounding devices have shown that different parts of the ocean vary enormously in depth — from no more than a metre (a few feet) where gently sloping beaches meet the sea, to the immense depth of about 11,000 metres (36,200 feet) in the Challenger Deep of the Pacific Ocean — a trench so great that if Everest, the world's highest mountain, were lowered into it, its peak would lie a mile below the ocean surface.

Careful plotting of the ocean depths has enabled cartographers to draw up maps of the sea bed. These show that instead of looking like the smooth bottom of a bath, the floor of the sea is broken up by underwater mountain ranges, volcanoes, cliffs, and valleys, as depicted by the diagram on these pages.

Off many of the shores of the continents, the sea bed starts as a gently sloping shelf which stretches outwards in some areas for several hundred miles. Then it ends abruptly in a steep underwater slope, gashed by great ravines. Beyond, lies the deep sea floor, broken here and there by great submarine volcanoes and underwater mountain ranges, including the enormous Mid Atlantic Ridge, 16,000 kilometres (10,000 miles) long. Great layers of mud cover the ocean floor, much of it made from decayed sea plants and shells, skeletons, and teeth of dead animals. Below this ooze lies a thin layer of hard basalt rock, 'floating' on the semi-liquid rock beneath the earth's crust. As our diagram suggests, this crust is far thinner beneath the oceans than beneath the continents, which rest upon thick granite layers.

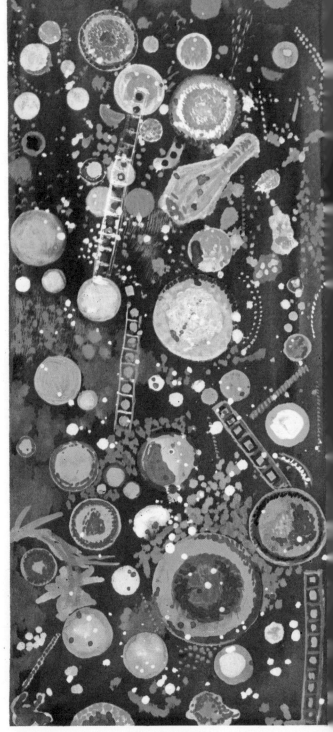

Section through the oceans and the earth's crust.

Plankton shown much magnified.

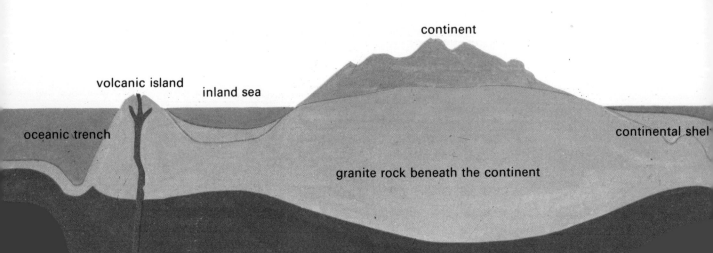

continent

volcanic island

inland sea

oceanic trench

continental shel

granite rock beneath the continent

LIFE IN THE OCEANS

By netting samples of plants and animals from different depths in the seas, scientists have detected different life zones.

Tiny plants and animals which drift about with surface tides and currents make up the life group known as *plankton*. Most of its life forms can be seen as individual organisms only with a microscope. With its help, a drop of plain sea water is transformed into a world of tiny geometric shapes like those pictured on the facing page. Most of the tiny plants in such a drop of water are the kind known as diatoms. Diatoms help to feed tiny planktonic creatures like copepods, radiolarians, arrow worms, and baby jellyfish, which range in colour from transparent to filmy blue and pink.

Among and below the plankton lives the life group known as *nekton*: free-swimming animals including fishes, squids, octopuses, whales and dolphins. Their differing needs for food, pressure, salt, temperature and so on mean that different nektonic creatures live at different levels — for instance flying fish at the surface; but luminous angler fishes in the dark depths.

Benthos, the third great life group in the oceans, consists of bottom-dwelling plants and animals. Seaweeds and other rooted underwater plants can grow no deeper than the sun's rays penetrate; but worms and other creatures of the sea bed flourish in the remotest depths of the oceans.

Although different members of the plankton, nekton, and benthos groups live at different levels in the ocean, they form part of a food cycle in which the larger creatures eat plants or smaller creatures, and plant and animal remains nourish plankton.

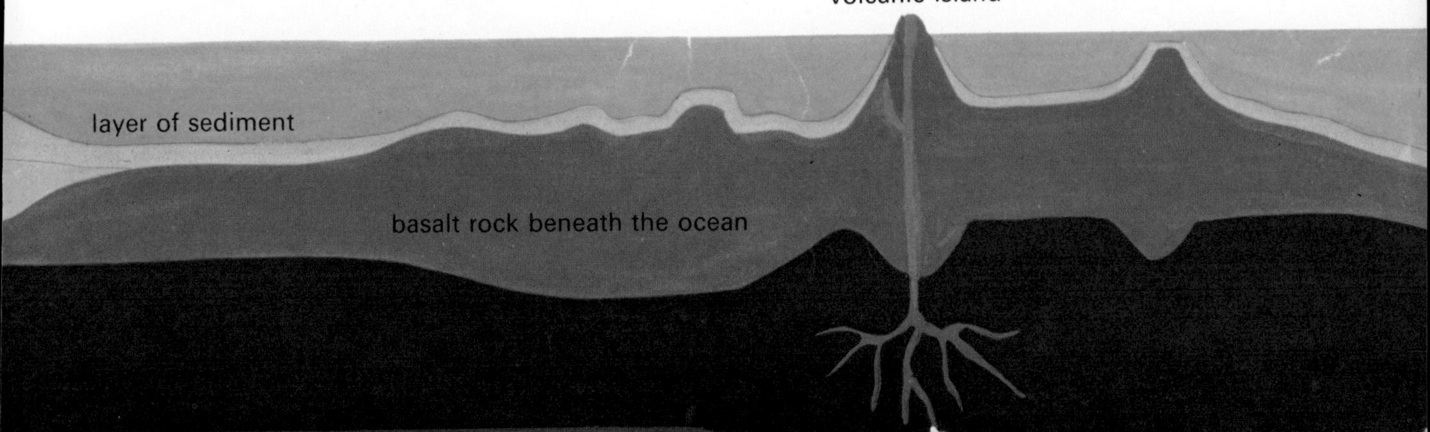

Fishes adapted for life at different levels in the sea.

volcanic island

layer of sediment

basalt rock beneath the ocean

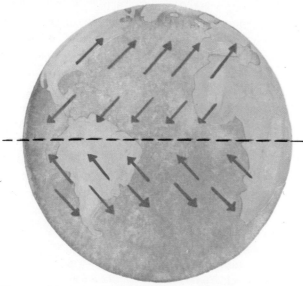

The earth's rotation (short black arrows) deflects winds and ocean currents (long black arrows) so that those flowing from the equator (broken line) trend east, those flowing towards it trend west — the so-called Coriolis effect.

THE RESTLESS OCEAN

On a calm day the glassy-surfaced sea may seem completely motionless, but this appearance is deceptive, for the seas are always moving.

Great belts of surface water endlessly circle the oceans north and south of the equator, rather like rivers in the seas, but far larger than any river found on land. Some of these currents start where the sun warms up the surface waters near the equator, making the surface water lighter than that deeper down. Winds blow the warm surface waters out over the cooler, heavier waters farther north and south of the equator. However, in the Northern Hemisphere, wind direction and the earth's spin deflect their northward flow so that they drift northeastward. Eventually, the water in such currents cools, mingles with cold polar water, and flows back southwestwards to the equator in a great curving path which rejoins the northeastern stream to form a ceaseless clockwise flow. In the Southern Hemisphere the same kind of movement take place, but in an anticlockwise direction. Some of the water lost in outward flowing surface currents is replaced by surface counter currents from the opposite direction. Other surface water is replaced by colder water from the depths, which wells up even in the tropics and which brings vast amounts of salts that help to feed huge populations of fish and fish-eating seabirds.

Largest of all surface currents is the great Antarctic Circumpolar Current — a river of cold which sweeps ceaselessly round the frozen coasts of Antarctica. But the best-known current is the great Gulf Stream — a belt of warm water equal in size to one thousand Mississippis — which flows from Florida northeastwards across the Atlantic Ocean to warm the British Isles and parts of northwest Europe.

Top and bottom arrows show wind belts formed as warm air from the equator rises and flows out towards the poles; inner arrows show wind belts formed as cool air moves in to take its place.

Three forces (the sun's heat, winds, and the Coriolis effect) create a clockwise flow of surface currents north of the equator and an anticlockwise flow south of the equator.

This section through the oceans shows surface water heated by the sun's rays (red arrows) flowing from the equator towards the poles, and being replaced by deep, cold, polar water.

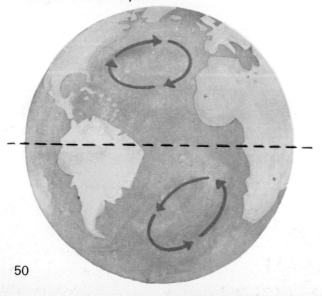

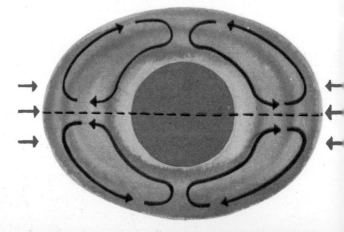

THE WAVES AND TIDES

Although the great ocean currents may be invisible to the watcher on the seashore, he cannot fail to notice movements of the sea's surface produced by waves and tides.

Waves are usually formed by the effect of wind on water and (as our diagrams show) they tend to travel *through* the water, moving its particles up and down rather than along. Waves can range in size from tiny wavelets raised by a light breeze, to great 18 metre- (60-feet) high storm waves piled up by the force of storm winds blowing unchecked across many hundred miles of open ocean. Even more dramatic are the waves called *tsunami*. Thrown up by earthquakes and volcanoes these devastating walls of water, up to 60 metres (200 feet) high and travelling at nearly 800 kilometres (500 miles) an hour, can cross oceans to engulf and destroy coastal areas. In 1883, more than 36,000 people died from the great waves unleashed by the eruption of Krakatoa, the Indonesian volcanic island. Ordinary waves are not so dramatically destructive, yet as they break on the sea shore they are powerful enough to shift sand and rocks, slowly but certainly erode some shorelines and build out others into the sea.

While waves merely riffle the surface of the sea, the tides imperceptibly alter the level of the oceans which rise and fall twice a day. These tidal movements result largely from the moon's gravitational pull upon the oceans. The water bulges outwards on the earth's side nearest the moon, and on the far side away from the influence of the moon, there is a compensating displacement. When sun, moon, and earth are all aligned, the combined pull of sun and moon causes full *spring* tides; when sun and moon are at right angles, weak *neap* tides occur.

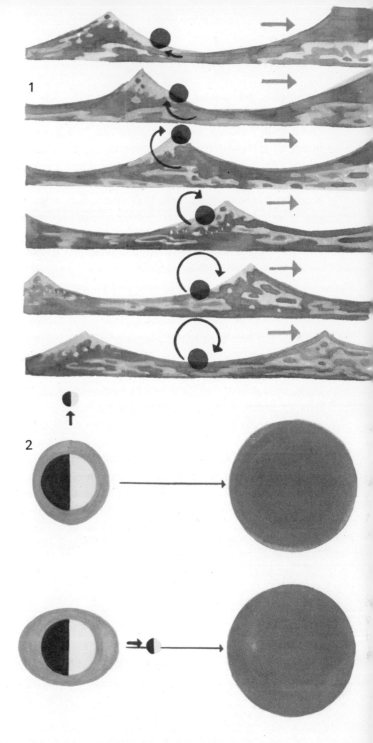

1. When the wave displaces the floating ball, the ball moves up, then down, rather than along, indicating how waves affect the water through which they pass.

2. Small neap tides occur when the tug of sun and moon cancel one another out (above); large spring tides result when both pull together.

3. A section through the sea, showing how waves change shape as they near a shelving shore.

UNWEAVING THE WEB OF LIFE

If you peer into a tidal pool at the sea's edge you will quite likely see the kind of plant life and animal community shown in the picture on this page: a forest of different types of seaweed, starfish creeping across the plants, and small fishes darting about.

If you examine a grassy bank, a heathy moor, a woodland grove, you will find that each type of place, or habitat, has its own community of plants and animals. Within each community the different plants and animals have their own special niche, all of them inter-relating to each other.

The incredible variety of the earth's living things can seem bewildering. Yet on closer study of the ways in which they are constructed, clear patterns appear. For example some plants and some animals have bodies made of one cell only; others have bodies made from many cells. A careful study of such similarities and differences has helped scientists to place them in special groups according to how closely they appear to be related to each other.

The first great division of the living world separates the plants and animals. All living things which have a cell wall as well as a membrane, have no fixed number of body parts, and take their food directly from minerals and gases, belong to the *plant kingdom*. Living things which have a cell membrane but no cell walls, have a special number of body parts, mostly move about, and can only obtain their food ready-made, belong to the *animal kingdom*. Scientists subdivide each of these great groups in many ways: on the next pages we shall be looking at some of the best-known subdivisions in the animal kingdom.

Not all scientists agree about just how to divide up the animal kingdom. Many split it into two great subkingdoms: the *Protozoa* (one-celled animals), and *Metazoa* (many-celled animals). Each of these subkingdoms is itself divided and its divisions subdivided. For example, instead of simply saying that man is a member of the *Metazoa*, we separate him from all other metazoan animals by saying that he belongs to the species *sapiens* in the genus *Homo*, of the family *Hominidae*, in the order *Primates*, of the class *Mammalia* (mammals), in the subphylum *Vertebrata* (vertebrates), of the phylum or tribe *Chordata* (chordates) — one of many into which the *Metazoa* are divided.

But man is one of the most complex creatures. At the lower end of the scale come 20,000 species of *Protozoa*, tiny one-celled creatures invisible to the naked eye. Protozoa have no special organs for eating, moving, reproducing, and so on, and they live mainly in water. They include amoeba, a tiny blob of jelly, and the slipper-shaped paramecium which swims by thrashing the water with tiny hairs, or cilia (more than two thousand of them).

A community of plants and animals in a shallow sea.

LOWLY CREATURES OF THE WATERS

We began our tour through the animal kingdom with its smallest, simplest members — the one-celled protozoans. The many-celled members of the *Metazoa*, the second animal subkingdom, are larger creatures. However, many of these are also simply constructed, especially the *sponges* which grow in colonies on the floor of the sea. Sponges are plant-like creatures with skeletons made up of fibrous cells that support and protect the soft, inner cells. Whip-like structures in the cell walls drive water-borne food particles through the tubes and cavities which are the sponge's digestive tract.

By comparison with the simple sponges, the *coelenterates* are rather more complicated, and their cells are grouped as tissues. The soft-bodied jellyfishes, colourful sea anemones and corals belong to this big tribe.

Anemones have tentacles covered with cells designed for stinging their prey, and a simple nervous system. The anemone's system of nerves ensures that they can extend their tentacles to capture prey (see illustrations 3 and 5), retract them to avoid danger (2) or to pull a captured fish into the mouth of their digestive cavity (4). Anemones spend their lives rooted to one spot; but a jellyfish (1) can move upwards by closing its umbrella-shaped body and squirting water downwards.

1. JELLYFISH
2, 3, 4, and 5. SEA ANEMONES

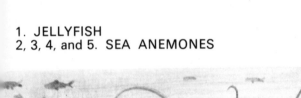

53

The sponges and coelenterates which we have just described represent two of many tribes of invertebrates (without backbones), which also include the *comb jellies*, *bryozoans* (plant-like animals that grow on underwater rocks), *brachiopods* (certain two-shelled shellfish), and *annelids* (worms whose bodies are made of many segments). But among the best known tribes of invertebrates are those represented on this page.

At first glance, the sea urchin and starfish could scarcely look less alike: the sea urchin has a ball-shaped body protected by long, sharp spikes bristling out from a limestone shell made up of hundreds of interlocking plates. The starfish on the other hand has five tapering arm-like projections. However, both are *echinoderms* — creatures whose common features include spiny skins, bodies encased in a leathery skin or limestone shell made up of small plates, the same sort of overall symmetrical design, separate male and female sexes, a simple digestive system and nervous system, and often hollow tube feet which they use to move about for food-gathering. Many echinoderms are beautifully coloured.

The squid (like the octopus) is a *mollusc*, although unlike most of these soft-bodied creatures it has ten feet instead of one. Instead of growing a protective limy shell as do the clams, oysters, and snails, for protection it relies upon rapid swimming.

Our crayfish represents the *arthropods*, a huge tribe of creatures with jointed limbs, outside skeletons, and a developed nervous system with eyes; it includes not only sea-dwelling crabs, shrimps, and barnacles, but also the largely land-dwelling spiders, centipedes and insects.

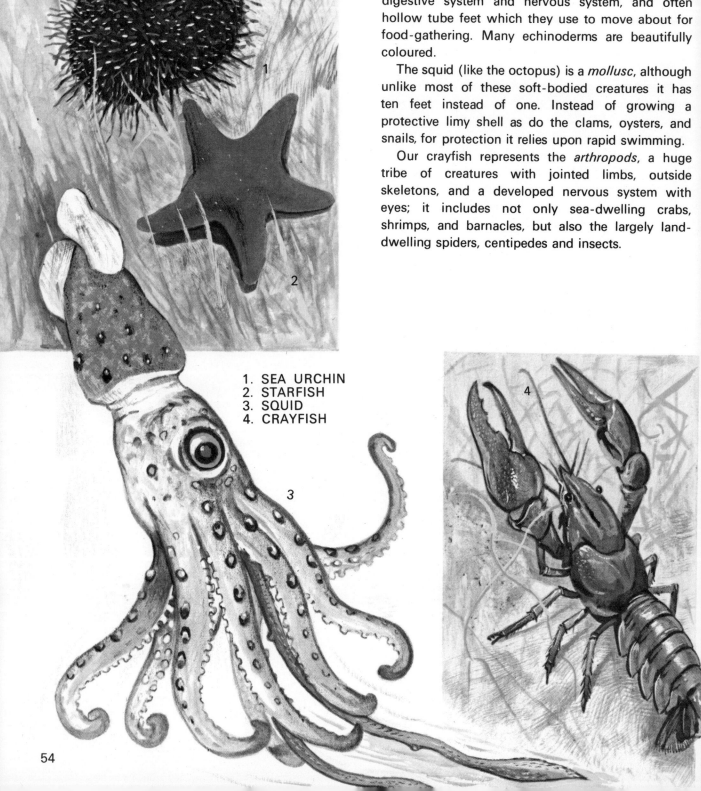

1. SEA URCHIN
2. STARFISH
3. SQUID
4. CRAYFISH

THE FISHES

Compared with the crayfish, starfish, and other spineless creatures that live in water, the fishes with backbones are superbly designed for swimming. Generally speaking, fishes are cold-blooded creatures with backbones, and a scaly torpedo-shaped body with fins, which spend their lives entirely in fresh or salt water breathing dissolved air by means of gills. By no means all fishes fit into this pattern exactly, but all belong to the vertebrate sub-tribe of the tribe *Chordata* (animals with a notochord – a cord-like precursor of the backbone). Four of the eight classes of vertebrates are fishes: *Agnatha* (jawless fishes), *Cyclostomata* (fishes with fixed open mouths, like lampreys and hagfishes), *Chondrichthyes* (fishes with cartilage rather than bone), and *Osteichthyes* (bony fishes). Most of the 30,000 living fish species belong to the last two groups.

The cartilaginous fishes include the sharp-toothed sharks, renowned as savage killers that live in the seas – eating anything from small fishes to any swimmer unlucky enough to cross their path. The white and blue sharks are sometimes man-eaters. By contrast the huge whale shark, which grows up to 18 metres (60 feet) long and is the largest fish in the world, is entirely harmless to man, browsing only on small sea creatures and plants.

The bony fishes include all those that man commonly hunts for food and keeps in aquariums. The four shown on this page give some idea of the immense variety of shapes and colorations of bony fishes. Most have colours that serve as perfect camouflage for their particular habitat and most are also perfectly streamlined for rapid swimming. Fastest of all is reckoned to be the big Atlantic sailfish, which has been timed at over 96 kilometres (60 miles) an hour.

5. EEL
6. CHAR
7. MACKEREL
8. BLUE SHARK
9. TETRADACHIRUM MELANURUS

SEA MAMMALS

Rather misleadingly, some of the most fishlike of sea-dwelling creatures are not fishes at all but mammals which have become ideally adapted for life in water (for *mammals*, see page 68). In the slow course of adaptation to life in water, the limbs of whales and dolphins have evolved into flippers or tails. The water's buoyancy has also allowed some to reach a weight and size greater than that achieved by any land-dwelling animal. For instance, the blue whale, or rorqual, measures up to 30 metres (100 feet), and weighs as much as 152 tonnes (150 tons). It is not only the largest animal alive today, but probably the largest animal that ever lived.

Sea mammals belong to three different orders: the *cetaceans*, *carnivores*, *sirenians*. Cetaceans are almost hairless, fish-shaped mammals with a thick fat layer called blubber beneath their skin, flipper-like forelimbs, no hind limbs but a tail with fins. They breathe air through lungs but spend their entire lives in the sea, where their young are born alive and fed with their mother's milk. The sperm whale, narwhal, killer whale, porpoise and dolphin are known as toothed whales. The last three are among the most intelligent of all animals: captive dolphins readily learn to obey simple commands and to perform fairly complex acrobatic tricks.

Instead of teeth, the baleen whales have horny plates fringed with bristles which strain from the water the shrimps and other small sea creatures which form their food. Baleen whales include the huge-headed right whale, and they range in size from the great blue whale, the largest and fastest-swimming of all, down to the pygmy right whale, less than one-thirtieth the weight of the blue whale.

Seals, sea-lions, and walruses all belong to the *Pinnipedia*, a suborder of the order *Carnivora*. Unlike cetaceans, these torpedo-shaped sea mammals always return to land for breeding; indeed sea lions can move quite quickly overland on their muscular flippers, but the short stubby limbs of the seals make them poor land travellers. Of all seals the largest is the elephant seal which weighs over 3 tonnes (3 tons) and can be 6·5 metres (21 feet) long.

The dugong and manatee both belong to the *Sirenia* — the third sea-mammal order. They have flipper forelimbs, no hind limbs, and a tail fin; their curiously human shape perhaps gave rise to the old legends of mermaids.

1. SEA LION
2. WALRUS
3. SEAL
4. RIGHT WHALE
5. PYGMY RIGHT WHALE
6. BLUE WHALE
7. KILLER WHALE
8. NARWHAL
9. DOLPHIN

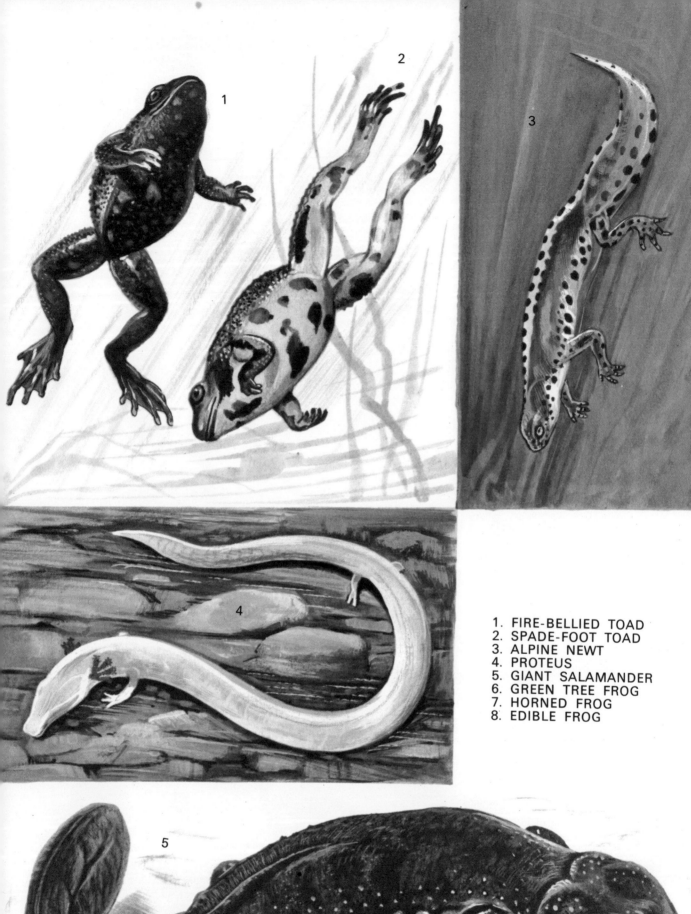

1. FIRE-BELLIED TOAD
2. SPADE-FOOT TOAD
3. ALPINE NEWT
4. PROTEUS
5. GIANT SALAMANDER
6. GREEN TREE FROG
7. HORNED FROG
8. EDIBLE FROG

THE AMPHIBIANS

The sea mammals shown on the two previous pages are descended from land animals which took to the water. Amphibians, on the other hand, form a class of animal descended from bony fishes which took to the land.

Like fishes, amphibians have backbones, and a temperature which changes with that of their surroundings. Also like fishes, amphibians hatch or are born in water or damp surroundings, and start life as fish-like gill-breathing tadpoles. But instead of hard scales, most possess soft, moist skin. As they mature they lose their fish-like shape and grow limbs, develop lungs, and lose their gills. Many adult amphibians leave the water, to return only for breeding.

Scientists place amphibians in three orders: *Apoda* (small, limbless burrowing creatures called caecilians which live in the tropics); *Caudata* (tailed amphibians like newts and salamanders, which have legs); *Salientia* (frogs and toads: short-bodied amphibians in which the adults are tailless, and have long back legs for hopping).

Tailed amphibians range in size from the 76 millimetre- (3-inch) long alpine newt which lives in ponds and streams of mainland Europe, to the 305 millimetres (5 feet) giant salamander, found in mountain streams of China and Japan. The tailed amphibians also include the curious olm or proteus, a blind, eel-like cave dweller that grows limbs but keeps its gills.

Frogs and toads are also very varied. In Europe they range from the tiny 25 millimetre (1 inch) fire-bellied toad and green tree frog to the 100 millimetre edible frog and 125 millimetre marsh frog (4 and 5 inches respectively); tropical frogs and toads are often much larger. The South American horned toad is big enough to eat mice and birds.

6

7

8

THE REPTILES

Lizards, snakes, tortoises, and crocodiles are all reptiles — a class of vertebrates midway between fishes and mammals. Like fishes, reptiles are cold-blooded backboned creatures with scales; but they breathe with lungs not gills, and most kinds have four well developed legs and live on land. Unlike their amphibian ancestors they have *dry* skins, and many lay eggs which are protected by limy or leathery shells. Therefore, while amphibians must live and breed in damp surroundings, reptiles can live and breed in warm dry places — indeed, without warmth most would die, although those adapted to cool climates survive the winter by hibernating.

Of the 15 reptile orders that developed, only four have survived, but they embrace about 6,250 species. Of these, some 6,000 belong to the *Squamata* (snakes and lizards), over 200 to the *Chelonia* (turtles and tortoises), over 20 to the *Crocodilia* (crocodiles and alligators), and only one (the tuatara) to the *Rhynchocephalia*.

The *Squamata* include an astonishing variety of creatures. For instance, although most lizards have four well developed legs, the slow worm and some other lizards are legless and move and look like snakes. Lizards also vary enormously in size, from tiny geckos of 76 millimetres (3 inches) to the fierce dragonlike Komodo monitor which grows longer than a man and weighs up to twice as much. Perhaps the most intriguing of all lizards are the swivel-eyed chameleons which change colour to blend protectively with their surroundings. Unlike lizards, snakes are limbless reptiles with loosely linked jaw-bones that allow them to swallow creatures larger than their own heads. Snakes range in size from the South American anaconda, measuring over 9 metres (30 feet), to the West Indian worm snake, fully grown at under 127 millimetres (5 inches). Many snakes are harmless to man, but some, including the cobras, have poison fangs.

Chelonians include the land-dwelling tortoises and aquatic turtles, both encased in protective shells. Giant land tortoises can weigh over 400 kilograms (900 pounds), leatherback turtles twice as much.

Crocodilians are great lizard-like creatures with tough hides, long saw-toothed jaws, and tails flattened for swimming in the warm tropical waters where they live.

Unique among all reptiles is the lizard-like tuatara, last survivor of the order *Rhynchocephalia* (beak heads), and now found only on remote islands off New Zealand.

1. TUATARA
2. CHAMELEON
3. GIANT TORTOISE
4. COBRA
5. CROCODILE

1. EMERALD CUCKOO
2. SHAG
3. DELALANDE'S GREEN PIGEON
4. FRANCOLIN
5. OSTRICH

6. WHITE-BREASTED WATERHEN
7. SOUTHERN CARMINE BEE-EATER
8. WHITE-FRONTED OWL

THE BIRDS

Few creatures are more beautifully adapted for their way of life than the birds, whose graceful aerobatics can make man's aircraft seem almost clumsy. Birds are warm-blooded, backboned animals with feathers, beaks, long forelimbs evolved as wings, clawed hind legs designed for walking, perching, or swimming, and lightweight bodies with air sacs and bones with air spaces. Many have deeply keeled breastbones to which their powerful flight muscles are attached. All birds lay eggs and most birds can fly.

Since the first bird feebly fluttered in the air about 150 million years ago, the great class of *Aves* (birds) has produced over 30 orders with more than 200 families. Eight orders and 41 families have died out, but the rest total over 8,500 species.

More than 5,000 of these species belong to the order of perching birds (*Passeriformes*), birds with three forward-pointing toes and one backward-pointing toe on each foot. They range in size from the minute sunbirds and wrens to the much larger crows, and include the brilliantly coloured birds of paradise, and such splendid songsters as blackbirds, nightingales, and larks. Some species feed on insects (the flycatchers for instance); others (such as the finches and buntings) are seed-eaters. By no means all perching birds belong to the *Passeriformes* order: the pigeon, cuckoo, and bee-eater shown here represent three other orders. For the sake of convenience, people often group birds in ways that do not always tally with family relationships. Thus carnivorous birds, armed with sharply hooked beaks and powerful claws, are commonly grouped together as birds of prey — a heading which covers the nocturnal owls, and the eagles which hunt by day, although owls and eagles belong to two separate orders.

Game birds embrace not only the closely related pheasants, grouse, and partridges (including francolins), but the ducks and geese which simply share their rôle as creatures hunted by man.

Flightless birds include the equally unrelated ostrich, kiwi, emu, and penguin.

Such headings of convenience often overlap — for instance ducks and penguins can also be listed as water birds (which heading includes pelicans, waterhens, cranes, and shags), or they can be listed with web-footed birds (including pelicans but not waterhens).

Sometimes people talk of tropical birds as a group, although few birds are more unalike than the macaw and the crowned crane.

In some cases unrelated birds look alike because they have evolved similar bodies to fit similar modes of life. Thus from a distance a soaring white stork and Egyptian vulture may be confused because both have long broad gliders' wings. Equally, related birds with different habits may look entirely dissimilar, such as the massive-billed seed-eating hawfinch and the needle-billed insect-eating treecreeper.

1. GOLD AND BLUE MACAW
2. SWINHOE'S PHEASANT
3. BLEEDING HEART PIGEON
4. WHITE TAILED EAGLE
5. GREEN MAGPIE
6. KIWI
7. PELICAN
8. CROWNED CRANE

THE INSECTS

To many people the word insects conjures up a picture of hordes of small creatures that buzz, sting, or bite and spend their lives tormenting picnickers or gardeners. This picture contains some truths. Insects certainly exist in hordes; in fact no other class of animal is so numerous. More than 800,000 insect species have so far been identified (100 times as many as the stars which you can see without a telescope), and this may represent no more than one quarter of the world's grand total of living insect species. Insects are also certainly *small* compared with many animals: some beetles are tiny enough to walk through a needle's eye, and the largest insects are stick insects, which are no more than 300 millimetres (12 inches) long.

It is also true that fast-flying insects may *buzz* as their rapid wingbeats make the air vibrate; but not all insects fly. Wasps *sting* and ants *bite*; but some insects do neither. Colorado beetles and cabbage butterflies can be classed as pests, but the harmless ones far outnumber the pests, while ladybirds and honey bees are beneficial to farms and gardens. Clearly, then, the popular idea of what constitutes an insect is far from accurate.

Scientists have more precise ways of deciding which animals fall within the class *Insecta*. Scientifically speaking, adult insects have a three-part body with a *head* which contains a pair of feelers or antennae, a *thorax* which supports six legs and very often two or four wings, and an *abdomen* which contains organs for digestion, excretion, and reproduction. The whole body is encased in tough horny armour made of chitin: an outside skeleton akin to those of the insects' arthropod relatives, the crabs and spiders.

Insects cannot grow inside such outside skeletons but they can and do grow by shedding them from time to time. After hatching from its egg the soft-bodied larva grows larger, eventually forming a hard-skinned pupa from which a very different looking adult insect emerges.

Some insects are wingless, for instance the little silverfish which sometimes streak across a kitchen floor, and the curious springtails including so-called snow fleas that can leap about on snow. But twenty of the twenty-four insect orders belong to the great subclass of winged insects or *Pterygota*.

Perhaps the most beautiful of all winged insects are the butterflies and moths, called *Lepidoptera*, or scale wings, because thousands of tiny scales cover their wings. Three common European butterflies are pictured here.

Easily the most numerous kinds of insect are the beetles or *Coleoptera*, whose 300,000 species outnumber the *Lepidoptera* by three to one. Beetles' forewings are hard sheaths folded back to guard their soft hind wings. Beetles vary greatly in shape, size, and colour as the three on the opposite page show.

1. RED ADMIRAL
2. PHILOTES VICRAMA
3. TORTOISESHELL
4. MECYNORRHINA TORQUATA
5. LADYBIRD
6. CICADA
7. SPHEX paralysing a caterpillar
8. PSOA DUBIA
9. HORNET

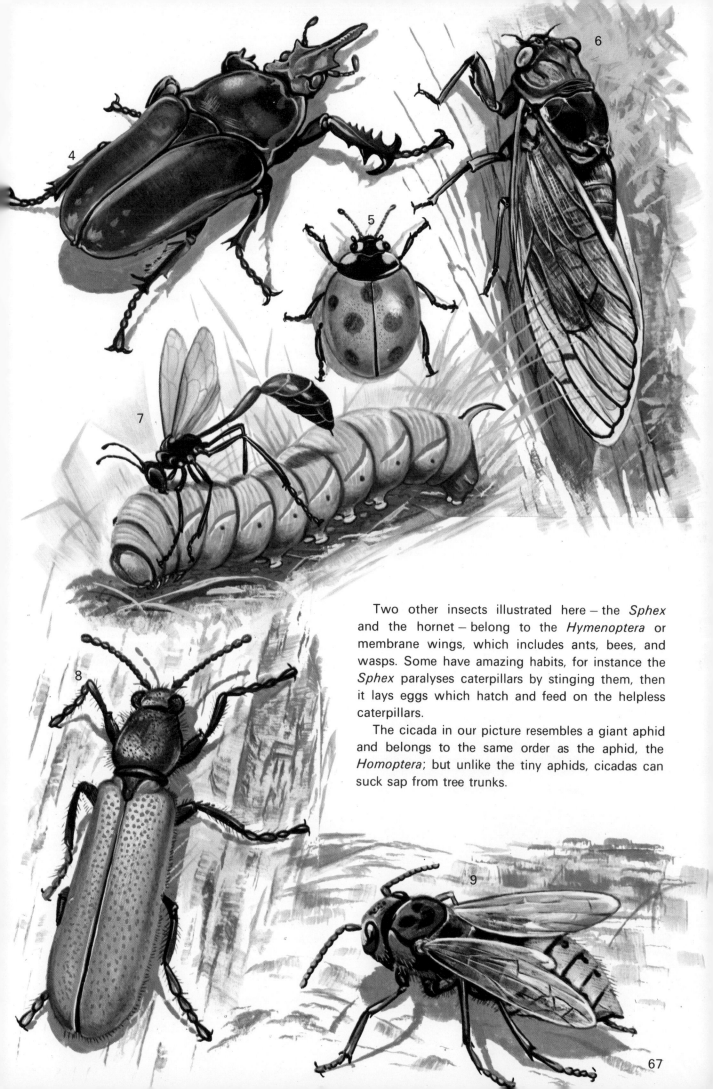

Two other insects illustrated here – the *Sphex* and the hornet – belong to the *Hymenoptera* or membrane wings, which includes ants, bees, and wasps. Some have amazing habits, for instance the *Sphex* paralyses caterpillars by stinging them, then it lays eggs which hatch and feed on the helpless caterpillars.

The cicada in our picture resembles a giant aphid and belongs to the same order as the aphid, the *Homoptera*; but unlike the tiny aphids, cicadas can suck sap from tree trunks.

1. PLATYPUS
2. ECHIDNA
3. BANDED ANTEATER
4. KOALA
5. GREY KANGAROO
6. DASYURE

THREE KINDS OF MAMMAL

Our brief survey of the animal kingdom has already included not only creatures without backbones like insects but all except one of the five main groups of backboned animals. In looking at the whales and seals we also had a brief preview of this fifth and most highly developed group, the mammals.

The great animal class *Mammalia* takes its name from the Latin word *mamma*, meaning breast, because all mammal mothers feed their babies with milk produced by special milk glands in their breasts. Mammals are also warm-blooded backboned creatures with hair, a well-developed brain housed in a bony skull, and lungs. There are over 4,200 mammal species, and they start life inside their mothers' bodies, feeding from a special organ called a placenta through a supply line called an umbilical cord. Such babies grow inside their mothers until they are completely formed.

But not all mammals develop like this. Some kinds begin life in ways that remind us of their reptile ancestors. These belong to the curious Australasian group of monotremes which lack placentas and are hatched from eggs. The only living examples of these strange mammals (which incidentally have beaks instead of teeth) are the platypus and the echidna, shown on this page. With its webbed feet and broad, flat tail, the platypus is an excellent swimmer. It lives in Australian streams, using its leathery bill to rummage for underwater worms and shellfish. The echidna shuffles about the forests of Australia, Tasmania, and New Guinea, flicking out its long tongue to catch insects. Like the hedgehog it can roll itself into a ball, and it wards off its enemies with the help of a coat of sharp protective spines.

Unlike the monotremes, the creatures pictured on the right-hand page are born, not hatched from eggs. But their young are born in a very undeveloped state. Such animals are called marsupials because most of the mothers carry their newborn young in a protective *marsupium* or pouch. Best-known of all marsupials is the kangaroo. When born it is only one inch long. It creeps up its mother's fur and into her pouch where it attaches itself to a nipple to suck her milk. Not all marsupials have such well-developed pouches as the kangaroo; the banded anteater is pouchless and its undeveloped young must cling grimly to its mother's nipples. These marsupials (also the cat-like dasyure and bear-like koala) come from Australia; but opossums and some other species of marsupialia live in the Americas.

3

4

5

6

MAMMALS THAT EAT MEAT

Many placental mammals differ from one another in various ways, for instance dogs and cats belong to an order of mammals specially adapted for eating flesh, and are named *Carnivora* from two Latin words that mean flesh and eating. All carnivores have long, sharp, cutting teeth with which they can tear mouthfuls of flesh from other animals. Most land carnivores are also armed with sharp claws, keen eyes and noses, and long, strong, agile limbs to help them hunt their prey. Many also have a thick body covering of fur. As we noticed earlier when we looked at some of the sea-dwelling mammals, the fin-footed water-living carnivores, including seals and walruses, are somewhat differently designed.

The pictures on these two pages show five mammals belonging to four of the seven families of land carnivores. The spotted snow leopard and the striped tiger both belong to the cat family which includes the formidable lion and jaguar as well as the domesticated cat. Big cats are among the strongest and fiercest of all land animals, easily able to kill a cow or a man.

The shaggy-coated black Himalayan bear on the facing page is one of the eight living species of the bear family. These ferocious yet playful-looking beasts range from the tiny 91 centimetre-long (3 feet) sun bear of Asia to the 275 centimetre (9 feet) Alaskan brown bear, weighing up to eight times as much as a man and the largest flesh-eating land animal.

Although the giant panda in our picture looks like a bear, most experts consider it an outsize member of the raccoon family, which includes the small, bushy-tailed North American raccoon and the monkey-like kinkajous of South America. The panda's favourite food is bamboo shoots, although it sometimes eats meat.

In spite of its slightly dog-like appearance the African aardwolf belongs to the hyaena family whose other members are the hyaenas themselves: massively jawed hunter-scavengers with powerful teeth, which often live in packs.

Three families of carnivores not represented in these pictures are the dog, weasel, and civet families. The dog, or canine, family includes foxes, wolves, jackals, and all the modern breeds of domesticated dog. The weasel family embraces such different looking beasts as badgers, otters, weasels, and skunks; and the civet family includes both the cat-like civets and otter-like mongooses — both from Africa and Asia.

1. SNOW LEOPARD
2. AARDWOLF
3. HIMALAYAN BEAR
4. TIGER
5. GIANT PANDA

MAMMALS THAT EAT PLANTS

The creatures upon which the fierce carnivores prey are chiefly herbivores. Unlike the carnivores with their sharp claws, many of the herbivores have feet ending in toes shaped as hoofs. Instead of dagger-like flesh-tearing teeth, theirs are designed for cropping leaves. And because herbivores obtain their food in a more bulky, less concentrated, form than the flesh-eaters they have a more complicated digestive system for coping with it.

Many herbivores are grouped largely by differences in their hoofed toes. Ungulates (hoofed herbivores) with two or four toes on each foot belong to the order of even-toed herbivores *Artiodactyla*. Ungulates with an odd number of toes sheathed in a horny hoof belong to the odd-toed herbivores, or *Perissodactyla*.

Four of the five creatures shown on these two pages (the rhinoceroses and the tapir) are odd-toed ungulates. Even the most powerful carnivore would seldom risk tangling with the massive rhinoceros, protected as it is by a thick, almost armour-plated skin, and one or more hard horns of compressed fibres. The Indian rhinoceros in our picture weighs up to 2 tonnes (2 tons) and lives in marshy jungles. The black and the white rhinoceroses are both actually grey; each has two horns and lives on dry African plains. The white rhinoceros can reach a height of 2·5 metres (8 feet) at the shoulder and weigh as much as 3 tonnes (3 tons); the white is the largest rhinoceros of all. Tapirs are much smaller mammals with a trunk-shaped nose. Different kinds live in the forests of South and Central America and South-East Asia.

1. INDIAN RHINOCEROS
2. WHITE RHINOCEROS
3. BLACK RHINOCEROS
4. MALAYAN TAPIR
5. HIPPOPOTAMUS

Tapirs are strong swimmers but spend less time in water than the great river hippopotamus, the even-toed ungulate shown on the right-hand page. This huge bodied beast is the heaviest of all land animals after the elephant, and lives in the swamps and rivers of tropical Africa.

1. GERENUK
2. OKAPI
3. BONGO
4. ELAND
5. GEMSBOK
6. RETICULATED GIRAFFE

MAMMALS WHICH CHEW THE CUD

All the mammals on these pages are even-toed ungulates called ruminants. Ruminants have four-chambered stomachs. They soften the swallowed food in their first two stomachs and regurgitate to chew the cud before it passes into the third and fourth stomachs. Animals that chew the cud, or ruminate, include the deer, antelopes, giraffe, okapi, cattle, goats, and sheep. In fact ruminants are easily the most abundant of all kinds of ungulate.

Although all of them have similar digestive systems, different ruminants are adapted for finding food in different places. The four antelopes shown here help to illustrate this point. All four live in Africa (the home of most of the world's antelopes). But the slender gerenuk feeds by standing on its muscular hind legs to nibble the leaves of low-growing branches in the park-like open country of East Africa. The larger, more thick-set bongo, on the other hand, browses in the forests of western and central Africa. The big gemsbok feeds in the dry grasslands of southern Africa, where it paws the dusty ground to dig up thirst-quenching bulbs. The eland of west-central Africa feeds both on grassland and in the forest fringe; weighing over 850 kilograms (17 hundredweights) and standing up to 182 centimetres (6 feet) at the shoulder this is the largest antelope in Africa.

Unlike the antelopes (creatures with hollow, unbranched horns), the okapi and giraffe belong to the giraffe family of ruminants. But they too are specially adapted for eating certain kinds of vegetation. The okapi is a large mammal standing 152 centimetres (5 feet) high at the shoulders, and has long front legs and a long neck which help it to reach upwards to browse high vegetation. Okapis are shy creatures that live in the dense Congo forests.

The giraffe is a splendid example of an animal designed for eating special kinds of plants. The tallest animal in the world, with the longest neck, the giraffe is perfectly equipped for tearing twigs and leaves from the tops of trees in the park-like grasslands of Africa, south of the Sahara Desert.

6

TWO KINDS OF HORNS

The four animals on these pages belong to two different families of ruminants. The ibex (a wild goat), the bighorn Sheep, and the African buffalo, all with hollow unbranched horns, belong to the family, *Bovidae*. This family includes wild and domesticated goats, sheep, cattle, and antelopes. The red deer, on the other hand, belongs to the *Cervidae* or deer family: ruminants which have mostly solid, branching horns called antlers.

Most of us think of sheep, goats, and cattle as placid animals; but their wild relations are often muscular and agile.

Ibexes, for example, roam the almost inaccessible peaks of the European Alps and Asian Himalayas, in small herds. They wander down from the snows at night to browse in high mountain woodlands.

Several races of bighorn sheep live in North America's western mountain ranges; climbing, leaping, and plunging from dizzy ledges with astonishing agility to escape wolves and other enemies. The bighorn sheep is also found in the Old World, mainly in Asia, and it seems likely that this is the area of their origin.

1. ALPINE IBEX
2. DALL BIGHORN
3. RED DEER
4. AFRICAN BUFFALO

The African buffalo often chooses fight instead of flight, relying upon its powerful body and formidable horns for defence; a cornered buffalo can be just as dangerous as a lion or tiger. Other kinds of cattle include the Asian water buffalo, the bison of North America and Europe, the Tibetan yak, and the domesticated breeds found throughout the world.

Red deer are large but usually timid beasts that browse at dusk and dawn in forests from Europe to Iran. Other kinds of deer live in Europe, Asia, Africa, and the Americas. They range in size from the tiny pudu of Ecuador, which grows no larger than a dog, to the great moose of North America, which stands as high as a horse.

1. AFRICAN ELEPHANT
2. DROMEDARY
3. LLAMA
4. GRÉVY'S ZEBRA
5. WILD BOAR

MORE MAMMALS THAT EAT PLANTS

The three animals at the foot of these pages belong to the same order of even-toed herbivores as the sheep, goats, and cattle. But scientists group none of them with those cud-chewers, although dromedaries, llamas, and other members of the camel family all have stomachs designed for rumination. The one-humped dromedary and its close relative the two-humped Bactrian camel of Central Asia have feet adapted for difficult terrains — rocky deserts and soft sand. The fat stored in their humps serves as a food reservoir for long desert journeys. Because they seldom sweat dromedaries can go for days without a drink, even in hot weather. Llamas, on the other hand, are designed for life among the cool Andes Mountains of South America — the continent where their relatives the alpacas and guanacos also live.

The wild boar belongs to the swine family, as do our farm pigs, the ugly African warthog, and other kinds of wild swine found in Africa and Asia. All have long, cone-shaped heads ending in a snout, teeth that curve up as tusks, and bristly hair; they grub in mud for roots and other delicacies. Their near relatives include the hippopotamus and the pig-like peccaries of South America.

To end our look at the odd- and even-toed orders of herbivores let us turn back to the odd-toed herbivores with which we started. Unlike in appearance as they are, the lumbering rhinoceroses on page 72 fit into the same order as the swift-footed zebra, as both are members of the horse family, or *Equidae*. The horse, the wild and domesticated asses, zebras, tapirs and rhinoceroses all have toes fused into a single hoof. Zebras roam much of Africa; wild asses live in Africa and Asia; and a few wild horses survive in Mongolia.

The elephant — the largest land animal alive — belongs not to the odd-toed or even-toed ungulates but to the *Proboscidea* or trunk-nosed mammals. Its trunk is a long, muscular, yet sensitive nose which also serves as a hand. Its massive (sometimes 6-tonne) body is sheathed in leathery, almost hairless skin, and it has pillar-like legs with club-shaped feet. The world's largest ears warn it of danger, while two huge tusks serve as valuable tools for digging up roots and stripping bark. Hundreds of kinds of elephant evolved but only the African and Indian species have survived. Perhaps their nearest living relatives are the rabbit-like hyraxes of Africa and Asia.

4

5

MAMMALS WITH NAILS OR CLAWS

Unlike the mainly hoofed plant-eating mammals which we have just described, squirrels, lemurs, pangolins, anteaters, bats, shrews, and pikas all have claws or nails. But each represents a different order of mammals.

Squirrels are rodents – gnawing mammals with chisel-like incisor teeth. Rats, beavers, prairie dogs, and hamsters are rodents and they range in size from tiny harvest mice to the capybara of 120 centimetres (4 feet) long of South America. Over 1,800 species of rodent have been classified; they are more numerous and widespread than any other mammal order.

Pikas, hares, and rabbits make up the order of lagomorphs, or hare-shaped mammals. Like rodents, they have chisel-like incisor teeth which grow continuously to make up for heavy wear caused by gnawing grass and bark.

The flying lemur, shown here hanging from a branch, has a web of skin between its limbs allowing it to glide from tree to tree. Flying lemurs are the only members of the order *Dermoptera* (skin-winged). They are capable only of gliding and are not true fliers like the bats.

The flying foxes of India and South-East Asia are also fruit-eating bats, and they too have skin stretched between their limbs. But unlike the gliding lemurs, flying foxes really fly. Flying foxes are furry, skin-winged mammals of the hand-winged order *Chiroptera*, so-named because bats' wings are stretched over their forearms and elongated fingers. Most of these nocturnal mammals eat fruit, fish, or insects; but the South American vampire bat bites and laps up blood.

Although the giant anteater of South America and the pangolin of Asia and Africa both have long pointed snouts with long sticky tongues for catching ants, they fit into different orders. The giant anteater belongs to the *Edentates*, toothless and near-toothless mammals which include the sloths and armadillos. The pangolin is also toothless but its body is protected by overlapping horny plates, and it belongs to the *Pholidota* or scaly anteaters. Yet another long-nosed ant-eating mammal – the aardvark of Africa – forms its own order, the *Tubulidentata*.

Like the anteaters, the shrews, hedgehogs, moles and tenrecs are all insect-eaters, though most eat a much more varied diet than the anteaters. They make up the order of *Insectivora* comprising small mammals with a long snout, sharp teeth, and five-toed feet.

1. RED SQUIRREL
2. COBEGO, OR FLYING LEMUR
3. PANGOLIN
4. GIANT ANTEATER
5. FLYING FOX
6. WATER SHREW
7. PIKA

THE PRIMATES

Zoologists believe that tiny five-toed insectivore-like creatures may have been the ancestors of modern primates. The word *primate* means first, and scientists consider that primates make up the highest order in the entire animal kingdom. Most kinds have big brains, nails not claws, and hands capable of grasping objects. Most also live in trees in the warmer countries of the world.

There are two main sub-orders of primates, the *Prosimii* and *Anthropoidea*. Prosimians include the tree shrews, tarsiers, lemurs, lorises, and galagos. Tree shrews are tiny mammals, 152 millimetres, with shrew-like snouts and squirrel-like bushy tails. These little fruit- and insect-eating primates live in Indonesia and mainland Asia, and their remote forebears may be ancestral to all other primates.

The rat-sized tarsiers have huge eyes, and sucker discs on their toes and fingers for clinging to branches. Like owls they can swivel their heads completely round. Tarsiers live in Indonesian forests, leaping from tree to tree in constant search of the insects and small reptiles that form their food.

True lemurs (whose name incidentally means ghosts) have pointed muzzles, soft fur, often bushy tails, and live on the island of Madagascar eating fruit, eggs, and small animals caught in the trees. Closely related animals include the huge-eared, small-bodied bushbabies, or galagos, of Africa and the big-eyed, squirrel-sized, slow-moving lorises of Africa and Asia.

The mandrill, gibbon, chimpanzee, and orang-utan shown here, and the gorilla on page 84 all belong to the second primate sub-order *Anthropoidea*, which gets its name from the Greek word *Anthropos*, man. As their name suggests, anthropoid primates are more man-like than other kinds. This sub-order is divided into three so-called superfamilies: the

1. LEMUR
2. MANDRILL
3. GIBBON
4. CHIMPANZEE
5. ORANG-UTAN

Cenoidea (New World monkeys), *Cercopithecoidea* (Old World monkeys), and the *Hominoidea* (apes and men).

The New World monkeys of Central and South America are smaller and weigh less than many Old World monkeys but have more teeth and frequently a grasping tail that helps them to swing through trees. Woolly, howler, and capuchin monkeys are all New World kinds.

The Old World superfamily of monkeys lack grasping tails, and tend to have a long, narrow muzzle producing an almost dog-like face in creatures like the mandrill, a big colourful baboon which lives in West Africa; and a curious cucumber-like nose in the proboscis monkey of Borneo. Like the mandrill, some other Old World monkeys are brilliantly coloured.

The superfamily *Hominoidea* is split into two families: the pongids (named from the African word *mpungu* meaning ape) and the hominids (named from the Latin *homo* meaning man). The four members of the ape family are the gibbon, chimpanzee, orang-utan, and gorilla. These tailless, hairy mammals closely resemble man, but have longer arms, shorter legs, thicker skulls, and a less developed brain than man. Gibbons, the smallest apes, stand only 91 centimetres (3 feet) high, and use their long arms to swing through the tree-tops of South and South-East Asia. The orang-utan (whose name means 'man of the woods') is found in Borneo. Chimpanzees are large forest apes from Africa intelligent enough to use simple tools. The African gorilla, which weighs twice as much as a man, is the biggest and most powerful of all the apes.

GORILLA

Mongoloid
(straight hair)

Caucasoid
(wavy hair)

THREE VARIETIES OF MAN

Unlike the apes, man walks upright on two legs, which are longer than his arms. He is also less hairy, has relatively smaller teeth, and a larger brain developed well enough to help him reason and speak — abilities that make man more intelligent than any other animal.

All men on earth today are members of *Homo sapiens*, the only surviving species of the several kinds of man that have evolved at different times. Yet the world's peoples are by no means all identical. Differences in shape, size, and colour suggest that there are three main varieties or race of man called white or Caucasoid; yellow or Mongoloid, and black or Negroid.

Besides their white to brown skins, Caucasoid peoples tend to have fine blond to dark brown wavy hair, light blue to dark brown eyes, a long to round head, a narrow nose with a high bridge, a prominent chin, thin lips, and large broad feet. Most are tall or of medium height.

Besides their often yellow skins, the Mongoloid peoples tend to have coarse black or dark brown straight hair, brown eyes with lid folds that make their eyes appear to slant, a round head, a flattened face with a slightly broader flatter nose than the Caucasoids, a moderate chin, thin lips, and small narrow feet. Most are medium in height.

Negroid
(frizzy hair)

Negroid peoples have light brown to black skin, coarse black frizzy hair, brown eyes, a long head, a broad flat nose with flared nostrils, a weakly pronounced chin, thick turned-out lips, big teeth, and large narrow feet. Most are tall but the groups called Pygmies are tiny.

Possibly the different races evolved because man had to adapt himself to life in different climates. For instance, the dark skin, eyes, and hair of Negroes protect them from the strong radiations of the tropical sun, while the Caucasoids' pale skin allows a beneficial amount of weak northern sunlight to penetrate their bodies.

Australian aborigine

African herdsman
(Negroid)

Icelandic fisherman
(Caucasoid)

WHEN RACES MINGLE

In some parts of the world most people clearly represent one of the three main racial types that we have just described. For instance, the African herdsman on this page is typical of many Negroes in Africa south of the Sahara Desert. Almost all Icelanders share the distinctive Caucasoid features of the Icelandic fisherman. The Laotian waterman is characteristic of most Mongoloid inhabitants of his part of South-East Asia.

But the Australian Aborigine fits neatly into none of these three main racial groups. Instead, many anthropologists place him in a fourth racial group which they believe represents an old-fashioned form of Caucasoid stock.

While such ancient racial types as the Australian Aborigines persist in remote corners of the world, areas in close contact with one another have seen a rich intermingling of different racial stocks, so that many of the world's more than 3,500,000,000 people are neither strictly speaking white, black, nor yellow but a mixture of two or more stocks. In fact some anthropologists recognise as many as 27 races, living in the more than half a dozen anthropological areas into which they divide the world. On the next few pages we shall take a look at these areas and the kinds of people who inhabit them.

86

Laotian waterman
(Mongoloid)

Pole

Russian

Nordic
(Sweden)

Alpine
(central France)

Dinaric
(Yugoslavia)

THE PEOPLES OF EUROPE

The white-skinned Caucasoid peoples of Europe have mingled relatively little with Negroids and Mongoloids. But all Caucasoids do not look alike, for groups separated from one another by seas, mountains, languages and other barriers have tended to develop in noticeably different ways. Anthropologists often divide Caucasoid stock into five separate groups, centred in different parts of Europe.

Nordics are usually thought of as tall, long-headed, fair-haired people with pale skins and blue eyes. Many people of this kind live in the Scandinavian countries, especially Norway and Sweden.

Peoples of the *East Baltic* type have broad, round heads, fair hair, pale skin, blue or grey eyes, and thickset bodies. Many Poles, Russians, Finns, East Germans, and some others fit this description.

Central France, south-west Germany, Switzerland, northern Italy, are among the chief homes of *Alpine* peoples, who have broad heads, fair skins, brown or chestnut hair, light-coloured eyes, and generally medium or thickset bodies.

Most of the *Dinaric* group live in south-east Europe, for instance in Yugoslavia and other Balkan countries, east to Ukrainian Russia, and north to southern Poland, Dinarics have large, round heads, often flattened at the back, dark hair and eyes, hooked noses, and tend to be taller than the Alpines.

Mediterranean peoples are long-headed and dark-complexioned, with black hair, dark brown eyes, and a much browner skin than, say, the Nordics, and lighter in build. As their name suggests, most live around the Mediterranean shores.

Millions of people from all five groups have intermingled, and their descendants now share the features of several different European groups. Millions of Europeans have also emigrated to Australia and the Americas.

Mediterranean
(Italy)

Moroccan Berber

Egyptian

PEOPLES OF NORTH AFRICA

In prehistoric times, Caucasoid peoples seem to have moved west into North Africa. Since then, trade, war and emigration have brought Europeans south across the Mediterranean Sea, peoples with Negro blood north across the Sahara Desert, and sharp featured Caucasoid Arabs west from Arabia.

The Berber represents one of the oldest kinds of inhabitants of North Africa. Many Moroccans and Algerians look like this dark-skinned member of the Caucasoid stock, whose features suggest he may be related to the Alpine and Mediterranean Europeans.

Most Egyptians are dark-complexioned Caucasoid peoples like the Egyptian in our picture. Egypt also has nomadic Arab herdsmen, while in the south many Egyptians have much Negro blood.

The seated group represents three kinds of semi-nomads living in the great Sahara Desert. Moors are of mainly Berber stock: tall, slim, dark-skinned people usually with wavy hair and hooked noses. Tuaregs, also chiefly of Berber stock, are tall, long-headed people with brown skin, dark hair and eyes. But some have crinkly hair, and certain Moors and Tuaregs have some Negro blood. The broad-nosed Tebus are Berber-Negroes.

1. Moor
2. & 4. Tuaregs
3. Tebu
5. Young Tuareg

88

Iranian

Turanian from
Russian Turkestan

PEOPLES OF SOUTH-WEST ASIA

Walking through the city streets of Tehran, Merv, Haifa and Kabul you might well see peoples very like those illustrated here, for they represent varieties of dark-complexioned Caucasoid people of the Armenoid type found in different parts of South-West Asia.

Many Armenoids look much like the Dinaric type mentioned earlier, but some anthropologists consider there is a distinctive Armenoid racial group of medium height, stocky build, with broad heads, flattened at the back, and large fleshy hooked noses. People fitting that description are certainly common in Turkey, Syria, and Iran among the Armenians, Kurds and Jews.

Other Jews more closely resemble the Arabs of the Arabian peninsular, Palestine, and Jordan — peoples of medium height, with lean bodies, long heads, dark hair, fine aquiline noses, and dark eyes. Indeed so similar are the Jews to their South-West Asian neighbours that knowledgeable people reject the old idea that the Jews make up a race of their own. Jews share a common faith, tongue, and culture: they make up an ethnic, not a racial group.

As we travel east through South-West Asia we still find peoples surprisingly like the Mediterranean Europeans, for instance in Afghanistan, where more than half the population are Pathans — people of medium height with sallow skins, dark hair and eyes, large, long heads, well developed at the back. But lying near Central Asia, Afghanistan also has peoples with Mongoloid features. So does its neighbour, Russian Turkestan, whose Turanians often have hooked Armenoid noses but prominent Mongoloid cheekbones.

Palestinian Arab

Afghan woman

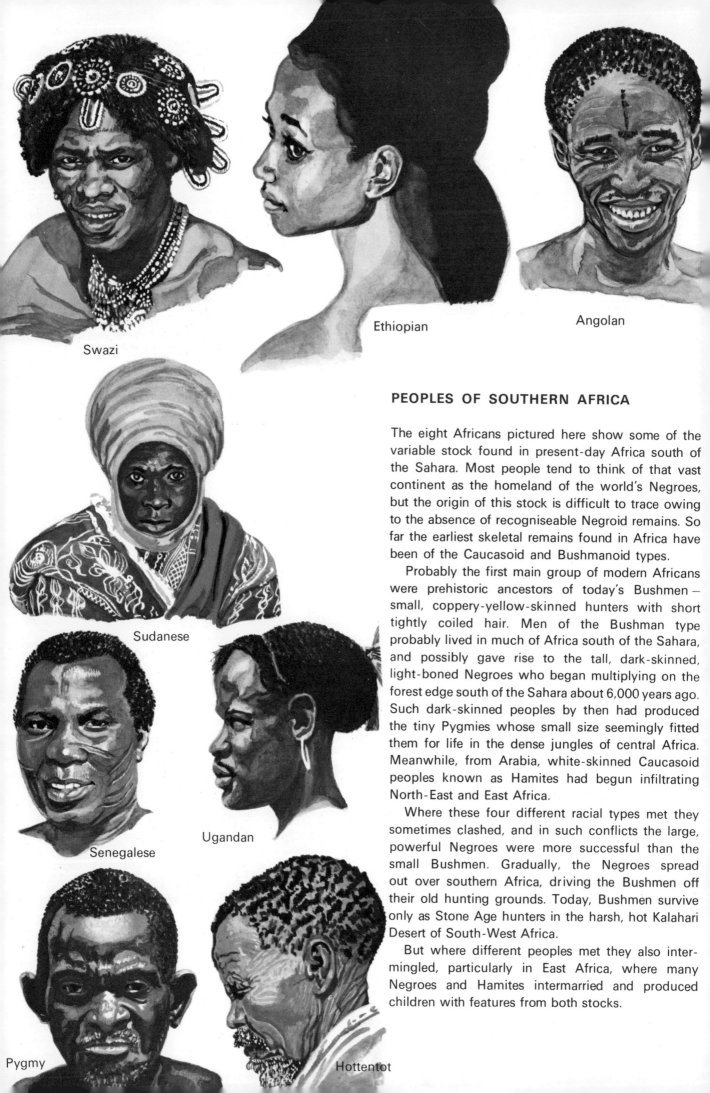

Swazi

Ethiopian

Angolan

Sudanese

Senegalese

Ugandan

Pygmy

Hottentot

PEOPLES OF SOUTHERN AFRICA

The eight Africans pictured here show some of the variable stock found in present-day Africa south of the Sahara. Most people tend to think of that vast continent as the homeland of the world's Negroes, but the origin of this stock is difficult to trace owing to the absence of recogniseable Negroid remains. So far the earliest skeletal remains found in Africa have been of the Caucasoid and Bushmanoid types.

Probably the first main group of modern Africans were prehistoric ancestors of today's Bushmen — small, coppery-yellow-skinned hunters with short tightly coiled hair. Men of the Bushman type probably lived in much of Africa south of the Sahara, and possibly gave rise to the tall, dark-skinned, light-boned Negroes who began multiplying on the forest edge south of the Sahara about 6,000 years ago. Such dark-skinned peoples by then had produced the tiny Pygmies whose small size seemingly fitted them for life in the dense jungles of central Africa. Meanwhile, from Arabia, white-skinned Caucasoid peoples known as Hamites had begun infiltrating North-East and East Africa.

Where these four different racial types met they sometimes clashed, and in such conflicts the large, powerful Negroes were more successful than the small Bushmen. Gradually, the Negroes spread out over southern Africa, driving the Bushmen off their old hunting grounds. Today, Bushmen survive only as Stone Age hunters in the harsh, hot Kalahari Desert of South-West Africa.

But where different peoples met they also intermingled, particularly in East Africa, where many Negroes and Hamites intermarried and produced children with features from both stocks.

Nepalese

Kashmiri

Woman of Jaipur

The peoples shown here are living reminders of these events in Africa's unwritten history. The closest of all to the original Negro stock are possibly the Sudanese and Senegalese (whose face incidentally is scarred by ceremonial tribal cuts). Both live just south of the Sahara Desert in or near the first homeland of the Negro race. Both have very dark brown skin, long heads, frizzy hair, broad flat noses, thick lips, narrow hips, broad shoulders and other strongly Negroid features. The dark-skinned Ugandan from East Africa and the paler-skinned Swazi from South-East Africa are also clearly of Negro stock.

The pale-skinned Ethiopian woman from North-East Africa certainly has some ancestors of Caucasoid stock – perhaps among the many Arabs who long ago migrated from Arabia to Ethiopia. Many Ethiopians and some nearby peoples are nearly as dark-skinned as pure Negroes but have narrow, aquiline noses and wavy, not frizzy, hair.

The Pygmy represents the third of the four main racial types in southern Africa. Pygmies grow only 137 centimetres (4½ feet) tall, have round heads, broad noses, tightly curled red-brown hair, brownish-yellow skin, and they live in small hunting bands in the Congo forest area.

The other people pictured here are examples of interbreeding. The coffee-coloured Angolan may well be of mixed Negro and Bushman blood, while the short, woolly-haired reddish-yellow-skinned Hottentot from South-West Africa could be of mixed Bushman and Caucasoid ancestry.

Other kinds of Africans include the Dinkas and Nuers of the hot upper Nile area: peoples whose immensely tall lanky bodies have relatively little volume in relation to surface area – an ideal arrangement for heat loss.

PEOPLES OF INDIA

Few parts of any continent are so sharply cut off from its neighbours as is the pear-shaped subcontinent of India from the rest of Asia. North, north-west, and north-east lie great mountain barriers. South, south-west, and south-east stretches the Indian Ocean. But at different times in India's history, peoples have filtered through the mountains and settled in the lush alluvial plains of the north: chiefly Caucasoids from the north-west, and Mongoloids from the north and north-east.

Today nine out of every ten Indians are Caucasoids of the Mediterranean type. These range in colour from the tall, fair-skinned Indo-Aryans, who make up most of northern India's population, to the shorter, dark-skinned Dravidians who are most numerous in southern India. Although these peoples tend not to intermarry much today, clearly the two types have intermingled in the past.

In northern India, intermingling has also often taken place between the Caucasoids and their Mongoloid neighbours living north of the great Himalayan mountain barrier.

The three women on this page give some idea of how these events have shaped the peoples of northern India: the broad-faced Nepalese woman looks at least partly Mongoloid; the rather pale-skinned Kashmiri woman tends toward the Indo-Aryan type; and the dark-skinned woman from Jaipur is probably of Dravidian stock.

The hills and jungles of Central and Southern India are also the home of small but distinctive groups of peoples, including the short, dark, wavy-haired, flat-nosed, fleshy-lipped Veddas, who are perhaps descended from an ancient Caucasoid type.

Siberian

Mongolian

Chinese

Japanese

Javanese

PEOPLES OF THE FAR EAST

About one in three of the world's peoples belongs to the yellow or Mongoloid race which can be divided into about 7 groups: Classic Mongoloids, Japanese, Northern Chinese, Tibetan, Indonesian-Malay, Turkic and the American Indian. Mongoloids are easily the most numerous group in Asia outside India and the south-west. The race takes its name from the yellow-skinned, round-headed peoples of Mongolia who have black straight hair, slanting eyes, broad cheeks, and flat noses. But as our illustrations suggest, Mongoloids are not all alike.

The Mongolian is somewhat differently built from the slighter Chinese and Japanese who live farther east, and even these are not identical. The pronounced nose of the man from northern Siberia suggests mixed Caucasoid and Mongoloid blood; while the wavy hair, full lips, and lack of a marked eye-fold in the slightly-built Javanese again suggest mingling of Mongoloid with other races. Although this Javanese is rather pale-skinned, southern Mongoloids tend to be dark.

No one is sure when or where the yellow race began. Some anthropologists suggest that the slanting almond-shaped eyes, protected by a fleshy fold of skin, are adapted to cope with the glare of sun or light on snow. They also point out that the Mongoloids' rather short limbs help to conserve body heat. Both facts suggest that the first Mongoloid peoples lived in cold, north-eastern Asia.

As they spread south and west, Mongoloids evidently met other groups of peoples. Some were the ancestors of the modern Ainus, a group of short, pale-skinned, brown-eyed, wavy-haired, long-headed peoples thought to be descended from an early type of Caucasoid once widespread in northern Asia. Ainu men are more heavily overgrown with body hair than any other people, and their rather coarse, heavy features suggest relationship with the distant Aborigines of Australia.

Pushing down into warm South-East Asia, the Mongoloids must also have found groups of Negroid peoples, including tiny Negritos much like the Congo Pygmies of Central Africa. Just as in Africa where the Negroes thrust the Bushmen into the harsh Kalahari Desert, so in East Asia the Mongoloid peoples seem to have driven the Ainus and Negroid peoples into remote islands and forests. Today, the few remaining Ainus live in the cold northernmost islands of Japan, and Negritos persist in the Andaman Islands and the forests of Indonesia and the Philippines. Mongoloids also spread west across the plains of Central Asia to intermingle with the white Caucasoids.

92

PEOPLES OF THE PACIFIC

The world map shows the big islands of Indonesia and New Guinea set like stepping stones between South-East Asia and Australia. East of these islands lie strings of much smaller ones flung thousands of miles out into the Pacific Ocean and forming the groups called Melanesia, Micronesia, and Polynesia. The first Europeans to reach these remote places must have been astonished to find that many of them were already inhabited by Stone Age peoples.

Geographers think that the first men to reach the large islands of Indonesia and Australia walked there from South-East Asia in the last Ice Age when sea levels were low, and land bridges linked Australia with Malaya. Two main kinds of people may have migrated: ancestors of today's Oceanic Negroes and Australian Aborigines.

The Oceanic Negroes were perhaps produced from a Negrito, Caucasoid, Australoid mixture, and are unlike African Negroes in often having reddish curly hair, thin lips, more body hair, and a strongly pronounced nose. Perhaps under pressure from Mongoloid Malays moving in from mainland Asia, Oceanic Negroes eventually built big sea-going canoes and peopled Melanesia or the 'black islands', so named from the islanders' black skins (our pictured Melanesian is paler than most).

Meanwhile, more than 16,000 years ago, Australoid peoples had walked into Australia, where they became isolated by the rise in sea level, and where some of their descendants still pursue a Stone Age hunting life: chocolate-skinned peoples with low, sloping foreheads, beetling brows, deep-set eyes, big noses, heavy jaws, and curly or wavy hair.

But the most remarkable of all peoples in or near the Pacific Ocean are the islanders of Polynesia, the remotest island group forming a great triangle with Hawaii, Easter Island, and New Zealand at its tips. Polynesians are tall, strongly built, light-skinned peoples with straight or wavy black hair, probably stemming from early Caucasoids related to the Ainus of Japan but with Oceanic Negroid and Mongoloid blood. Several thousand years ago, the Polynesians' ancestors evidently lived in southern China, but sailed off in search of island homes under pressure from the expanding Chinese. By 1000 B.C. some had settled parts of Melanesia. Over the next 2,500 years — navigating by stars, clouds, birds, and ocean currents — they sailed their big double-hulled canoes all over Polynesia.

Some anthropologists challenge this explanation of the peopling of Polynesia, and in 1947 the Norwegian Thor Heyerdahl successfully sailed a balsa log raft 4,300 miles from Peru to Raroia in Polynesia to prove that the Polynesians had originally come from South America. But few scientists accept his theory, reminding us that almost all Polynesian tools and food plants show strong links with Asia, not America.

Negrito

Australia Aborigine

Melanesian

AMERINDIANS AND ESKIMOS

Today Negroes, Caucasoids and Mongoloids all live in the great connected continents of North and South America. But both the Negroes and Caucasoids are really newcomers. The first white men to make any lasting contact with America were the Spaniards who discovered it about five centuries ago. Soon, white colonists, living in a climate too hot for their own comfort, had imported Negroes from West Africa as workers for their farms. Peoples of white or Caucasoid stock, and black or Negro stock now make up the majority in the Americas.

But this was by no means always so. The first men and women to set foot inside America, perhaps 20,000 years ago, seem to have been peoples of an early form of the Mongoloids. Before oceans rose to their present level, these ancient hunters trudged into north-western North America from Asia along a land bridge now buried by the chilly waters of the Bering Sea.

Over the centuries, some of these people funnelled through the high valleys of the Rocky Mountains and fanned out across the broad plains of North America. Others thrust southwards through the narrow neck of land that links North and South America. Some of these primitive explorers pushed on south to make their homes on the high plateaux of the Andes or in the low, steaming jungles of the Amazon basin. A few kept on to the cold southern tip of South America and settled on the windswept shores of Tierra del Fuego.

These Amerindians share the high cheekbones, straight black hair, and lack of body hair found in most Asian Mongoloids. But their eyes usually lack a slanted appearance and their skins tend to be coppery or brown, not yellowish.

Moreover, different parts of the Americas have Amerindians of very different appearance. For instance, tribes living in central and eastern North America are tall, slim, and rugged featured; tribes in western North America and in Central and South America tend to be short and stocky with finer features.

Four of the people shown here reflect something of these regional differences. The Sioux lives in eastern-central North America; the Navaho in the south-western United States; the Bolivian and the Jivaro girl both live in South America — the first on the high Andean plateau, the second in the hot Amazonian forest.

But the very Mongoloid-looking Eskimo belongs to a completely different group from the Amerindians. As recently as 2,000 years ago his ancestors were Asians who crossed the Bering Sea by boat to Alaska and began carving out a foothold in the cold Arctic lands of Alaska, northern Canada, and Greenland. Eskimos have paler skin, smaller hands and feet, and shorter arms and legs than the Amerindians. Their short, thickset bodies and flesh-padded faces help them to conserve body heat and so to survive in a climate far too cold for many of the peoples we have been describing. The unusual plan of an Eskimo's body is a reminder that each main racial type is no freak of nature but is a process of evolution which has fitted him for life under certain conditions.

Bolivian Indian

Eskimo

Navaho

Sioux

Jivaro girl

Man Masters the Earth

MAN AT THE DAWN OF HISTORY

Earlier in this book we saw how thousands of millions of years passed after life began before the first man-like creatures appeared on earth. We saw how millions more years passed before men like ourselves began to flourish, perhaps 30,000 years ago during the last Ice Age. We saw that by 15,000 years ago different races of modern man had probably colonised all of the world's great land masses except cold Antarctica.

By then man had slowly and laboriously learned how to fashion tools from stone, wood, and bone; and how to make fire. But perhaps only 10,000 years ago did people discover how to produce an assured food supply by farming.

If we think of the last million years since the days of early tool-making man as the twelve hours on a clock face, the last 10,000 years represent only 36 seconds. Yet in that tiny sliver of time man has transformed himself from a rather rare animal to the master of his planet. Ten thousand years ago the world probably held only 5,000,000 people; today the number is heading quickly towards 4,000,000,000. Ten thousand years ago disease and hunger killed off most people by the age of 30; today people live more than twice that long. Ten thousand years ago staying alive was a full-time task; today people have leisure time to enjoy themselves. Ten thousand years ago all men slowly plodded about the world on foot and knew little of what lay beyond the skyline; today men can walk on the moon.

These and other such changes which transformed savages into civilised citizens can be traced back to the invention of farming and to the poor, primitive riverside villages like the one in our picture, with its lean cattle, razor-backed pig, and patch of poppy-infested wheat. As the pictured storage jar reminds us, even such Stone Age farming communities could often produce more than enough food for their farming inhabitants. In time farmers began exchanging spare food for tools fashioned by expert craftsmen who were thus freed from the need to produce food for themselves. These beginnings of trade and division of labour set barbarian villages on a momentous path.

A farming village in the New Stone Age with domesticated animals, and plants, and a jar for storing grain.

THE WORLD'S FIRST CITIES

In some parts of the ancient world, New Stone Age farmers found the soil particularly rich. One such area was Egypt's Nile Valley. Another was the fertile crescent: a belt flanked by mountains and deserts which runs through Palestine, Syria, Lebanon and Iraq. To the south-west of the crescent the River Nile annually floods, dumping tons of rich warm mud along its banks. At the crescent's eastern end, the rivers Tigris and Euphrates water a great dry plain. In both areas, by 6,000 years ago, villagers were learning to band together under leaders to dig ditches and canals, diverting river waters to their rich but thirsty fields. To help them work these fields, they improved upon the farming methods of the early New Stone Age by harnessing oxen to a plough so that each farmer could tend more land.

These changes meant that in the fertile crescent and Egypt fewer people than elsewhere had to produce food and more were freed for full-time work away from the land. Such specialists came to include skilled smiths, potters, builders, weavers, merchants. There were also priests: religious leaders skilled in mathematics and astronomy who helped to fix field boundaries and predict the best times for sowing crops. Then there were warrior kings who defended their communities against raiding nomads from the nearby deserts.

By 5,500 years ago, thousands of Egyptians and Sumerians (early inhabitants of Iraq) were no longer living on the land that fed them but occupying towns and cities. Man, first a savage, then a barbarian, was becoming civilised.

THE BRONZE AGE

In the early cities of ancient Egypt and Sumer, kings, priests, merchants, craftsmen formed a great human pyramid supported by the farmers. Only the food surplus that farmers produced made possible the thriving trade that kept the cities going. But without the metalsmiths trade may never have begun at all, for it was largely to buy tools that the farmers first started producing enough spare food with which to trade.

No one knows exactly how metal working started, but the first metal to be used was possibly copper – a rather soft reddish metal sometimes found in lumps pure enough to be beaten into useful shapes with no other kind of treatment. Peoples in the Middle East probably began working copper in this way as much as 10,000 years ago. Then – perhaps 8,000 years ago – someone made the remarkable discovery that copper could be melted out of certain rocks.

Perhaps the accidental inventor of copper-smelting was an ancient Egyptian exploring rocky country for coloured stones thought to hold magical powers. One such kind of stone which the Egyptians prized was malachite – a mineral rich in copper. Perhaps the collector accidentally dropped a lump of malachite in the red-hot ashes of his camp fire. As he watched, brightly shining globules of liquid metal ran from the malachite. The startled onlooker must have been even more astonished to notice that as the globules cooled they hardened. His chance discovery meant that by heating copper-bearing rocks men could extract pure copper in a liquid form; and that if they poured this molten copper into a mould it would cool and harden in the mould's shape – as a knife blade, axe-head, or some other weapon, tool or ornament.

Once men understood this fact (and they were slow to do so) they could begin to manufacture tools

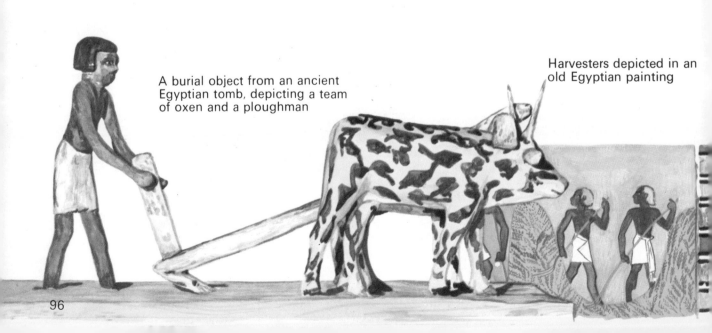

A burial object from an ancient Egyptian tomb, depicting a team of oxen and a ploughman

Harvesters depicted in an old Egyptian painting

with all and more of the advantages of stone. For like stone, copper tools are hard and can be sharpened. But copper tools are less brittle than stone, and once blunted they can be remelted and recast.

But making copper tools proved a particularly complex process calling for the invention of two-piece moulds, crucibles, tongs, furnaces, and above all bellows to provide the blast of air for heating the furnaces to 1200 degrees Centigrade — the temperature at which copper melts. The demanding tasks of finding and mining copper ore, then smelting and moulding copper also called for well-trained miners, smelters, and smiths, working full time in the copper-bearing mountains often far from the food-rich valleys. Only when the valley farmers began trading food with the mountain peoples were enough people freed from food production to start making useful quantities of metal tools, ornaments, and weapons.

About 5,800 years ago a great new incentive for trading in metal objects appeared when metal workers learned that by melting copper with tin they could produce a substance that was both easier to cast than copper and was harder. They had developed the alloy bronze which gives its name to the Bronze Age — the period after the New Stone Age when bronze began replacing stone for tools and weapons.

It was trade in bronze tools more than any other factor which sparked off the inventions of the early civilisations, of which writing was perhaps the greatest. Different kinds of writing included the hieroglyphics which Egyptians inked on flattened stems of papyrus, and the wedge-shaped or cuneiform script which Sumerians impressed in soft clay tablets with reed tips. Such systems were vital for recording trade transactions in the Bronze Age civilisations that took root in the Middle East, then spread west across the Mediterranean and east to India and China.

Egyptian hieroglyphic writing on papyrus

Babylonian cuneiform inscription in clay

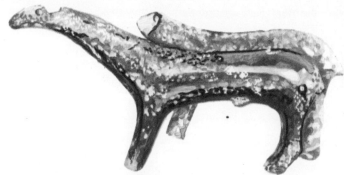

Two animals cast in bronze

Golden jewellery from Bronze Age Crete

Bronze figurines from Sardinia

Sumerian war chariot pulled by onagers.

INVENTING THE WHEEL

A Bronze Age invention which almost more than any other was to revolutionise trade and transport was the wheel, but its development was the climax to a chain of earlier discoveries. Back in the Old Stone Age hunters had discovered that it was easier to drag slaughtered deer than to carry them on their backs. In 5,000 B.C. men were pulling loads along on sleds whose smooth runners helped to overcome the braking effect of friction, and by 2,000 B.C. teams of sled-hauling Egyptians were moving statues and stone blocks weighing several tons.

The main drawback to sleds is the fact that slight roughnesses in the ground produce friction along the entire length of the sled's runners. The wheel largely overcomes this problem, for its round surface rolls instead of slides, reducing the effects of friction, and so requiring less effort for moving a given load.

The Sumerian inventors who built the first wheels about 5,500 years ago may have taken the idea from log rollers used for shifting heavy stone blocks. But for every 30 centimetres (one foot) moved by a roller 122 centimetres (4 feet) in circumference, its load travels 61 centimetres (2 feet) and falls off. This does not happen when the rollers are wheels separated by an axle which supports the load. The world's first carts, which were hauled by asses had four wheels made of solid three-piece discs. Later came two-wheeled war chariots with lightweight spoked wheels; the horses which eventually pulled these ancient middle eastern battle tanks were, incidentally, first tamed by the wild nomadic tribes of Central Asia.

MAKING MUD AS HARD AS ROCK

The use of wheels for transport could have arisen from the potter's wheel. Pottery is a far older craft than either wheelwrighting or copper smelting. Indeed it can be traced back to the very dawn of farming: to the times when people began to settle down and collect useful possessions that would have been too heavy for their nomadic ancestors to carry about. The first pots were perhaps simply waterproof clay linings for baskets. Perhaps the baskets accidentally caught fire, leaving behind a hard-baked clay shell — a hollow vessel which could store not only grain but water and which withstood heat well enough to hold boiling water used for cooking purposes. Baked clay storage and cooking pots became essential to almost all farming peoples.

Most likely it was women who first discovered how to make pots. By laboriously hand-moulding lumps of wet river clay, or building up the pots from worm-like strips of clay, they would sun-dry or bake the finished results in an open fire to produce drab brown, grey, or red ware according to the local clay colour and the kind of fuel.

By 3,500 B.C. some potters of the Middle East were able to produce a large pot in minutes instead of days by shaping it upon a spinning, horizontal wheel, at first by hand, then by a foot-pedal that left both hands free for moulding. They had also learned to produce harder, more durable pots by firing them in ovens instead of placing them directly in the flames. And they were learning how to give pottery attractive glazes and pictorial designs. Vessels which had begun as purely useful containers thus gave rise to superbly shaped and coloured works of art, for instance the ornately patterned three-legged Chinese vessels, and Cretan vases bearing designs of fish and octopuses. Eventually Middle East peoples also learned to bake beautifully enamelled bricks designed rather like pieces of a jigsaw puzzle which they built up to make a picture wall. But as we shall now see, peoples of the the early civilisations also used baked-clay bricks to raise large impressive buildings.

Enamelled brickwork from ancient Persia.

A group of Egyptian pyramids at Giza.

Realistic donkeys sculptured in an old Egyptian tomb

TEMPLES, TOMBS, AND PALACES

Back in the New Stone Age a few simple buildings sufficed to make a village. But a large Bronze Age city needed not only more, but specially designed buildings to satisfy special needs.

Rulers of such cities as Harappa and Mohenjo Daro in the Indus Valley therefore began organising granaries to store food against times of famine, reservoirs (some fed by aqueducts), highways, drainage systems, thick protective city walls, gigantic royal tombs and palaces, and temples to proclaim the power of the gods. Building on such a scale shows that city rulers could call upon the resources of huge teams of workers and vast quantities of raw materials. Such rulers included the pharaohs who dominated Egypt, and the kings of Babylonia who mastered much of what is now Iraq.

But large buildings such as these called for more than the co-ordinated efforts of thousands of labourers. Building could not begin without surveyors able to draw plans, mark out sites, and reckon the quantities of materials required — skills which furthered the young study of mathematics. Knowledge of what could be done with available materials was also essential: in Egypt builders spanned doorways with huge slabs of quarried stone, but in Mesopotamia, where stone was scarce, builders began to span spaces by fitting bricks together to produce the world's first arches. Building also called for the development of special tools to hew, shape, and shift heavy blocks of stone.

Little remains of the ancient Egyptian cities but the great stone tombs of the ancient pharaohs remain among the wonders of the world. Scores of these man-made monumental structures, called pyramids, line the River Nile. Perhaps the most impressive of all is the immense Great Pyramid of the Pharaoh Khufu who died over 4,500 years ago. Nearly 2,500,000 stone blocks, each weighing about 2·5 tonnes (2½ tons), went into the making of this massive structure whose topmost block originally stood 146·7 metres (481 feet) above a great 5·25 hectare (13-acre) base measured so accurately that it is only a fraction of a centimetre outside a true square. To build the pyramid, some 100,000 men spent 20 years quarrying the rocks, ferrying them across the Nile, and raising them into position with the aid of rollers, ramps, ropes and levers.

Nothing but mounds of rubble remain to remind us of the lost splendour of such Bronze Age Mesopotamian cities as Ur, Lagash, and Larsa, but, patient excavation has helped archaeologists to reveal how they must have looked. Greatest of all ancient cities to be excavated was Babylon, a wealthy trading centre in Mesopotamia astride the cross-roads of the ancient world. Three miles of mounds strewn along the River Euphrates in Iraq mark the site of this mighty city which Hammurabi made the capital of Babylonia some 3,800 years ago, and which the Chaldean king Nebuchadnezzar II magnificently rebuilt before he died in 561 B.C.

Nebuchadnezzar's Babylon was a vast square of colossal outer walls enclosing fields and the main city, which was protected by an inner wall pierced with great bronze gates. Inside, mud-brick houses lined the grid of streets. One of the palaces within the city was noted for its Hanging Gardens, an ornamental collection of decorative plants placed on top of tall arches.

Above all else towered an immense stepped pyramid, crowned by a temple dedicated to the god Marduk. Priests reached the temple by a great stairway which climbed the seven stages of the pyramid like a ladder leading to heaven. Each stage was coloured to represent one of seven levels between heaven and the underworld. It was such a *ziggurat*, or 'high point' as these stepped pyramids were called, that inspired the famous Tower of Babel bible story.

Sometimes a ruler's palace might be almost as large as a city. One such sprawling maze of corridors and rooms was the Bronze-Age Palace of Minos at Cnossus, in Crete. Far larger was ancient Mari in northern Syria: a palace complex with nearly 300 rooms. But among the most splendid of ancient eastern palaces were those built after the Bronze Age ended, at Nineveh by the Assyrian ruler Sennacherib after 700 B.C. and at Persepolis by Persia's Darius the Great (about 520 B.C.).

The greatest ancient structure of all, however, was the 2,200 kilometre-long (1,400-mile) Great Wall of China, built in a vain attempt to protect the Chinese from barbaric hordes who roamed Central Asia.

Ruined brick walls in the Sumerian city of Ur.

about 5,500 years ago — some 4,500 years after farming began in the Middle East. Another great time lag separated the start of metal working in the Middle East from its introduction into Western Europe.

For thousands of years most Europeans lived in small Neolithic villages; some were built on high well-drained hills; others were raised on wooden piles driven into the marshy edge of Swiss and German lakes.

Europe's Neolithic villagers lived mainly in rectangular huts clustered about small clearings in the great forests which then covered much of the land. Villagers lived by growing wheat and barley, harvesting wild apples, fishing, and hunting. They also wove baskets and simple clothing, worked with wood, moulded simple pots, and travelled with the help of sleds, skis (in Scandinavia), eventually carts, and dugout canoes.

Although Europeans still used stone tools (such as axes, hoes, sickles, and daggers) they gave many of these objects a finely ground and polished finish. And to get the best stone, peoples in chalk country learned to tunnel down until they reached rich seams of flint.

Backward though they undoubtedly were, the Europeans were by no means isolated. A thriving trade in stone axe-heads made by 'factories' in Ireland, Wales, and northern England linked the peoples of the British Isles, while Danes, using a long route that crossed the Alps, traded 'magical' yellow amber with Mediterranean peoples.

THE BACKWARD EUROPEANS

Long after the ancient city-dwelling Egyptians were building their colossal pyramids, and the Sumerians had raised their first ziggurats, European peoples remained for centuries in Stone Age conditions.

Only gradually did the New Stone Age skills of farming filter through the Mediterranean and up the Danube Valley to north-west Europe, to reach Britain

THE AGE OF IRON

Soon after bronze tools had at last reached north-west Europe they were being outdated in the Middle East by iron. The Egyptians had made beads from iron meteorites as long ago as 3000 B.C., but it was not until about 1200 B.C. that iron ore became widely known and used. This might seem surprising, since iron ores are much commoner than copper ores. Its usefulness remained unknown largely because iron melts at a far higher temperature than copper, and Bronze Age smiths were unable to produce such high temperatures.

CITY STATES OF SOUTH-EAST EUROPE

In the Middle East bronze weapons had helped ambitious rulers to weld the city states of Sumer and Akkad into the powerful nation of Babylonia; iron weapons later helped the Assyrians to scoop Babylonia inside their empire. Then by 500 B.C. the iron-using Persian armies under Cyrus of Persia had seized Egypt and Asia Minor and made Babylonia the heart of the largest empire then known in south-west Asia. Babylonia was later overrun and conquered by Alexander the Great, then by the Romans and, finally, by the Parthians.

Above: *ancient ironwork from the Hittite Empire.*
Right: *Greek vase painting of Dionysus, god of wine, bringing the grape vine to Greece.*

However, about 1400 B.C. peoples living in the Hittite Empire based on Turkey learned to heat iron ore red hot, and to separate the iron from the slag residue by hammering. Then, they learned to harden this soft wrought iron by hammering it in contact with bits of charcoal to produce a kind of hard, tough steel, which could be hardened further by quenching in cold water.

About 1200 B.C. the Hittite Empire broke up and the smiths were scattered, taking with them their great discovery of an abundant kind of useful metal far cheaper than bronze. By the 8th century B.C., the warlike Assyrians were proving the value of iron weapons by battering their neighbours into submission. Soon, too, peasants unable to afford bronze tools began to benefit from iron hoes, axes, picks, and ploughshares. The age of iron was dawning.

While iron helped ambitious kings to forge powerful empires in the Middle East, it had a very different effect in Greece — a rocky peninsula in south-east Europe, where small fertile valleys alternate with barren mountains. Here there were no big rivers to provide a linking highway as in ancient Egypt and Sumeria; the Greeks depended instead upon the open sea. This landward isolation helped the city states that sprang up round the coasts to keep their independence.

Iron tools certainly brought changes to the Greeks, however. Iron-bladed hoes and other implements allowed peasant farmers to open up stony ground for cultivation, enabling them to produce larger crops of wheat, grapes, and olives — food plants which, in turn, supported a rise in population. By 750 B.C., however, population was outstripping

1

peoples, Greek thinkers used their powers of reason as never before to detect important similarities and differences between objects, numbers, shapes, and abstract ideas. Thus by about 400 B.C. Democritus had theorised that the entire universe consisted of millions of tiny particles of the same material differently arranged in different objects; in other words he predicted the existence of atoms some 2,300 years before it could be proved. Studying mathematics for its own sake (rather than to solve building problems as the Sumerians and Egyptians had done) Thales of Miletus, in 600 B.C., helped to found geometry as we know it. Pythagoras, another brilliant mathematician, who lived in the 6th century B.C., proclaimed that the earth was round. Probing the natural world, the philosopher Aristotle, who lived in the 4th century B.C., recognised that living animals range in an orderly way from simple lowly creatures to the complex apes and man. Hippocrates (about 460–377 B.C.) rejected magic and pioneered scientific medicine.

The Greeks, then, developed science and mathematics as we understand them; yet to Greek thinkers no sharp line divided science from art. Greek architects built mathematical rules into the designs of temples to provide harmony of line and beauty of proportion. Greek architects supported buildings like the gleaming marble Parthenon in Athens on beautifully tapered and fluted columns which were crowned by delicately carved stone slabs or scrolls. Similarly Greek sculptors made a mathematically calculated perfect human figure which was the framework for their statues of muscular warriors and athletes, the fine proportions of which have never been surpassed in art.

food supply, and overcrowded city states were forced to send colonies of landless peasants overseas. In western North Africa and Spain the Greek emigrants found their landings blocked by Phoenician settlers from the eastern Mediterranean; and in northern Italy the Greeks found the civilised Etruscans firmly entrenched. But the people of the Greek city states successfully threw a necklace of colonies round the Black, Ionian, and Aegean seas.

Living a freer life than the subjects of their rival autocratic oriental empires, Greek thinkers at home and abroad were able to push human knowledge outwards in new directions.

Building upon the discoveries of Middle Eastern

2

3

4

The Greeks also excelled in other arts — drama, lyric poetry and history.

Many of the great Greek accomplishments in the arts and sciences were produced in the small city state of Athens which we remember chiefly as the first nation with a democratic form of government. But while we recall Athens as the fountain-head of Western civilisation we must remember too that only one in seven of Athens' 315,000 inhabitants had the privilege of voting and still fewer were probably rich enough to devote their lives to the pursuit of learning and beauty. Most of the rest were slaves, and it was slave labour which propped up the proud fabric of the Athenian state. Many slaves were war prisoners who worked in cruel conditions to win silver from the mines of Laurium, where they toiled by lamplight, picking out the silver ore which was then piled into baskets, hauled up by ropes and pulleys, and processed into coins — a form of money probably invented in nearby Asia Minor only after 700 B.C.

Coins (discs stamped with a government's guarantee of weight and value) assisted the development of trade, as did the Greek alphabet — a system of signs representing sounds which had been adapted from the even older Phoenician alphabet.

Assisted by coinage and the alphabet, trade was the secret of survival for overpopulated Athens, which produced far too little food to feed itself. Instead, it lived by shipping out such goods as wine, olive oil, metals, cloth, and pottery; it imported grain and fish from the Greek colonies round the Black Sea.

To supply this thriving economy hundreds of Greek potters worked in small factories mass-producing wine containers in the form of Grecian urns, many of them beautifully glazed and painted

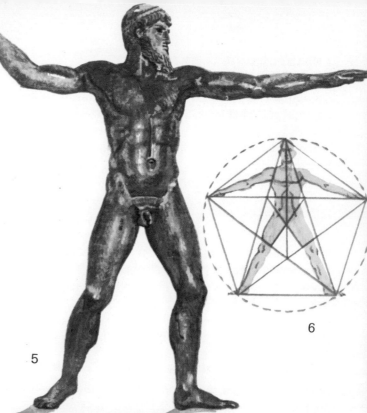

5

6

with human figures. Meanwhile factories of up to 100 smiths beat out iron shields and swords, rope makers slowly trod their walks, and in tiny textile factories weavers wove cloth, some of it coloured with the rare purple dye obtained from the murex shellfish. Elsewhere Athenian shipwrights were building the two main types of Greek vessel: roomy, wooden-hulled, slow-moving merchant sailing ships, and sharp-prowed warships manned by teams of oarsmen and armed with sharp metal rams projecting from the bows. No products were more important to Athens than its ships, for the entire prosperity and defence of this city state hinged on sea trade and naval warfare.

1. The temple of Athena Nike built on the Acropolis at Athens in 424 B.C.
2, 3, 4: columns and their crowning capitals representing the three orders of Greek architecture.
2. Doric (heavy), 3. Ionic (elegant and simple),
4. Corinthian (ornate).
5. Greek bronze statue (5th century B.C.).
6. The canon of human proportions in Greek art.
7. Early (8th century B.C.) Greek vase with geometric designs.
8. Greek vase of the 5th century B.C.

7

8

103

ENGINEERS OF ALEXANDRIA

By 300 B.C. a rich new city was emerging in Egypt south of the Mediterranean Sea — Alexandria. It was founded in 332 B.C. by the Greek-educated Macedonian, Alexander the Great, whose whirlwind conquests had made him, first, master of Greece, then master of the known world east to India.

Alexandria stood at the mouth of the Nile delta near old land routes from Arabia and Mesopotamia, and Alexander had judged that its position would make it the leading centre for a rich new trade between the conquered cities of the Middle East and Greece in south-east Europe. War-torn Athens lost its old proud leadership of the Greeks, and under Alexander's general, Ptolemy and his successors, Alexandria flourished and became the hub of a much enlarged Greek-speaking world.

The Egyptian city's broad highways, large warehouses, ship-lined quays, and unique lighthouse, all spoke of huge prosperity. But what most attracted Greek scholars to Alexandria were its library and university. These study centres brought together not only the riches of Greek learning, but the ancient knowledge of the Middle East. It was in Alexandria that the Greek mathematician Euclid worked out a system of geometry that would be taught in schools more than 2,000 years later. Here, Eratosthenes combined geometry with astronomy to compute the earth's diameter at about 12,560 kilometres (7,850 miles) — only 120 kilometres (76 miles) less than its diameter at the equator. Here, too, astronomers pondered Aristarchus's declaration that the earth revolved round the sun; and the great anatomist Herophilus described the brain.

But the greatest figure of the Alexandrian age was the mathematician-inventor Archimedes, who studied in Alexandria but worked largely at Syracuse in Sicily. Called the world's first true engineer, Archimedes has been credited with explaining the

Ships like this sailed from Alexandria.

principle of the lever. All machines that reduce the effort needed for moving heavy loads, including the pulley, screw, wedge, and wheel are based on the principle of the lever. Archimedes also discovered the principle by which objects placed in a liquid float or sink. And his method for working out the ratio of a circle's circumference to its diameter helped him to tackle hitherto unsolvable problems dealing with the areas of circles, and the volumes of cylinders. He also pioneered methods now employed in the branch of higher mathematics known as calculus.

Archimedes used some of his discoveries to make or improve upon certain practical inventions such as the capstan (systems of toothed interlocking gear wheels), the Archimedean screw (a screw which revolves inside a cylinder to raise water for irrigation purposes), and a crane with grappling hooks for lifting hostile ships from the sea. For King Hiero of Syracuse he built the *Syracusan*, one of the largest and most sumptuously appointed ships of ancient times, featuring an iron balustrade, and said to be capable of carrying several thousand tons of merchandise, passengers in lavishly designed cabins, a crew of 600, and a guard of 300 marines.

But Archimedes was not the only great inventor linked with Alexandria. In the 2nd century B.C. Ctesibius evidently made an improved water clock and devices worked by air pressure, including a type of air gun, a force pump, and a fire engine. Hero, who lived there in the 3rd century A.D., seemingly developed siphons, water organs, and even a simple kind of steam engine.

Astonishing as it may seem, Greek inventors looked on such remarkable contraptions as no more than toys, and ignored the possibilities that they offered for easing the hard labour of the workers and raising industrial output. In an age when slave labour was cheap and abundant most wealthy Greeks could see no reason for replacing men with engines.

Early gear wheels: the slowly turning big wheel spins the small one quickly.

THE AGE OF ROME

We have seen how civilisation began in the Middle East and spread westwards to the Greeks of southeast Europe whose colonists helped to carry it round the Mediterranean shores. By the 3rd century B.C. another European people, the Latin-speaking Romans of central Italy, were building their own Iron Age culture, and expanding.

Determined and well disciplined, Roman troops steadily subdued the peoples around them – by 264 B.C. they had first conquered other Italian tribes, and by 146 B.C. they had overthrown the powerful Carthaginian Empire built up by Phoenician settlers in the western Mediterranean. By A.D. 14 Roman rule and Roman civilisation embraced France, Spain, southern Central Europe, and the Greek-speaking lands around the eastern Mediterranean. When the Roman Emperor Trajan died in A.D. 117 much of what are now Great Britain, Rumania and Iraq had been added to the empire.

The Roman troops who won the empire were infantry who fought with spears and short swords made of better steel than most of their enemies possessed. They carried shields, and wore protective helmets, breastplates, and often jointed leg-guards. For artillery they used big mobile catapults capable of shooting heavy iron-headed arrows several hundred feet, or hurling rocks as heavy as a man for shorter distances.

To crush the Carthaginians, the Romans built a battle fleet and developed cavalry, although less effectively than Alexander the Great had done. But

*Roman officer
(from a bas-relief)*

STAGES IN ROME'S IMPERIAL EXPANSION

BRITANNIA
• Eburacum
• Londinium
Lutetia
Augusta Treverorum
GERMANIA
Burdigala
Lugdunum
Mediolanum
Sirmiur
Narbo
Massilia
Roma
Augusta Emerita
Tarraco
Carthago Nova
MAURETANIA
NUMIDIA
Carthago

their general success was due mainly to the infantry and its tactics of abandoning the old-style solid phalanx formation and fighting in three divisions subdivided into mobile sections. Roman victories of course also owed a great deal to the leadership of brilliant generals like Julius Caesar.

For centuries the Romans cleverly ruled the huge empire which they had won. Although they were brilliant soldiers and administrators they lacked, however, much of the inventive genius of the Greeks and Middle Eastern peoples. Indeed, they relied largely on Greek architects to help in the design of their buildings.

Even so, the comfort-loving Romans carried many inventions and discoveries much further. For instance, they warmed their homes with complex hot-air central heating systems; became the first people to fit their windows with glass (a product first invented perhaps about 3000 B.C.); arranged sheets of calf-skin, lambskin, and kidskin in layers to produce some of the world's first books; and in 46 B.C. invented a calendar which remained in use for over 1,500 years.

But above all we probably remember the Romans as the first people to take the ancient idea of the arch and use it for spanning space in new ambitious ways. Mighty arched aqueducts like the one pictured here helped to carry piped supplies of lifegiving water to cities, many miles from the source of streams and springs. Similarly, great arched bridges provided highways across rivers that had once been barriers to travel. Romans also used the arch technique to roof colossal public baths and support the tiered seats of huge amphitheatres.

A 720 metre long Roman aqueduct built at Segovia in Spain over 1,800 years ago. It was still in use in the 20th century.

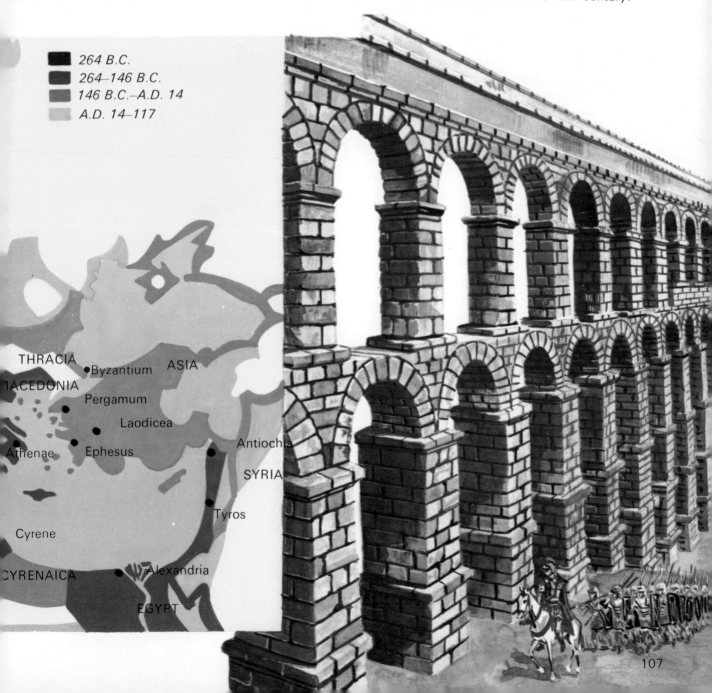

264 B.C.
264–146 B.C.
146 B.C.–A.D. 14
A.D. 14–117

THRACIA
MACEDONIA
•Byzantium
ASIA
Pergamum
Laodicea
Athenae
Ephesus
Antiochia
SYRIA
Tyros
Cyrene
CYRENAICA
Alexandria
EGYPT

Nowhere were Roman buildings more impressive than in Rome itself, possibly the world's first city to hold more than a million people, many occupying multi-storey flats. A great system of aqueducts supplied them with water, while underground drains carried waste matter from the city out into the River Tiber. The citizens of Rome worshipped Jupiter and their other gods in fine stone temples. The great round, domed Pantheon raised over 1,800 years ago in honour of all Roman gods is still standing.

The centre of city life was the forum, a great open space flanked by government offices and a large assembly hall, or basilica, where bankers, lawyers, and merchants met for business. Roman citizens could pass their leisure time bathing, chatting, exercising, shopping, and even dining inside great vaulted public baths, some capable of accommodating several thousand people. Even more capacious were the huge public hippodromes and amphitheatres such as the Colosseum, where as many as 45,000 people enjoyed colourful and often gory spectacles. These ranged from chariot races and life-and-death struggles between gladiators and wild beasts to naval battles made possible by flooding the entire arena.

To feed Rome's teeming thousands, an army of slaves and poor labourers was kept constantly at work, ploughing, harrowing, sowing, reaping, flailing ears of wheat to separate grains from husks, grinding grain into flour in dreary rows of hand-mills, or kneading dough and baking loaves in public bakeries. Workers also made olive oil and wine, squeezing the juice from olives and grapes by turning a screw which moved a heavy press. Meanwhile weavers were busy making linen, cotton, and silk textiles, and metal workers were producing alloys.

Rome's huge demands for food and manufactured goods could scarcely be satisfied by its adjacent fields and mines. Instead, miners throughout the empire toiled for the copper, iron, lead, silver, gold, and marble which Rome needed; and North Africa became a great granary, exporting huge quantities of wheat to Italy.

Such large-scale trade was only possible because Rome had a superb communication network. The fine port of Ostia was its springboard to the western Mediterranean. Paved roads ran north before fanning out across western Europe, and the great Appian

Street scene in a Roman town.

Chariot race in a Roman hippodrome.

A Roman temple based on Greek designs.

Way struck southeastwards to Brundisium, from where ships ferried troops and traders across the narrow Adriatic Sea to the Via Egnatia — a highway linking Rome with Asia Minor. Policed by Rome's army and navy, roads and sea routes were made safe for the merchants who brought to the city not only the necessities of life but highly prized oriental luxuries such as silk from China, and spices from south-east Asia. For the first time ever, the peoples of western Europe and east Asia were put in touch, although indirectly, through Indian, Persian, and Arab middlemen.

Throughout the Roman Empire trade enriched the towns — many of them new settlements founded by the Romans. Places like *Lugdunum* (Lyons), *Lutetia* (Paris), *Londinium* (London), and *Eburacum* (York) grew large and prosperous — the birth of many of Western Europe's great modern cities was taking place.

Yet the powerfully organised Roman Empire survived for less than five centuries against over 30 centuries for Egypt's and over 20 for that of imperial China. For several reasons, its government, trade, and towns were in decay by A.D. 400. By A.D. 500 Goths, Vandals, Huns and other so-called barbarians had stormed inside its frontiers from eastern Europe, many fighting on horseback using stirrups — a device which made it difficult to dislodge a rider from his horse, and an Asian invention which the Romans did not possess. Sweeping west and south through western Europe, they splintered the western Roman Empire into small barbarian kingdoms. Only the eastern Roman Empire centred on the great new city of Constantinople survived.

Oared warships of the Roman battle fleet.

EUROPE'S DARK AND MIDDLE AGES

The Barbarian invasions which toppled the West Roman Empire by A.D. 500 were the first of many attacks that ravaged Europe in the next five centuries. From the north, fierce Viking sea raiders harried western Europe's shores. From the east, Slavs and Magyars struck at Germany. From the south, Moslem Arabs invaded Spain.

Such onslaughts helped to keep western Europeans divided and poor — so poor that their cities shrank into towns, and the towns into villages. The peasants sank back into an almost New Stone Age way of life, producing barely enough to feed themselves and leaving only a small surplus to barter for salt and iron tools. The five centuries that followed the collapse of the Roman Empire are deservedly called Europe's Dark Ages.

But although the flame of European civilisation flickered, it was never snuffed out completely. Those who did most to keep it burning were the missionaries and monks of the young Christian Church at Rome who spread their faith and founded churches and monasteries all over Western Europe. Church school teachers helped to keep alive the skills of reading and writing. Farmer monks began clearing forests and draining swamps. They cultivated heavy northern soils with iron-bladed ploughs fitted with wooden mould boards for overturning the sliced strips of sod. In time, they learned to harness teams of horses to the plough and to replace the old ox-yoke (which half choked the horses by pulling on their windpipes) with the horse-collar which rested comfortably against their shoulders, so making much better use of the creatures' traction power. Monks also knew how to rest the soil to preserve its fertility, and they ground grain with labour-saving mills worked by running water.

Surprising as it may seem, some of the inventions that made Dark Age life a little easier were brought by the destructive barbarian invaders. For instance the Huns — peoples who lived on horseback — have been credited with inventing or developing the bit, the spur, the stirrup, the saddle, the horseshoe and other equipment which altogether made horses extremely manageable and useful animals.

By about A.D. 1000 Europe's Dark Ages were giving way to the much more prosperous Middle Ages. Big changes now affected the Europeans' lives. By now the worst waves of barbarian invasion had been thrown back or absorbed. In the more peaceful atmosphere that followed, the young nations of modern Europe began emerging. At first their kings had little power over their warrior nobles who controlled large estates from their castle fortresses, and cowed the serfs, or peasants, who

Stained-glass windows from Chartres show how knights fought on foot and horseback.

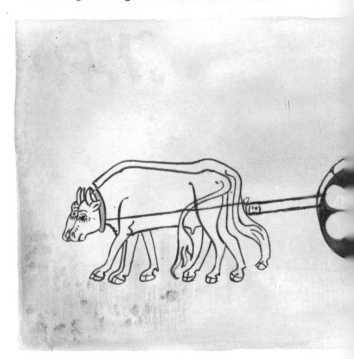

A 12th century peasant ploughman.

lived in huts and made up the majority of the population.

Under the so-called feudal system nobles held land from the king in return for promising him knights in time of war; serfs provided nobles with food in return for protection against roving bands of thieves and murderers. In some countries, everyone

chants formed powerful groups called guilds. By 1400, many towns had bought trading rights from the kings, who used the cash to hire standing armies which crushed rebellious nobles and so helped the kings to forge strong national governments.

Much of the trade that made these changes possible was in different products from different parts of Europe, for instance in English wool, Flemish cloth, French wine, Scandinavian fish, Italian glass, Prussian amber, and Russian furs.

A network of great trading centres grew up to handle this rich international exchange. Six big trade fairs a year were held in Champagne (now part of France). In the north, German cities formed the powerful Hanseatic League; in the south Venice and Genoa were the leading trading rivals.

Besides trading in their own products, the big Venetian and Genoese galleys brought Western Europe much-coveted luxuries from the East, especially silks, spices, perfumes, precious stones, fragrant woods, ivory, and Damascus steel blades. Some of this merchandise came from the Byzantine Empire (as the East Roman Empire became known). But, after the religious wars known as Crusades had put Europeans in close trading touch with the Arab lands, much came from the great area which the Moslem Arabs had overrun in and after the 7th century. This stretched from Spain to India, embracing the old heartlands of Middle Eastern civilisation and touching the great medieval civilisations of India and China.

Contact between Christians and Moslems was to have an everlasting effect on European civilisation. From the Arabs, Europeans acquired many eastern food plants including rice, sugar cane, shallots, artichokes, cotton, and apricots. Through Arab middlemen they also learned of the Chinese inventions of paper-making and gunpowder; and they learned how to use the simple Indian system of numerals (including the sign for zero) which made calculating easier than it had ever been. From the Moslems, Europeans also gradually rediscovered the long-lost writings of Aristotle and other ancient thinkers whose works had been preserved in Syria and Egypt. Indeed, while Europe had been sunk in Dark-Age ignorance, Arab scholars in their universities had been extending ancient learning; so much so that by 1100 the poet-mathematician Omar Khayyam was pioneering modern algebra. Discoveries like these also trickled into Europe.

Such civilising influences gave medieval Europeans a taste for a more comfortable way of life.

By 1400 the wealthy wore finely woven wool or linen clothes, and enriched their homes with chimneys, glass windows, wax candles, and carpets. But better clothes and homes were only part of the achievements of medieval Europe.

was tied together in this complex system of rights and obligations.

Gradually, though, the bonds of feudalism slackened. As life grew less warlike, trade revived, money circulated, and many peasants began to buy their freedom from serfdom and move off the land into the now expanding towns where craftsmen and mer-

MEDIEVAL ART AND ARCHITECTURE

Easily the finest monuments to Europe's medieval civilisation are its churches. Early Christian churches were little more than barn-like buildings with stone walls and wooden roofs, but over the centuries they became more complex. Many were built in the shape of crosses; they contained chapels and apses and were surmounted by tall bell towers.

Soon after A.D. 1000, French architects had

supported on tall, slim columns joined to buttresses outside the walls. The buttresses helped to prevent the main columns collapsing under the huge outward thrust of the roof. Now that they had replaced massive walls with slender pillars, the architects filled the tall pointed arches between the pillars with huge stained-glass windows made from pieces of coloured glass joined by lead strips.

Because this graceful style of architecture owed little to the Romans, people condemned it as bar-

Romanesque column

A chapel of the Knights Templar: a 12th-century Romanesque building at Laon in northern France.

ceased to roof these large buildings with a framework of wooden beams. Instead they built a solid stone vault whose great weight was supported by massive columns and thick stone walls pierced by small windows with rounded tops. First built in France, but recalling the great vaulted buildings of the Romans, this type of architecture became known as *Romanesque*.

About A.D. 1150, however, architects were experimenting with new and daring kinds of church design in which immensely tall churches were roofed by sharply arching vaults. The roof was

baric or *Gothic*. Now, however, almost everyone admires the magnificent vaults, towers, and spires of such great Gothic churches as Notre Dame in Paris and Salisbury in England. Stained glass windows depicting events in the Bible and beautifully carved stone figures helped to teach simple Bible tales to the many medieval churchgoers who were unable to read or write.

Such churches are monuments to the religious devotion of their builders; they are also reminders of their medieval designers' astonishing ability to solve difficult problems in physics and mathematics.

HARNESSING THE WINDS AND WATERS

To build their great Gothic cathedrals, medieval architects relied upon skilled manpower. For heavier work, people used mostly horses and oxen.

Such strong, docile animals ground grain into flour, operated windlasses for hauling buckets from mine-shafts, worked water pumps for irrigating land, and performed many more such tasks. But medieval people were also replacing the muscle power of men of two large wooden-headed mallets that alternately rose and fell, pounding cloth as part of the thickening process called fulling. There were also water-driven saw-mills, and eventually mills with revolving grindstones for polishing and sharpening weapon blades, mills for crushing ores, and mills for working windlasses.

In medieval times, water-mills became so important that industries tended to concentrate close to fast-flowing streams and rivers. To make the best

Gothic capital

Gothic architecture: the choir of Beauvais Cathedral (13th century).

and beasts with machines that harnessed the natural forces of running water and moving air.

From the Romans they inherited the idea of the water-mill, in which flowing water turns a wheel whose motion is transmitted to a grindstone by a system of interlocking wheels capable of altering the speed and direction of movement so that the grindstone can be used for crushing grain.

Developing the idea of the water-mill in different ways, medieval engineers built a variety of water-driven machines. One of those was the fulling-mill in which a water-wheel engaged tappets in the shafts

possible use of these natural supplies of energy engineers learned to regulate the flow of water by building dams and dredging and canalising rivers.

In the Low Countries, where streams flow only sluggishly, the Dutch became experts at harnessing wind instead of water by building windmills — possibly a Persian invention which reached Europe in the 12th century. Equipped with systems of cog wheels enabling the sails to catch the wind from any direction, windmills helped the industrious Dutch to drain low-lying areas and to reclaim great tracts of land from the sea.

A mobile muzzle-loading cannon

CANNONS AND CARAVELS

Warfare was one of the greatest spurs to developments in medieval metal making. Primitive artillery probably dates from 1250, and some of the first bronze cannons were first fired at the Battle of Crécy in 1346. Such weapons were made by pouring molten metal into three-piece moulds of baked clay — a process based on casting big church bells. Later, new ways of making blast furnaces hotter helped armourers to produce cannons from cast iron. The early cannons were muzzle-loaded with a charge of gunpowder, followed by a heavy iron or stone ball; ignited through a tiny hole in the base of the barrel, the gunpowder exploded forcing the cannon ball out of the mouth. After cannons came the invention of the first hand-guns, known as arquebuses.

Until firearms became accurate enough to make protective clothing useless, armourers were kept busy equipping knights with increasingly heavy suits of metal armour made from riveted plates or interlacing chainmail; such spear- and sword-proof suits weighed up to 100 pounds and so encumbered their wearers that a fallen knight could be as helpless as an upturned tortoise.

Developed for purposes of war and trade, shipbuilding and navigation made huge strides in the Middle Ages. However, the hardy Viking seamen had long been sailing the rough northern seas in their slim longships in which a skin of overlapping planks was fastened to wooden ribs nailed to a central keel. Steered by a stern oar, and propelled by oars and a big square sail, Viking longships from Scandinavia had reached Iceland before A.D. 900, Greenland by 932, and America by A.D. 1000 — nearly 500 years before Columbus made his famous rediscovery.

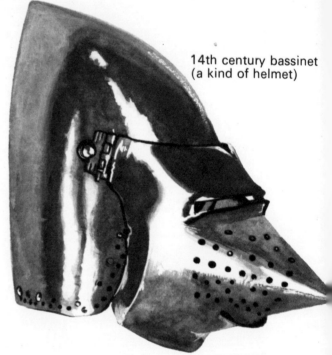

14th century bassinet (a kind of helmet)

Part of a medieval miniature showing armed knights and infantry.

An early type of caravel.

The developments that made possible this last event included Portugal's invention (at the close of the medieval period) of the caravel, a ship with two triangular lateen sails, perhaps based on the sails used by Arab dhows. Unlike Europe's traditional square-rigged ships, caravels could make good headway against a wind; and unlike the oar of the Viking longship the caravel had a much more convenient steering device in the form of a rudder hung from the sternpost.

By the 1400s such ships were not only more manoeuvrable than earlier types but they carried better navigation aids. One was the astrolabe, an Arab invention which allowed navigators to measure the sun's altitude and so to work out their latitude or north-south position. Another important navigation aid was the magnetic compass, possibly invented by the Chinese. By 1400 the free-swinging compass needle mounted on a card marked off in compass points enabled seamen to make a precise reckoning of their direction of travel. By this time map-making was also progressing, and sailors navigated the Mediterranean with the help of the so-called portulan charts. New ships and navigational aids were to bear rich fruit in the great age of geographical discovery which dawned in the 15th century.

PAPER AND PRINTING

When the Middle Ages began few people could read or write, largely because books were scarce and costly. They were costly partly because they were made from sheets of expensive parchment, but their high price also reflected the fact that each volume had to be painstakingly hand-copied, and making one volume like this could take a copyist several months. Indeed 45 copyists working for an Italian prince took nearly two years to turn out just 200 volumes.

As the Middle Ages ended, two inventions were about to make books more plentiful and much cheaper. The first of these was paper making. For centuries the Chinese wrote mainly on awkward slips of bamboo and wood, and on expensive silk. Then, about A.D. 100, some inventive Chinese discovered that by separating the fibres in mulberry bark and softening them by soaking before drying the flattened mass, he had produced a sheet of material that could be written on. Later, the Chinese learned to make fine paper from pounded rags.

After Arab troops captured some Chinese paper-makers in Central Asia, the art of paper making reached Baghdad in A.D. 795, from where it spread to Spain and Sicily. By about A.D. 1200 scribes in Christian Europe were learning that paper was better and cheaper for writing upon than parchment. Later the Europeans developed sizing and other techniques to give paper the fine, smooth finish with which we are familiar today.

Meanwhile the Europeans were evidently learning of another Chinese discovery: printing. Printing may have begun from the old practice of stamping goods with seals bearing their owners' mark. The Chinese developed this idea for stamping coloured designs on textiles and playing cards, and about A.D. 770 they were carving characters and pictures on blocks of wood and printing a page of text from each block. Carving out each Chinese character separately was a slow, cumbersome process, but in the 1400s the Europeans were also mastering wood-block printing and producing not only printed playing cards and pictures of saints, but whole books in which each letter of every page had been separately hand-carved.

Then, about 1440, some European changed the whole history of printing with movable type. Different experimenters have been credited with its invention, but the first big printing firm to use movable type was that of Johann Gutenberg, a goldsmith of Mainz in Germany. By 1448 Gutenberg seems to have learned how to use his goldsmith's tools to punch out letter shapes in soft metal and to mass produce metal type with the help of moulds. A compositor could then pick up the metal letters separately with tweezers and lay them in rows to produce pages of type held together in a frame called

A printer's workshop, showing the compositor (right) and the press operator (centre).

a chase. By fixing the chase to a screw printing press (perhaps adapted from a wine or cheese press), Gutenberg could quickly press inked lines of type against many sheets of paper, thus printing faster than ever before.

But he could only do this once he had perfected yet another invention: an ink sticky enough to cling to the metal type. The kind of ink that he used was made by grinding boiled linseed-oil with powdered charcoal or lampblack — an idea which Gutenberg may have gleaned from the oil-paints invented early in the 15th century.

Paper, movable type, the printing press, and printing ink together made books so cheap that printed text books on gunnery, navigation, arithmetic, and other subjects began spreading across Europe at an unprecedented speed.

MECHANICAL CLOCKS

Time-keeping devices date at least from about 1450 B.C. when the Egyptians made shadow clocks; time was measured by the length of a shadow cast by the sun. Other ancient time-keepers were the water clock and the hour glass — devices in which the passing of time was measured by the amount of water or sand which had flowed from a large container through a small hole. Thousands of years passed before such devices were improved upon by mechanically driven clocks.

Europe's first known mechanical clocks date from the 14th century. In these devices, an hour hand was linked by gear wheels to the shaft of a drum. A weight hung from a rope wound round the drum kept it turning. As it turned, toothed gear wheels connected to the drum turned a toothed crown wheel, which, in turn, engaged two vanes projecting from a shaft so as to rotate the shaft to and fro. Weights hung from a beam attached to the shaft made the vanes act as brakes, keeping the crown wheel turning slowly and steadily.

Clocks made on these simple lines were being installed in churches by the late 1300s. Some were extremely ornate, for instance at Wells Cathedral in England moving figures struck the hour; at Strasbourg in France an iron cock flapped its wings and crowed three times in memory of Peter's denial of Christ.

But early clocks kept poor time, for the slightest mistake in shaping their toothed wheels increased friction, producing daily errors in time-keeping. More accurate clocks appeared only after the Middle Ages, when, in the late 1600s clockmakers began replacing the old braking mechanism with a swinging

The fundamental parts of a clock: weights, pendulum, escapement wheel (which sets the other wheels in motion), and the regulator.

pendulum attached to a curved piece of metal called an escapement. This tilted up and down as the pendulum swung to and fro, interlocking with a toothed wheel so as to permit it to move only one tooth at a time. Even earlier than this clocks had appeared which worked by slowly uncoiling a spring, and the spring-driven watch dates from about 1500.

1. *Flying machine designed by Leonardo da Vinci.*
2. *Astrolabe for determining latitude.*
3. *Spanish caravel of the 15th century.*

THE AGE OF DISCOVERY

By the early 1400s, the inventions of the Middle Ages were giving western Europeans a new confidence in man's ability to mould the world to his will. By first-hand observation and experiment, thinking men now began rejecting long-held teachings about the scientific workings of the world and testing old-established authorities like Aristotle. Often this brought them into conflict with the Church, whose powerful Inquisition imprisoned and even executed people for teaching theories that ran counter to officially held belief.

But the thinkers persisted and their efforts help to give the name *Renaissance*, or rebirth, to the period between 1400 and 1600; although this term was first applied to the reawakened interest in the ancient arts of Greece and Rome that took place at this time. By 1600 the pace of scientific discovery was quickening as scholars began turning to the craftsman's newly developed tools to observe and measure the world about them; at the same time printed books

were encouraging the craftsman to learn to read, write, and reckon. As scholars and craftsmen began pooling their skills and knowledge they became better able to discover the rules which govern the workings of the natural world; and once they understood these rules men became far better placed to use them to their own advantage. Historians refer to this great burst of scientific discovery which lit up the 17th century as the scientific revolution.

One of the most outstanding figures of these times was the Italian painter-engineer Leonardo da Vinci (1452–1519), whose restlessly inquiring mind led him to make detailed sketches of subjects ranging from the bone structure of the human foot to flying machines. But perhaps the first truly scientific thinker was Galileo Galilei (1564–1642) who developed scientific method: the sequence of setting out a problem, forming a hypothesis or possible explanation of it, testing this by observation and experiment, interpreting the results, and drawing conclusions from them. Galileo's experiments led him to prove that heavy objects tend to fall at the

Vasco da Gama

Christopher Columbus landing in the Bahamas in the mistaken belief that he had reached East Asia.

same speed as light ones, and to confirm the theory of Copernicus (1473–1543) that the earth is not the centre of the universe. Later came other great discoveries in astronomy, including gravity, detected by Isaac Newton (1642–1727). Meanwhile other scientists were probing the mechanism of the human body, and in 1628 William Harvey's discovery that the heart pumps blood round the body put medicine on an entirely new footing.

Many such discoveries were assisted by new aids to calculation, observation, and measurement.

In mathematics, logarithms and decimals were now developed. The Frenchman René Descartes added an important contribution to geometry as taught by Euclid, and Newton and Leibniz devised calculus systems capable of solving hitherto baffling problems.

Spectacles had been made as early as the 13th century. By 1608, Dutch spectacle makers had discovered how to use glass lenses for making compound microscopes and telescopes. Microscopes opened up a whole new world of hitherto invisible

life; telescopes turned man's old ideas of the universe upside down.

Besides these aids to observation came many aids to precise measurement, for instance thermometers for gauging temperature; barometers to measure air pressure; the surveyor's theodolite to make map-making more accurate.

This was not only a great time of scientific discovery but a great age of geographical exploration. Already by the early 1400s the Portuguese had the ships and navigation aids needed for long-distance voyages. Soon, Portugal and Spain also gained the incentive for exploration.

After hostile Moslem rulers curtailed the rich east-west trade passing through the Mediterranean, Portuguese caravels began seeking a sea route round southern Africa to the rich spice islands of the East. By 1488 Bartholomew Diaz had rounded Southern Africa's tip; by 1492 Christopher Columbus – sailing west across the Atlantic – had discovered the un-suspected continent of America; by 1498 Vasco da Gama had sailed by way of Southern Africa to India.

But perhaps the greatest voyage of all was the first circumnavigation of the world led by Portugal's Ferdinand Magellan. Beginning in 1519, it lasted three years, and only one of the five Spanish ships and 18 of some 240 men survived to sail back to Spain under the command of Sebastian del Cano (Magellan had been killed by natives in the Philippines).

Hostile natives, shipwreck, starvation, and scurvy caused by a dried-food diet made long voyages hazardous; but the rewards were tempting. For instance, Sebastian del Cano's tiny ship *Victoria* returned with a spice cargo which more than paid for the huge losses of the whole expedition. More importantly, Columbus and other early explorers of the Americas brought back reports of gold and Stone

Peru who had ruled a mountain empire that ran more than 2,000 miles along the Andes Mountains from Ecuador to Chile.

As they spread out over the world, Europeans were learning that no native peoples had weapons to withstand their firearms. And where European conquerors triumphed, European colonists soon followed. By the early 1500s Spain was master of most of Central and South America and southern North America. Portugal laid claim to Brazil, huge stretches of the African coast, and Asian territory from India to Indonesia. But by the 1600s European rivals were contesting the Spanish and Portuguese colonial possessions: France and England were colonising North America, and the Dutch were edging the Portuguese from south-east Asia.

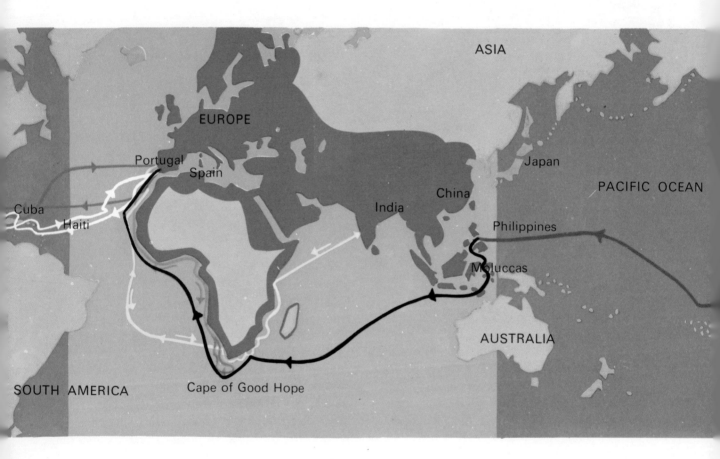

Age civilisations ripe for the taking. So in the footsteps of the explorers came conquerors like Hernando Cortes. Helped by firearms, rebellious Indian tribes, and the ravages of smallpox (an Old World disease that the Spanish took to the Americas) Cortes and his 650 troops crushed the huge Aztec Empire of Mexico in 1519 and 1520. Farther south, Francisco Pizarro repeated Cortes' success by toppling the Incas of

For the first time the peoples of one continent were discovering and mastering the rest of the world. In many ways the results were devastating for the countries that the Europeans overran. Millions of Amerindians died in smallpox epidemics; millions of Africans were enslaved to work the colonists' farms; everywhere Christian missionaries stamped out old tribal faiths and smashed and burnt fine statues and temples built in honour of heathen gods; while the conquistadores melted down tons of magnificent gold ornaments to turn the metal into coins.

But while the Europeans brought destruction they also introduced many of the benefits of their own advanced civilisation. They enriched the New World with valuable food plants such as wheat and sugar cane, and animals such as horses, cattle, chickens, and pigs. At the same time Europe's craftsmen introduced metal tools, ploughs, printing, the wheel, and the arch, while missionaries began to spread the skills of reading and writing and introduced Spanish as a common language to areas divided by hundreds of different dialects. In just a few years the fruits of thousands of years of Old World invention and discovery were flowing into

nourishment helped to support a steady rise in population.

By 1700 the resulting growth in seaborne trade had led European countries to build bigger, stronger ships. From the tiny two-masted caravels had evolved the larger three-masted carracks and proud galleons. A further helpful development in 1568 was Gerhardus Mercator's new way of showing the round world on flat paper. This greatly assisted the plotting of compass courses for long transoceanic voyages. As oriental gems and spices from India, and huge shiploads of gold and silver from America, began streaming into Europe the old Mediterranean powers of Genoa and Venice weakened. The new Atlantic sea lanes shifted the centre of gravity of Europe's trade west to Portugal, Spain, and France. But in

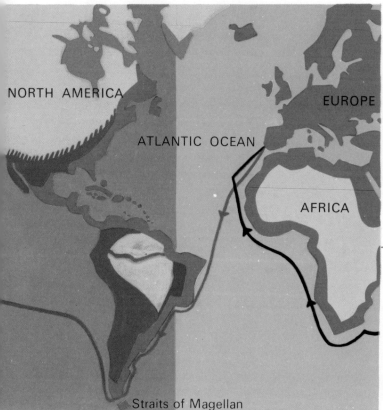

NORTH AMERICA

EUROPE

ATLANTIC OCEAN

AFRICA

Straits of Magellan

Colours represent stages in exploration.
Orange: areas unknown to the Europeans.
Red: areas discovered by the early 1520s.
Violet: areas discovered later in the 1500s.
Light blue bands show areas allocated to Portugal, *dark blue* bands show areas allocated to Spain according to the way in which Pope Alexander VI divided the world between these two powerful Catholic powers. This was done to prevent clashes between their respective explorers and colonists. Coloured lines represent major voyages of discovery in the late 1400s and early 1500s.

Green: Bartholomew Diaz (1487)
Yellow: Vasco da Gama (1497)
Blue: first voyage of Christopher Columbus (1492–1493)
White: second voyage of Christopher Columbus (1493–1496)
Brown: circumnavigation by Magellan (1519–1522), completed (*black line*) by Del Cano after Magellan's death in 1521.

countries still living largely in Stone Age conditions.

While the products of Old World civilisation were moving westwards across the Atlantic, cocoa, maize, peanuts, potatoes, tomatoes, turkeys — all produce of the Amerindians — were flowing eastwards into Europe, Africa, Asia, and eventually Australasia. A whole new range of foods was added to the diets of Old World peoples and, incidentally, this varied

these three countries close government control of trade eventually hampered merchants and manufacturers, and by 1700 Europe's leading ports lay farther north. In England and the Dutch Republic a freer way of life encouraged wealthy individuals and banks to lend capital to merchants and manufacturers in the hope that through trade and industry their investment would make them even wealthier.

BIRTH OF THE INDUSTRIAL AGE

It was to be in Britain that industry and trade brought the most far-reaching changes. In 1700 these changes would be hardly noticeable, but by 1800 they had brought about the explosive growth of manufacturing that we term the Industrial Revolution.

There were several reasons why the industrial revolution began in Britain. One was an increasing need for more manufactured goods to supply a population that had risen from 5,500,000 in 1700 to nearly double that by 1800. This rise partly followed public health improvements that had helped to cut the old high death rate to a lower level. But the rise in numbers was only kept up because British farmers began producing much more food. From Flanders, British agriculturalists adopted the four-year crop-rotation system. By growing flax, turnips, oats, and clover in turn they kept soil continuously productive. Moreover, the turnips provided valuable winter feed for cattle. From France, British farmers gleaned the idea of the seed-drill for sowing turnips in rows, permitting easy hoeing which removed weeds and so raised crop yields. And by breeding only from the meatiest sheep and cattle, Robert Bakewell produced strains of high-yield farm animals. By 1800, crop-rotation, seed-drills, hoes, turnips, and selective breeding were boosting sharply British food supplies and supporting a rapidly accelerating growth in population.

While more people meant a larger market and a bigger labour force to satisfy it, industry could only start expanding once huge sums of capital became available. These too flowed in as the 18th century progressed and Britain gained mastery of Canada and India at France's expense and began tapping the rich resources of what rapidly became the biggest, wealthiest empire in the world.

The rising population and accumulating wealth encouraged British manufacturers to invest cash to find new ways of raising production, especially of such necessities as textiles for clothing.

Several inventions now came to their aid to speed up the different processes of cotton manufacture: first, weaving (through John Kay's flying shuttle of 1733), then spinning (through Richard Arkwright's water frame and James Hargreaves' spinning jenny by 1770). Faster, finer spinning and weaving followed with Crompton's mule in 1779, and Cartwright's loom in 1787. Cotton output also soared after 1793 when the American, Eli Whitney, invented the cotton gin for separating seeds from fibres.

Where an employer had once paid families to work independently in their scattered homes, he now hired hundreds of workers to toil in the big factories built to house the new machines. One man minding such machines could produce far more cloth per hour than several working by hand. Eventually such factories were flooding the shops of the new industrial cities with cheap mass-produced articles of all kinds. What had once been luxuries for the very rich became necessities in many million homes.

Left: *hand loom. Lengthwise threads (the warp) pass alternately through eyelets in heddles (1) which rise and fall, creating spaces between the warp through which a shuttle (2) takes a woof thread to and fro. The reed (3) presses woof threads together to produce cloth.* Right: *Richard Arkwright's water-frame spinning machine.*

IRON AND INDUSTRY

The machinery used for heavy mass-production work had to be strongly and precisely built, but the wooden frames and other structures which some 18th century factories employed tended to be weak and inaccurately shaped. The solution was to replace wood with iron.

Early in the 18th century, however, iron was a relatively costly product, largely because of an increasing shortage of fuel for smelting the ores. For centuries the British iron industry had relied upon the charcoal produced by felling trees and burning their timber in a limited supply of air. By the early 1700s, however, the once dense forests of south-east England, where the iron industry was centred, had largely disappeared under the axe, and charcoal was becoming scarce.

Then, in 1709, an ironmaster called Abraham Darby made the remarkable discovery that he could smelt ore with coked coal instead of charcoal. Using coal from nearby coal mines, Darby's tiny ironworks at Coalbrookdale in Shropshire gradually stepped up its production. Soon, other iron manufacturers turned to coal, and by the 1790s the Wilkinson family, armament and steam engine makers, and the Walker brothers, had made fortunes from iron. As the century advanced, the British iron industry shifted from the south-east to the coalfields of South Wales, the Midlands, and the Scottish Lowlands.

Based on rich supplies of coal and iron ore British 18th century iron-making became the envy of Europe. By remelting iron in foundry furnaces specially designed to keep impurities out of the iron, British ironmasters began producing cast-iron cannons which rarely burst. And by 1777 the Darby foundries had begun to make the world's first cast-iron bridge — the first of many large structures in

Raising a great iron bridge in the Industrial Age.

123

which iron began replacing the traditional building materials of wood, stone, and brick. Soon, too, gear-wheels, forge-hammers, and many more parts of the new industrial machines were being made from hard, rigid iron.

Meanwhile improvements were all the while making iron manufacture faster and cheaper. In 1776 John Wilkinson used a powerful steam engine to produce a continuous strong blast of air to make coke fuel burn more thoroughly. In 1783 Henry Cort devised grooved rolls for rolling wrought iron ingots into sheets and bars. A year later he was refining pig iron into wrought iron in a puddling furnace where molten iron was stirred about to burn out impurities. By 1829 ironmasters were also learning that a preheated blast of air helped them to produce three times more iron with the same amount of fuel – a fantastic increase in production.

As iron became increasingly abundant, iron structures began to alter the appearance of the man-made world. But the change was nowhere sudden. For instance, although an iron ship was built as early as 1787, for the next century the ship-building accent was on the wooden sailing ship, and around 1800 a warship still looked much like the wooden sailing vessel pictured here. Only such objects as its cannon and navigation instruments were made of metal. Yet the mass production of iron and other metal objects owed a great deal to the example of the craftsmen who made such fine precision instruments as ships' sextants (devices used for finding latitude by measuring the angle between the sun or certain stars and the horizon), and chronometers (accurate clocks used for finding longitude by helping sailors to compare local time with that of Greenwich or some other fixed locality). For it was the extremely accurate lathes, screw-cutting machines, and other devices used by instrument makers from the early 1700s which were the forerunners of the machine tools that allowed manufacturers to produce machine parts accurate to within a fraction of an inch. Without such accuracy the steam engines which provided power for the industrial age could not have been perfected.

Sextant

18th-century sailing sh.

HARNESSING THE POWER OF STEAM

By Bronze Age times people were using the muscle power of animals; in the Middle Ages they harnessed the energy of wind and flowing water. But oxen and horses can only perform a limited amount of work at a slow speed, while a drought and a calm day bring the wheels of water-mills and windmills to a halt. To drive the new factory machines, the British engineers of the 18th century badly needed an engine more powerful than muscles and more reliable than one depending on wind or flowing water.

People had sought such a device long before, and back in the 3rd century A.D. Hero of Alexandria had stumbled upon one answer to the problem when he used a steam jet to spin a wheel. But such devices remained little more than toys until the late 1600s, partly because people remained unaware of the immense force which steam and the gases that make up air can exert.

The first breakthrough came indirectly, through a problem raised by mining. As Europe's needs for minerals increased, miners began to tunnel deeper than ever inside the earth. The deeper they mined the more their workings filled with water. To keep them drained, miners devised pumps, but found that none raised water more than some 9 metres (30 feet). Galileo's pupil Torricelli had discovered the explanation in 1644 when he found that the atmosphere exerted a pressure capable of supporting a column of water 9 metres (30 feet) high. Ten years later Otto von Guericke showed that atmospheric pressure acting on a two-piece hollow metal ball emptied of air was so great that two eight-horse teams failed to pull its two halves apart.

Armed with these discoveries, seventeenth century engineers, desperate to make more effective pumps, began experimenting with engines which could use atmospheric pressure.

The first big advance was made by France's Denis Papin. By 1690 Papin had built a tiny engine in which a little water boiling in a tube produced steam; the expanding steam thrust a piston upwards inside the tube. By cooling the tube, he made the steam condense into water. The water occupied less space than the steam, thus creating a vacuum below the piston which was thrust down again by atmospheric pressure.

The first useful steam engine (built in the 1690s by Britain's Thomas Savery) worked rather differently: it was a steam pump in which condensing steam produced a vacuum which filled with water pushed up from a lower level by atmospheric pressure.

But the first steam engine capable of draining deep mines was developed by Thomas Newcomen in the early 1700s. In Newcomen's engine, which was based on Papin's, rods linked to a moving piston helped to pump up water from mine workings deep in the ground.

Newcomen engine: the boiler (1) produces steam that helps to raise a piston in cylinder (2). The rising piston and weight of pump rod (3) tilt the beam (4). Water from tank (5) cools the steam, making a vacuum into which atmospheric pressure thrusts the piston down again.

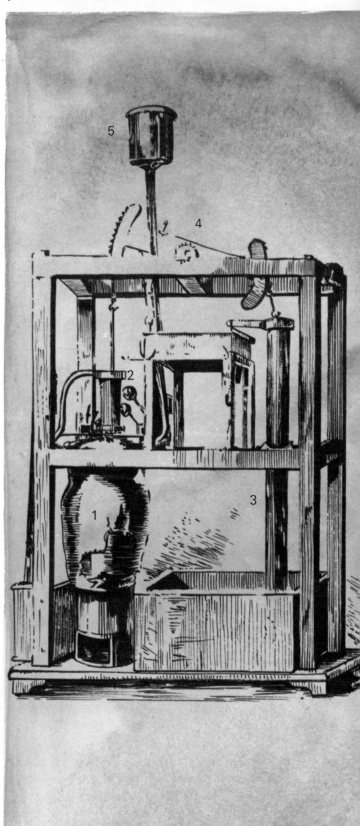

A high-pressure Watt steam engine using a piston's to-and-fro movement to spin a wheel.

STEAM POWER COMES OF AGE

The Newcomen atmospheric engine mentioned on the previous page was the first really successful steam engine. Producing about 5½ horsepower it could raise 545 litres (120 gallons) of water a minute as much as 46 metres (153 feet) by operating a relay of pumps at different levels. By the late 1700s, Newcomen pumping engines were keeping British tin and coal mines free of flooding.

But such engines were extremely inefficient and very wasteful of fuel for they involved alternately cooling and reheating a cylinder. The man who solved this problem was a mathematical instrument maker called James Watt. In 1763, while repairing a model Newcomen engine, Watt added a separate condenser – a chamber where steam drawn from the main cylinder by pump was cooled without loss of heat from the boiler or the piston in the cylinder. Watt's invention also reduced the time lag between piston strokes. The resulting fuel saving and increase in efficiency so impressed two Birmingham business-men that they helped Watt to make his engines.

Like Newcomen's engine, early Watt engines worked more by air pressure than steam pressure: the main thrust was that of atmospheric air pushing the piston down into the partial vacuum left in the cylinder as steam flowed out into the condenser. But by the early 1780s Watt had introduced improve-ments. One was the invention of a double-acting steam engine in which steam entered the cylinder from one end, pushing the piston to the other; then steam admitted from that end pushed the piston back again. Used steam escaped directly into the air, therefore there was no longer any need for a con-denser. But the high pressures created produced a risk of explosion which Watt avoided by inventing a centrifugal governor – two heavy balls fixed to a shaft linked with the boiler. High steam pressure moved the balls to open an escape valve.

Meanwhile Watt and others had invented cranks to turn the to-and-fro movement of the steam-driven piston engine into rotary motion. By 1800, double-acting steam engines were linked to giant wheels which operated machines in factories near the coalfields that supplied their fuel.

MAN TAKES TO THE AIR

Just as the new awareness of air pressure led to the invention of steam engines, so further studies of the nature of air helped men to realise their age-old dream of flight. By 1700 the Jesuit priest Francesco de Lana-Terzi had already recognised that Archimedes' explanation of why objects float or sink in water also applied to floating and sinking in air. And by the 1780s Britain's Joseph Priestley was publishing his discoveries about what he called different kinds of air.

In 1783, influenced by Priestley's writings, two French papermakers, the Montgolfier brothers, made a huge cloth bag lined with paper and lit a fire under a hole in the base of the bag. Hot air from the fire filled the bag and because bulk-for-bulk hot air weighs less than cold air, their hot-air balloon rose high into the sky.

Only days later, the French physics professor Jacques Alexandre Charles invented a balloon filled with the recently discovered lightweight gas hydrogen.

On 21st November 1783, Jean Pilâtre de Rozier and the Marquis d'Arlandes made the world's first free manned balloon flight in a Montgolfier balloon. Astonished Parisians saw them completing a five-mile flight over the French capital. Ten days later, Charles and a companion reached 610 metres (2,000 feet) and sailed 43 kilometres (27 miles) in a rubberised silk hydrogen balloon. Just over a year later two other balloonists completed the first aerial crossing of the English Channel. But because balloons were at the wind's mercy, controlled flight remained beyond man's reach.

Launching a Montgolfier balloon from Paris.

FROM ALCHEMY TO CHEMISTRY

For many centuries, dyers, tanners, iron smelters and glassmakers had known how to tailor certain substances at will. But their skills were based on chance discoveries, not on any systematic understanding of the chemical changes which their processes produced. Indeed, for centuries man's notions of the nature and properties of the substances about him were clouded by superstition and magic. Between about A.D. 300 and 1600 many people believed that the roots of all matter were earth, air, fire, and water; and the students of matter were alchemists whose chief aims were to discover the magical philosopher's stone which would change such cheap metals as iron and lead into valuable gold, and to find a recipe for everlasting life. Although they reached neither of these goals, the alchemists did accomplish much that was useful. For instance they learned how to make acids, discovered improved ways of extracting metals from their ores, and invented laboratory tools, including retorts, crucibles for melting metals, and fine balances.

By the 1600s, however, the new spirit of inquiry was replacing alchemy with the scientific study of matter which we call chemistry. The first true chemist was arguably Ireland's Robert Boyle (1627–1691) who experimentally proved that earth, air, fire, and water were not elements – basic substances which could not be subdivided into others.

Boyle also extended the study of gases and in the 18th century it was to be the discovery of the gas oxygen and its place in chemical reactions that gave birth to modern chemistry. Early in the century the Prussian chemist Georg Stahl had argued that burning and rusting released a substance called phlogiston, and in 1775 Britain's Joseph Priestley described how he had produced what he called dephlogisticated air by heating mercuric oxide. But in 1777 the French chemist Antoine Lavoisier disproved the phlogiston theory of combustion. He showed that rusting and burning were processes in which iron and fuel were combining with something already in the air, which he called oxygen (Priestley's dephlogisticated air) to form *compounds* – substances composed of two or more elements chemically combined. By the time of Lavoisier's discovery other gases were becoming known and studied: hydrogen in 1766, nitrogen in 1772, chlorine in 1774; and in 1784 Britain's Henry Cavendish showed that water consists of oxygen and hydrogen chemically combined. By 1808 John Dalton was able to declare that each element consists of a different kind of atom, and each compound of a special combination of elements.

Now that chemists were gaining a grasp of the true nature of matter they began to identify the more than 100 elements naturally present on earth, discovering their special properties, and finding ways of separating and joining substances to produce useful elements and compounds in useful quantities.

Part of the apparatus used by an eighteenth century experimental chemist for such processes as filtration (left) and distillation (right); based on an engraving made in 1770.

Precisely at this time the need for certain chemicals had grown particularly urgent, especially for alkali used in the textile, glass, and soap-making industries which were expanding fast by the late 1700s. As the demand for alkali increased, some countries began to run short of the old vegetable sources of supply.

It was in France in 1787 that the physician Nicolas Leblanc announced a way of making the alkaline substance soda from salt. By treating salt with sulphuric acid, mixing the resulting sodium sulphate with coal and limestone, roasting the mixture, treating it with water and, finally, evaporating the water he obtained a soda deposit. Leblanc's was the first industrial chemical process to be manufactured on a large scale. Moreover, by raising the demand for certain chemicals, it led to the mass production of others such as sulphuric acid, hitherto a costly product made only in small quantities. By 1830 new ways of mass-producing sulphuric acid inside corrosion-proof lead containers had cut its cost to about one-hundredth of the old price.

Meanwhile chemical manufacturers were experimenting with an embarrassment of hydrochloric acid produced as waste from the making of carbonate sodium by the Leblanc process. Finally, in 1868, a method was perfected whereby chlorine was set free from hydrochloric acid – thus a quick bleaching agent was made available to the textile industry.

But inefficiencies in the early 19th century soda and sulphuric acid manufacturing methods led to the new improved Solvay process for making soda, and a new way of making sulphuric acid. Thus a chain-reaction of inventions set the heavy chemical industry in motion.

Many products of 18th and 19th century chemical research now began to enrich people's daily lives, some of them affecting the food that people ate. For instance, in 1747, the German scientist Andreas Marggraf opened up an entirely new supply of sugar when he began to extract it from beets instead of sugar cane. In 1870 the French chemist Hippolyte Mège-Mouries invented margarine – a cheap butter substitute originally made from beef oleo oil, milk, water, and a vegetable dye. In 1810 the French confectioner François Appert proved that cooking food in sealed glass bottles preserved the contents for many months. This development (followed later in the century by refrigeration) meant that nourishing but perishable foods could now be eaten out of season.

Food output itself was to rise sharply after the 1840s when the German chemist Justus von Liebig discovered which chemicals nourished plants; so paving the way for the manufacture of synthetic fertilisers which (with such 19th century inventions as Cyrus McCormick's mechanical reaper) enormously increased crop yields across the Western World. Liebig's studies also helped to show which chemicals in foods build and energise our bodies. In fact Liebig largely pioneered organic chemistry – the chemistry of carbon compounds.

Meanwhile the scientific study of matter was bearing fruit in the development of many useful products. Three of the most important were coal-gas, synthetic dyes, and rubber.

In the 1790s the French engineer Philippe Lebon had shown that gas produced by burning wood burnt more brightly than tallow candles or oil lamps; but it was not until the middle 1800s that a plentiful supply of coal-gas was piped from the gas works to brighten homes and streets.

Burning coal to produce coal-gas also yielded coal-tar — a waste product which includes benzene. In the 1840s chemists began to discover that benzene could be used to make synthetic dyes. It was a first step towards the manufacture of a whole range of synthetic substances based on coal, including the 20th century development of nylon, that immensely useful fibre.

Europeans had known of rubber since the 1730s and by the early 1800s, British inventors had processed rubber for use in waterproof clothing. But it had the disadvantages of being brittle in cold weather, and sticky in hot weather. Rubber became a much more useful industrial commodity after 1839 when the American inventor, Charles Goodyear,

heated a sulphur-rubber mixture and produced vulcanised rubber. This type of rubber remained flexible at any normal temperature.

By 1900, then, chemical researches initiated by pioneers like Priestley, Lavoisier, and Liebig were enriching homes, offices, and factories with a wide variety of useful new materials.

Part of the apparatus used by an eighteenth-century experimental chemist for such processes as filtration (left) and distillation (right); based on an engraving made in 1770.

Three pioneers of modern chemistry:
1. Antoine Lavoisier (1743–1794) who explained that burning is the chemical combination of a fuel with the gas which he named oxygen.
2. Joseph Priestley (1733–1804) who discovered oxygen but called it dephlogisticated air.
3. Justus von Liebig (1803–1873) who showed that plants use inorganic chemicals as food.
Below: apparatus that helped Lavoisier (like Cavendish) to break down water into oxygen and hydrogen.

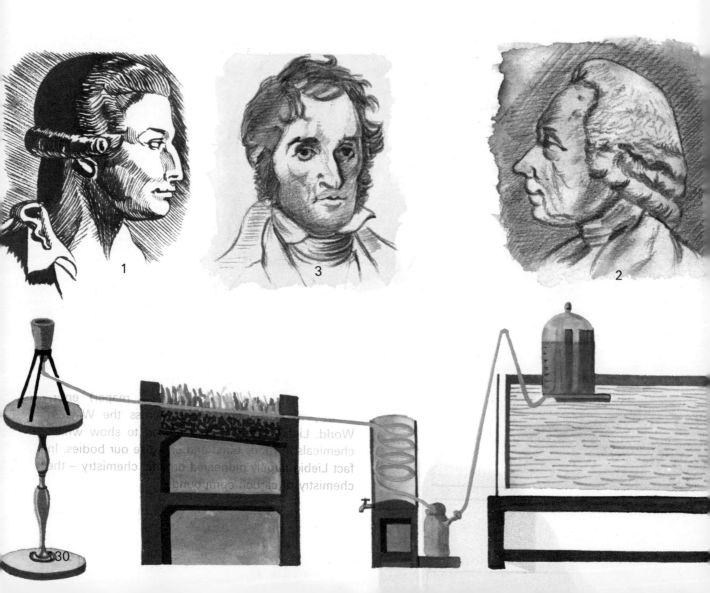

Nicolas Cugnot built this three-wheeled steam carriage in 1769 for hauling cannon over roads.

THE HORSELESS CARRIAGE

We have already seen how by 1800 the wheels of industry were being spun by steam, produced by stationary engines. But as early as the 1760s, the imaginative French engineer Nicolas Cugnot reasoned that it should be possible to develop steam for transport by harnessing a steam engine to a carriage. In 1769 he succeeded in building the first steam-powered vehicle to move about on land.

Cugnot's horseless carriage, designed for hauling cannon, consisted of a heavily constructed tricycle powered by an engine based on the Newcomen type, but modified in several ways. For instance, it was air cooled and had a double cylinder, each part of which was alternately filled with steam. In place of the heavy and cumbersome rocking arm of the Newcomen engine it used smaller devices to link its pistons with the forward drive wheel. The driver sat on a wooden seat nailed to the chassis, and steered by means of a tiller. Unfortunately, Cugnot's steam carriage could travel no faster than 4 kilometres (2½ miles) an hour, and it had to stop every 15 minutes so that its small boiler could be replenished.

In 1785 Britain's William Murdock improved on Cugnot's model by powering his version of the horseless carriage with a Watt double-acting steam engine. Then, in 1801, Richard Trevithick designed a four-wheeled passenger-carrying wagon with a chimney to increase furnace draught. And in 1804 America's Oliver Evans incorporated a high-pressure steam engine in a dredging scow which he drove overland to its river destination. It was the world's first amphibious vehicle.

In some ways the time seemed ripe for the steam coach and the steam carriage. For, with the increase in horse-drawn stagecoach travel, roads had begun to improve. Engineers were now building roads based on a waterproof mixture of asphalt and stone chips – a hard-surfaced road invented by the Scot, John Loudon Macadam (1756–1836).

But early nineteenth century steam coaches were slower than horses, they were noisy and their red-hot coals sometimes set fire to crops. Moreover they were so heavy that they broke up the road surface and the turnpike owners who controlled the roads began to charge extremely high tolls or else they refused to let the carriages pass.

Steam cars were actually produced as recently as the 1920s. But partly because steam road vehicles were often dangerous and difficult to start, most of these horseless carriages had disappeared by the 1840s. They were also being crowded out by competition from steam locomotives running on rails.

STEAMSHIPS SPAN THE SEAS

While some eighteenth century inventors experimented with steam-powered land vehicles, others were trying to harness steam engines to ships. The idea of building steamships was suggested as early as 1690 by the French physicist Denis Papin. But nearly a century passed before the first successful steamships were built, partly through lack of a suitable engine, partly because some early devices were smashed by angry watermen. They had reasoned that since steamships would need smaller crews than sailing ships, many sailors would be robbed of their livelihood.

At last, in 1783, the Marquis Jouffroy d'Abbans triumphantly sailed on the River Saône in France in his *Pyroscaphe* or fireship, a 182-ton vessel driven by a double-acting steam engine which turned two large web-footed paddle wheels.

But more experiments were needed before steamships became successful enough to persuade shipping manufacturers to build them. The next landmark came in 1801 when William Symington equipped the Scottish tug *Charlotte Dundas* with a horizontal double-acting engine in which he replaced the old-fashioned and awkward beam rocker with a connecting-rod linking piston with paddle wheel. But although this vessel hauled two 70-ton boats up the Forth and Clyde Canal against a strong headwind, people feared that her heavy wash would damage canal banks, and the invention was neglected by the British.

It was left to the American inventor Robert Fulton to make steamships pay. Impressed by the *Charlotte Dundas*, Fulton began to build his own steamships on the River Seine, and in 1807 his paddle steamer *Clermont* began plying up and down the Hudson River between New York and Albany.

In the wake of the first river steamers came steamships built for crossing oceans. The steam packet boat *Savannah* completed the first transatlantic crossing in 1819; but her engines were weak, and the *Savannah* relied heavily on sails to complete her slow, 25-day voyage.

The future of long-distance steamship travel still seemed by no means certain, and when sea speeds began to increase in the 1850s, the ships that broke old records were the long, lean-hulled clippers — sailing ships whose crowded canvas caught the lightest breeze. Built to race food supplies and gold prospectors to the new gold mines of California and Australia, and to rush the first of the new tea crop

from China to England, clipper ships halved the voyage time from London to Australia. They were the first vessels to exceed 400 sea miles in one day.

In the meantime, the wallowing steamships were slowly improving. In 1834 Samuel Hall patented a way of re-using steam; this meant that steamships need no longer replenish their boilers with sea water, which choked up boilers and pipes with salt. In 1838 the first successful screw-driven steamship, *Archimedes*, made her maiden trip. She helped to prove that screws were much more efficient than paddles, which wasted much of their energy in beating the waves. Steamships became not only more powerful they grew larger as engineers learned that hollow iron vessels over 300 feet long could resist the tendency to sag in the middle — a real hazard with long wooden ships when the ends were perched on a wave crest, and the centre hung over a trough. The year 1858 saw the launching of Isambard Kingdom Brunel's famous iron ship, the *Great Eastern*. Some 30,000 iron plates joined by about 3,000,000 rivets went into the making of this huge vessel which was over 183 metres (600 feet) long, displaced 22,500 tons and was designed to take 4,000 people between England and Australia. But her 12,000-ton coal bunkers and 6,600-horsepower engines proved too little to drive her great 36-ton screw and two 18 metre (60-feet) paddle wheels, and the biggest ship of the century ended her useful life cable-laying across the Atlantic Ocean.

The *Great Eastern* was ahead of her time. But by 1900 even bigger ships became possible as lightweight steel replaced iron, and new turbine engines sharply raised power capacities. By 1906 turbines developing 70,000 horsepower were thrusting Britain's 32,000-ton *Mauretania* through the waves at 27 knots. Since then the size of ships has increased dramatically, so that today shipbuilders can construct easily vessels of up to 500,000 tons.

Meanwhile, man-made waterways slashed the distances some ships had to travel. In 1869 Ferdinand de Lesseps opened Egypt's Suez Canal, which saved 3,500 miles on the voyage from England to Ceylon; and in 1915 the United States opened the Panama Canal which cut 10,000 miles off the sea journey from New York to San Francisco.

Thus in a bare century, travel by sea was unbelievably transformed by large fast steamships which cut voyage times from weeks to days; opened up new lands to settlements as never before; and shipped huge quantities of wheat and meat to Europe from new farms in America and Australasia.

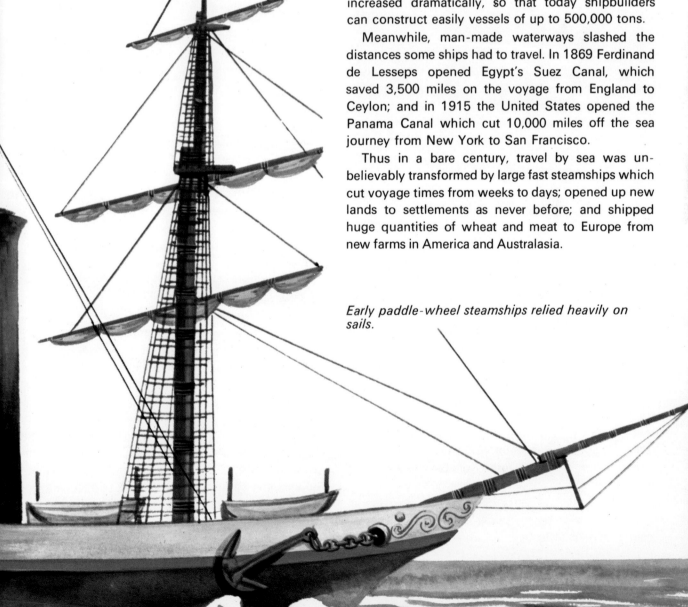

Early paddle-wheel steamships relied heavily on sails.

Above: *Richard Trevithick's locomotive of 1804.* Below: *George Stephenson's* Rocket *which ran in 1829.*

STEAM, RAILS, AND SPEED

What steamships accomplished for ocean travel, steam locomotives were to realise for travel on land, once inventors had discarded the idea of steam carriages which ran on roads in favour of steam-driven vehicles that ran on specially constructed iron rails.

The idea of the railway was already old – the ancient Greeks had rolled carts along ruts worn in solid rock. In the 16th century European miners had made the first rails in the form of raised wooden ruts along which they pushed small ore-filled trucks by hand. By the late 1700s British coal mines were equipped with flanged iron rails strong enough to bear heavily loaded carts pulled by horses.

The man who married steam locomotives to iron rails was the Cornish mining engineer Richard Trevithick. In 1804 – three years after constructing his first steam and road carriage – Trevithick tested a steam locomotive which pulled 5 wagons containing 70 men and 10 tons of iron along a 10-mile Welsh tramway at the modest speed of 8 kilometres (5 miles) an hour.

But perhaps the inventor who best deserves to be remembered as the founder of the railway was George Stephenson, an engineer working in the north of England. Partly because the Napoleonic Wars had made horse fodder expensive, a colliery paid Stephenson to build an iron horse or travelling

engine to shift coal from the pit to a port. By 1814 Stephenson had built a locomotive in which a steam blast injected into the chimney to reduce noise incidentally increased the draught in the boiler. A hotter flame was obtained which produced steam at higher pressure than before – so high that it almost doubled the power of the engine.

Stephenson steadily improved upon his locomotive designs, and by 1822 had persuaded the directors of the new Stockton and Darlington Railway to use his steam locomotives instead of horses on the world's first railway specially built to carry goods and passengers. In 1829 his famous engine *Rocket* moved only at an average speed of 24 kilometres (15 miles) an hour, but it won easily a contest to decide whose locomotives should be used on the Liverpool and Manchester Railway, the world's first major passenger railway which opened in 1830.

From then on railway progress was rapid. By 1850 new inventions like the multi-tubular boiler patented by France's Marc Seguin had helped to raise loco-motive speeds to 96 kilometres (60 miles) an hour. Spidery railway lines were now weaving a dense web across the countryside, binding cities and nations together as never before, while lines like the Union Pacific Railroad were soon spanning whole con-tinents and so opening up remote farmlands to trade and industry. For the first time man could travel faster than a horse, and at a price that almost every-one could afford.

SENDING INSTANT MESSAGES

The coming of fast railway travel made it important to devise a reliable, rapid system of long-distance signalling to warn of a train's approach. People had been sending simple messages across country for many centuries by lighting signal fires, beating drums, and waving flags. Indeed the first comprehensive telegraph was actually developed in the 1790s, before rapid rail travel had arrived. Its creator, the French engineer Claude Chappe devised it to speed up communication between the French revolutionary armies then fighting in widely scattered areas. Chappe's system was based on tall buildings placed roughly at 16 kilometre (10 mile) intervals. Each building was crowned by mechanically worked semaphore arms which could be operated to send specially coded signals. These were clearly visible to an observer at the next station keeping watch through a telescope. The first line of such telegraphic stations was between Paris and Lille (a distance of over 190 kilometres – 120 miles), and it began to work in 1794 with the news of the French recapture of Le Quesnoy.

The success of this first line encouraged the French government to build others, and by the 1840s Chappe stations were transmitting messages over a total distance of some 4,800 kilometres (3,000 miles). Meanwhile the United States, Britain, and other countries were adapting the Chappe telegraphic system. But although this was capable of sending short messages more than 160 kilometres (100 miles) in one minute it had great disadvantages. One was the high cost of employing its many operators; another was its vulnerability to weather – a patch of mist between any two stations in a chain could put it out of action.

The device which overcame these shortcomings was the electric telegraph. The idea for such an invention took root in the 18th century as scientists began to explore the mysterious force of electricity. As early as 1753 a contributor to the *Scots Magazine* suggested making a telegraph with 26 wires strung between the transmitter and receiver, each wire representing a different letter of the alphabet. When a device for producing static electricity touched one end of a wire it moved a pith ball connected to the other end.

Improvements on this idea were only possible with the arrival of better methods of transmitting electric current (first, as we shall see later, by batteries, eventually by generators). Improvements also followed the discovery that electric current could be used to magnetise a bit of iron or move a magnetic needle.

In the 1830s American and British physicists began to exploit such discoveries to make the world's first really practical telegraphic systems. In Britain, William Cooke and Charles Wheatstone patented a device in 1837 in which a current deflected up to six magnetic needles so that they pointed in turn to different letters printed on a dial. Meanwhile, the American inventor Samuel F. Morse was developing a simple system in which an operator pressing a switch key alternately made and broke an electric circuit. The electric impulses flowed through a single wire to produce, firstly, ink marks on a moving strip of paper, and, later, sounds in a receiver. By representing each letter and number with a different pattern of dots (short sounds) and dashes (long sounds), Morse could telegraph any message. Moreover he built relay devices along the line which meant that messages could cover almost any distance almost instantly.

Soon, the Morse code was being flashed across whole continents along a network of telegraph lines that followed the railways. Countries separated by seas and oceans were put in telegraphic touch, thanks to developments like the use of gutta-percha for insulating underwater cables. In 1851 the first submarine cable was successfully laid under the English Channel between Dover and Calais; by 1866 a transatlantic cable linked Europe with America; and by the early 1870s almost all of the Western world's great cities were in instant telegraphic contact. Today telegraphic messages flashed between them can be printed out in words by teleprinter.

a Morse receiver

a Morse transmitter

TELEPHONE AND PHONOGRAPH

Although, by 1870, coded telegraphic messages were speeding between continents, no one had by then produced a device for successfully transmitting the human voice.

The man who made a practical instrument of the telephone or far speaker was Alexander Graham Bell, a Scottish-born teacher working in America. In 1876 Bell built a device in which a voice set a diaphragm vibrating. The vibrations caused fluctuations in the current flowing through an electromagnetic coil, and the fluctuating current passed through a wire circuit to a distant electromagnet to vibrate a second diaphragm which produced sound waves matching the speaker's voice.

In 1876 David Hughes' invention of the microphone and Thomas Edison's new carbon transmitter strengthened the electrical signals so that the speaker need no longer shout. By 1900, cheap, plentiful electric current was helping to create telephone links between homes, offices, and factories throughout the world.

Only a year after the Bell telephone had begun to link people separated by space, Thomas Edison produced his invention — the phonograph — a device which recorded and reproduced the human voice. The voice vibrated a diaphragm joined to a cutting edge which scratched a wavy spiral groove on a revolving wax cylinder. If a soft needle was then placed in the revolving groove its vibrations moved a diaphragm which reproduced the recorded voice. Now much improved upon, this principle remains the basis of gramophone recording — an invention which permanently captures words, music, and other sounds that would once have been lost for ever.

an early telephone device built
by Alexander Graham Bell

a rival device
invented by Ader

early gramophone with horn speaker

STEEL AND ALUMINIUM

No substance was more valuable than hard strong iron when it came to the manufacturing of the factory machines and steam engines that underpinned the Industrial Revolution. In the 19th century, new machine tools, the hydraulic press and James Nasmyth's powerful steam hammer helped to produce iron structures of increasing size and variety.

But many of the inventions sparked off by steam and iron required metals with different properties from either cast iron (which is hard but brittle) or wrought iron (which is tough but relatively soft). The biggest need of all was for more steel, which is both tough and hard and is an alloy of iron and carbon with other substances.

People had been making steel for a very long time, but largely by hit and miss methods. They were not able to produce large quantities of steel with just the right amounts of carbon and other impurities.

The invention that above all others made steel plentiful and cheap was the Bessemer converter developed in 1856 by the British inventor Henry Bessemer. It consists of an egg-shaped furnace with an open top. Steel workers tilt the furnace, pour molten pig iron inside, then turn it upright and send a blast of high-pressure air up through the molten metal

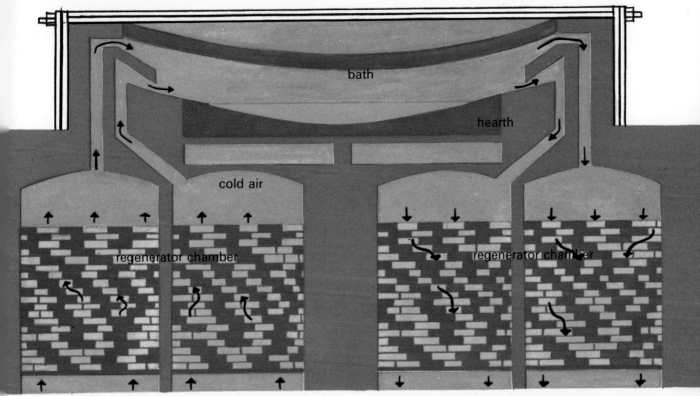

Open-hearth smelting: air and fuel heated in regenerator chambers burn above the hearth to make molten steel.

to burn unwanted impurities from the iron with flames which leap as high as over 900 centimetres (30 feet) into the air.

Before the century ended, two more new steel-making processes made it possible to produce steel by re-using scrap iron and scrap steel. The first of these was the Siemens-Martin open-hearth furnace perfected in the 1860s from inventions by the German brothers Siemens, and Pierre and Émile Martin of France. The second invention was the electric-arc furnace which France's Paul Héroult set working commercially in 1899.

Meanwhile, in 1875, the British amateur scientist Sidney Gilchrist Thomas and his cousin Percy Gilchrist were solving the serious problem of producing steel from iron ore rich in phosphorus – an impurity which rendered any steel containing it uselessly brittle. The cousins found that when limestone was added to the furnace phosphorus would combine with it to produce a harmless slag. It was a simple enough discovery but one which promised to double the world's output of steel.

Once these developments had made steel plentiful and cheap it began to replace iron in such forms as pipes, sheets, rails, and girders. The first great metal bridges designed by railway engineers like Robert Stephenson had been built with iron. For instance, in 1849, Stephenson had used huge wrought-iron tubes which he designed to rest on massive towers in his *Britannia* bridge, linking Wales with Anglesey. But in 1890 Scotland's Forth Railway Bridge, with

its colossal cantilevered spans, was completed from 50,000 tons of steel. At the same time steel was was giving rise to entirely new inventions ranging from barbed wire to bicycles.

Eventually, the larger industrial concerns began to employ teams of chemists and metallurgists to develop a whole range of steel alloys which combined iron with such elements as nickel, vanadium and cobalt to produce metals specially tailored to perform different tasks. For instance, technologists multiplied the useful life of certain tools up to six times by making them of steel alloyed with manganese and tungsten.

Meanwhile metallurgists were exploring new industrial uses for other metals. One of their greatest discoveries was aluminium – a silvery, lightweight metal which reflects heat, readily conducts electric current, will not rust, and can be rolled and stretched at will into almost any shape. Commercial manufacture (which requires huge quantities of electricity) was perfected in the 1880s, but only since the early 1900s (when electricity became plentiful) has aluminium really come into its own in objects ranging from saucepans to power lines, food packaging, and aircraft wings and bodies. Other new metals which we have today include lightweight heat-resistant titanium, used in aero-engines; and tungsten, with the highest melting point of any known metal, used for the filaments of electric lamps. The more than 3,000-year-old Iron Age has at last given way to an age of many metals.

SPEEDING THE PRESSES

While nineteenth century technologists were busy improving the established methods of producing metals, other old-established inventions and discoveries were being similarly transformed. One such invention was printing.

Although pioneers like Gutenberg had introduced in the 1400s, movable type, the printing press, and printer's ink, printing had changed surprisingly little by 1800. Founders still cast the type by hand, producing no more than six letters a minute, and setting was also hand-done in the old, slow way. Understandably, both the type-founders and type-setters resisted any invention likely to speed up their work for fear that many would lose their jobs.

But during the 19th century the situation sharply altered as rapidly expanding trade and industry catered for a large section of the community – the well-to-do middle class – and paid for schools where workers' children learned to read and write. These changes so increased the demand for books, magazines, newspapers, and advertisements that the printing industry had every reason to seek quicker ways of type-founding, type-setting and printing.

In 1838 an American designer built the first really efficient machine for casting type, and by the late 1860s one British newspaper, employing new type-casting machinery, could turn out as many as 60,000 letters in one hour. Type-setting machines appeared in the 1840s but it was in 1886, in America, that the German-born watchmaker Otto Mergenthaler devised the famous Linotype machine. With this machine a single operator typed keys on a keyboard to make matching impressions on a strip of papier mâché, thereby moulding a whole line of type at a time – a device which helped him to set type four times faster than the three-man team which worked less efficient mechanisms. By the 1890s America had also pioneered the Monotype machine which allowed the easy correction of one letter at a time.

Meanwhile developments in actual printing had run ahead of methods of founding and composing type. By the early 1800s, screw presses were producing no more than about 600 printed sheets an hour. But as the railway helped to make nationwide newspaper distribution rapid, the need for faster printing encouraged newspapers to explore rotary devices. In 1814 the German-born inventor, Friedrich Koenig, working in London, invented a revolving cylinder to press the paper against the type, and that year *The Times* of London stepped up output to 1,100 sheets an hour with his device. However it was in 1845 that the American inventor, Richard Hoe, was successful in fixing type to a revolving cylinder; this raised hourly output to 8,000 sheets. Modern high-speed printing dates from 1865, when a Philadelphia printer developed *stereotyping* by casting molten metal in a curved mould to fit the cylinder. Today, millions of copies of magazines richly illustrated with full-colour pictures are produced each week.

A FIRE INSIDE THE ENGINE

Even while great changes were revolutionising the old-established iron and printing industries, nineteenth century inventors were redesigning machines which had emerged only in the early 1800s. One was the powerful, heavy, steam locomotive.

We have seen how men like Trevithick had succeeded in building a steam locomotive to run on rails, but had failed to make the road-borne steam carriage much more than a curiosity. Their failure by no means discouraged others from trying to build a mechanical substitute for the horse-drawn carriage. To reduce weight and increase engine power, some tried to make a more compact firebox, boiler and cylinder with the help of metals lighter than iron. Those who finally succeeded kept the steam engine's piston and cylinder principle, but they discarded the idea of fire *outside* the cylinder in favour of controlled explosions of gases which burnt *inside* the cylinder to thrust its piston.

The first of these *internal combustion* engines

which really worked was developed about 1860 by the French inventor Étienne Lenoir. It featured a cylinder in which an electric spark ignited a mixture of air and the kind of gas used in street lighting. The spark exploded the gas-air mixture and pushed the piston. In 1862 Lenoir substituted petrol for the less concentrated gas fuel and in 1863 his first primitive automobile took to the road. But it developed less than two horse-power and proved so underpowered that it travelled only six miles in two hours.

Another early motor-car was built by the Austrian inventor Siegfried Marcus, when he attached a petrol engine to the rear wheels of a handcart in 1864. It ran only 180 metres (200 yards), although later Marcus models performed rather better.

The man responsible for putting real power into the internal combustion engine was France's Beau de Rochas, who did so in 1862 by compressing the gases before the moment of explosion to give far greater thrust to the piston. Beau de Rochas in fact pioneered the so-called four-stroke cycle used in modern car engines, in which (1) the piston descends, opening a valve which admits an air and petrol-vapour mixture into the cylinder; (2) the piston rises, closing the valve and compressing the air and petrol vapour; (3) a spark ignites the mixture, which expands and thrusts the piston downwards; (4) the returning piston opens an exhaust valve and thrusts out the burnt gases.

In spite of Beau de Rochas' achievement, this sequence of movements is often called the Otto cycle after the German inventor Nicolas August Otto who built the first successful stationary engine of this type in 1876. In 1885 it was Otto's former technical director Gottlieb Daimler and Carl Benz (working independently of one another) who became the first men to succeed in making four-stroke engines power a vehicle.

Even their vehicles were relatively slow and underpowered, and more developments were needed before cars as we know them took shape. Key inventions included multiple-cylinder engines; the float-feed carburettor developed in 1893 by Wilhelm Maybach to control petrol flow inside the cylinder; wheel instead of tiller steering; and, dating from 1895, pneumatic car tyres. Meanwhile, other important technical advances in the internal combustion engine included Rudolf Diesel's invention in 1893 of the oil-powered Diesel engine in which the heat developed by compressing gases was sufficient to cause ignition.

But it was the coming of cheap abundant petroleum and steel, harnessed to the mass production methods introduced by Henry Ford in the early 1900s, which transformed the automobile from a scarce luxury to a fast, reliable means of independent travel cheap enough for millions to enjoy.

1. *Étienne Lenoir's horseless carriage of 1862*
2. *Delamarre-Debouteville vehicle of 1883*
3. *Benz automobile built in 1886*

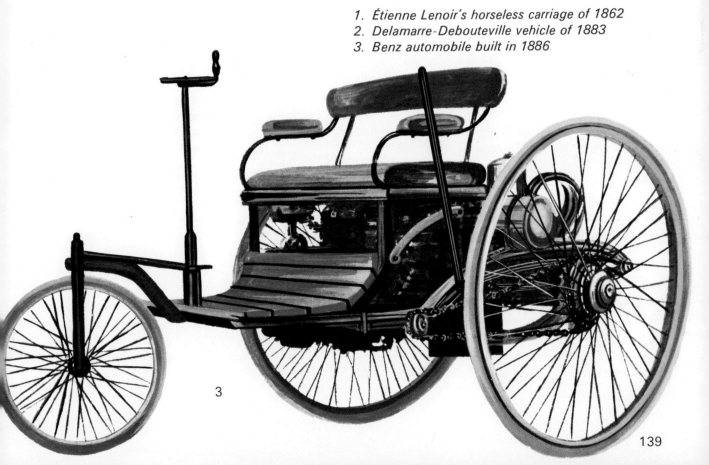

3

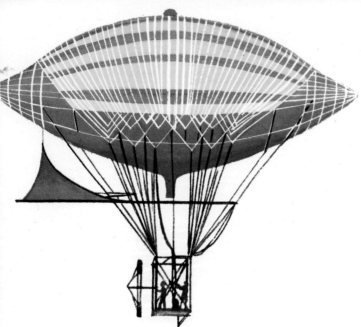

Henri Giffard's steam-powered dirigible of 1852

AIRSHIP AND AEROPLANE

By 1900 men had harnessed the power of steam and petrol to machines which carried them efficiently over land and sea. But mastery of the air still escaped them.

However, since the Montgolfier balloon made its first drift voyage in 1783, balloon enthusiasts had been working on ways of harnessing an engine to a balloon to control their journeys. The first man to produce a steerable powered balloon was France's Henri Giffard. In 1852 he successfully flew 28 kilometres (17 miles) out of Paris with a cigar-shaped balloon steered by a rudder and driven by a three-horsepower steam engine, which thrust the vehicle through the air at about 8 kilometres (5 miles) an hour. But Giffard's engine lacked the power to make headway against a stiff breeze.

The first really successful airship, which appeared in 1884, was built in France by Charles Renard. Featuring a 50-metre long (165 feet) gas bag, and driven by an 8½-horsepower electric motor, it accomplished an 8 kilometre (5 mile) circuit near Paris. In the 1890s the Brazilian, Alberto Santos-Dumont, was also trying out new designs.

But the type which attracted most interest was an airship in which a lightweight framework gave the envelope rigidity. The Austrian engineer David Schwarz flew the first rigid airship in 1897 but it was Germany's Count Ferdinand von Zeppelin who gave his name to a whole breed of rigid airships when he launched his first enormous vehicle in 1900. Over 120 metres (400 feet) long, and holding 9,800 cubic metres (350,000 cubic feet) of hydrogen inside a linen envelope supported by an aluminium frame, the cigar-shaped monster was powered by two 16-horsepower internal combustion engines spinning four propellers.

This airship and another early model built by Zeppelin, proved to be expensive failures. But by 1908 his designs were successful enough for the German government to help finance new Zeppelins to carry mail and passengers. The airship age reached its climax in the 1930s with the great *Graf Zeppelin* and *Hindenburg* – airships twice as long as the first Zeppelin, containing twice as much gas, carrying up to 50 passengers, and thrust by engines of over 2,500 horsepower at over 110 kilometres (70 miles) an hour on regular runs across the Atlantic Ocean.

But airships were fragile and dangerous: in 1937 exploding hydrogen destroyed the *Hindenburg*, and 37 people lost their lives. Airships were to prove no match for the heavier-than-air flying machines which began to appear in the early 1900s.

By the 19th century it had become plain that man lacked the muscle power for flying by flapping bird-like wings strapped to his arms. But careful study of the ways that birds soar and steer led experimenters to start making fixed-wing gliders. In 1852 or 1853 a coachman sitting in a glider built by Sir George Cayley completed the first manned glide when he sailed across a valley. In the 1890s the American civil engineer Octave Chanute built successful multi-wing gliders. The greatest pioneer of gliding, though, was Germany's Otto Lilienthal. He designed streamlined wings with slightly curved surfaces – convex above, concave below – which cleaved the air. The air was compressed beneath the wings to create a partial vacuum above which sucked them upwards, creating lift. Before Lilienthal died from a gliding accident in 1896, France's Clement Ader had made the first flight in a powered heavier-than-air vehicle. But his curious bat-winged machine, driven by an airscrew powered by a steam engine, merely hopped uncontrollably along the ground.

The first *controlled* powered flight by a heavier-than-air machine was made in North Carolina in 1903 by Orville Wright. His triumph owed much to gliding pioneers like Lilienthal, to the system wing-warping by which Orville and his brother Wilbur controlled stability, and to their use of the new, powerful, yet lightweight internal combustion engine which drove the propellers. The Wright brothers' biplane *Flyer* flew only 36 metres (40 yards) at its first attempt. But it had ushered in an age of fast, long-distance flight which was, in the future, to break down most natural barriers to travel.

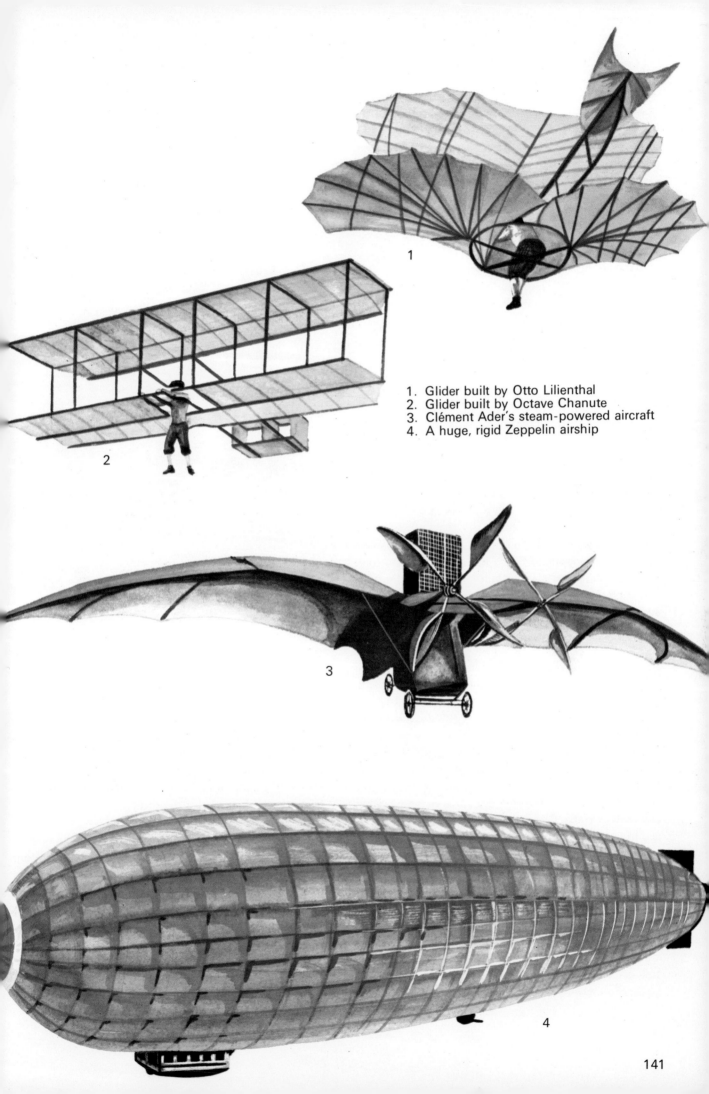

1. Glider built by Otto Lilienthal
2. Glider built by Octave Chanute
3. Clément Ader's steam-powered aircraft
4. A huge, rigid Zeppelin airship

PUTTING ELECTRICITY TO WORK

The developments of telegraphy and the internal combustion engine which we have already described depended at least partly upon electricity.

Until the 18th century little was known about this mysterious form of energy. The ancient Greeks had understood that amber rubbed on fur attracted bits of dust and feathers, and by the 1700s scientists knew that the act of rubbing some such substance as amber on certain materials produced electric sparks. Then, in 1746 Benjamin Franklin proved that powerfully destructive lightning was a similar but much larger spark. He flew a kite in a storm and a lightning bolt ran down the damp string to cause a spark in a key tied to the end.

By the late 1700s scientists realised that under certain conditions electricity would flow from one substance to another, but that while some substances (called conductors) transmitted electricity, others (insulators) did not.

But no one produced much more than an instant flash of electricity until 1800 when the Italian experimenter Alessandro Volta made the first electric battery by sandwiching cloths soaked in brine between paired zinc and copper plates. When he connected a wire to the outer plates (one zinc, one copper), electricity began to flow through the wire. Volta had shown that the chemical energy locked up in different substances could be released in the form of a steady flow of electric current. It was soon clear that such current could break down water into oxygen and hydrogen by the process called electrolysis, and similarly help to isolate new metals such as potassium, sodium, magnesium, as well as plating one metal with another.

Soon, scientists realised, too, that current passing between two carbon rods produced a brilliant light, and that current heated the conducting wires through which it passed. But heavy use quickly wore out Voltaic batteries, and scientists sought a longer-lasting, more powerful source of continuous electric current.

The clue to eventual success came in 1820 when Denmark's Hans Christian Oersted showed that an electric current magnetised a nearby piece of iron and made it move. From Oersted's discovery sprang the electric motor in which an electric current alternately magnetises and demagnetises nearby pieces of iron in a way that causes constant movement.

Meanwhile in 1831 Oersted's discovery led Britain's Michael Faraday to show that a moving magnet would produce electric current in a nearby coil of wire. From Faraday's discovery came the electric generator or dynamo, the source of electric

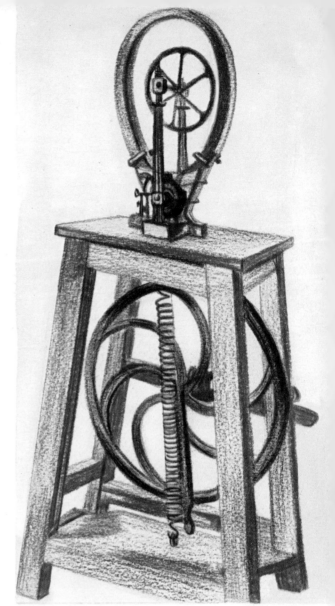

An electromagnetic device designed by Zénobe Gramme

energy which today lights and heats our homes, and powers the electric motors in our washing machines, vacuum cleaners, cake-mixers, and the much more powerful motors used in factories and trains.

But much remained to be done in the 19th century before electric current on a large scale could be effectively generated, transmitted across country, and transformed into useful quantities of heat, light, and mechanical energy.

By the middle 1860s Werner von Siemens had greatly increased the potential power of generators by replacing their ordinary magnets with electro-magnets to create generators needing no constant input of electricity from batteries. By the 1870s dynamos driven by steam engines and devised by Zénobe Gramme were producing useful quantities of current.

Meanwhile inventors were experimenting with new kinds of electric lamp with filaments made from

Volta demonstrating his Voltaic pile

'WINDMILL SAILS' SPUN BY STEAM

By 1900 the Western world's increasing appetite for electric power was giving new meaning to the turbine — one of the oldest devices for converting the energy of motion into useful work. Strictly speaking, a turbine is any kind of engine spun round by the force of a moving gas or liquid.

Probably the oldest form of turbine is the water wheel. However, the toy engine built by Hero of Alexandria, perhaps about A.D. 300, was worked by steam, not water. It comprised a hollow metal ball mounted on a hollow axle. Steam forced inside this axle entered the ball, escaping from two tiny pipes bent at right angles so that the force of the escaping steam produced a reaction in the opposite direction, spinning the ball round by jet propulsion.

But such early reaction turbines were far ahead of their time. For more than 1,000 years the only kinds of turbine which were usefully employed were water wheels and windmills; devices which inefficiently let much of the water and air slide uselessly off the sides of their turning blades.

The first really efficient turbine, an enclosed water wheel, was designed by the French engineer Benoît Fourneyron in 1832: it developed 500 horse-power and drove powerful hammers in an ironworks.

The next great landmark came over 50 years later, when, in 1884, Britain's Charles Parsons patented a reaction steam turbine in which steam striking rows of angled blades enclosed in an outer casing, spun the big shaft or rotor, from which the blades projected at a rate of 18,000 revolutions per minute. Although this was the first effective turbo-generator, Sir Charles Parsons' work on the turbine had to wait almost thirteen years for recognition. But in 1897 a Parson turbine was installed in the ship *Turbinia*, and before the astonished gaze of the thousands gathered for the British Jubilee Naval Review the *Turbinia* steamed past at the unsurpassed speed of $34\frac{1}{2}$ knots. Within 10 years such turbines, generating 70,000 horsepower, were installed in large ocean liners.

Meanwhile, in the 1880s, the Swede, Gustav de Laval had built an impulse or direct-thrust turbine which worked like a steam windmill. Now, too, French and Swiss engineers were busy. But the future of the vibration-free steam turbine for generating electricity owed much to America's Charles G. Curtis. In 1903 he built an improved multi-wheel steam turbine for generating electricity, so efficient that it was equivalent to a steam piston engine eight times heavier, ten times larger, and three times costlier. Today, big steam turbines are so efficient that one of them can produce enough electricity for 3,000,000 people.

electrical conductors which would glow brightly without melting or burning. By 1880 Joseph Swan and Thomas Edison had solved both problems with a carbon filament sealed into a glass bulb from which all air had been removed.

Filament lamps and industry's increasing demands for electrical energy set physicists searching for ways of transmitting electricity over many miles and without much wastage from the generators to the consumers. They found that power losses were reduced by stepping up by means of a transformer, the voltage or pressure at which the current travelled. The transformer was a device pioneered by Faraday, in which current in one coil of wire induces current in a nearby coil at a voltage determined by the number of turns in its coil. But high voltage direct-current generators proved difficult to build, and most modern ones produce alternating current — current which reverses direction many times a second.

POWER WITHOUT SMOKE

While some engineers developed electric generators worked by steam produced by heating coal or oil, others began to improve upon the old water-wheel idea. They designed three main kinds of turbine spun by the force of falling water.

One is the Pelton wheel, in which high-pressure jets of water strike cup-shaped paddles. Another is the Francis reaction turbine in which guide-vanes channel water under moderate pressure to its 16 blades simultaneously, to spin them by reaction. The third kind of water-driven turbine is the propeller or Kaplan type which has four huge blades that can be angled according to the water pressure. Kaplan turbines work efficiently at low pressures.

In the early 1900s in order to produce a sufficient and constant flow of water to drive the turbines of electric generators, engineers set about as never before to harness streams and rivers. They built concrete dams across river valleys to block the rivers and the water gathered and spread out to produce great artificial lakes. This had two great advantages. In dry lands, the water provided irigation, so that huge areas which had once been desert now blossomed with farm crops. At the same time, the reservoirs provided the turbines with the necessary constant flow of high-pressure water through small holes near the base of the dams.

In narrow mountain valleys, the higher the dam the deeper the lake behind it, the deeper the lake the greater the pressure of water at the base, and so the greater the force with which its water spurted past the turbines. At night, when the demand for electricity was low, the turbines could be used to help pump some of the falling water back up into the lake, thus storing electricity for future use.

In such mountainous lands as Norway, Switzerland, and Canada, hydroelectricity (as electricity generated by water turbines is called) provided a cheap source of energy, which allowed factories to mass produce aluminium and other substances requiring a lavish use of electric current. In some countries, hydroelectric generators, and electric motors also helped to keep industrial cities far cleaner and quieter than the first factory towns, where coal-fired steam engines, kilns, and furnaces blackened the sky with soot and smoke.

Water penned back by this dam escapes through tunnels to spin turbines before spurting into the valley below.

UNLOCKING NATURE'S SECRETS

In the 1900s man began not only to unleash ever greater sources of energy with which to mould his world; he made huge new discoveries about the ways in which the world worked. Big new telescopes showed astronomers that our sun is just one star of 100,000,000,000 stars in our galaxy, and that the universe has at least a million such galaxies. Studying the earth itself, scientists like Alfred Wegener suggested that its continents drift about over many million years.

In biology, the American geneticist Thomas Hunt Morgan working on studies done by the Austrian monk Gregor Mendel, showed that parent plants and animals transmit their own characteristics to their offspring in tiny structures called genes. By the early 1900s other scientists were learning of the vitamins, special substances that man needs in tiny quantities in food to help build, repair, and energise his body. Probing deep into body chemistry, biochemists later unravelled the complex chemical reactions which keep our bodies alive.

Studying atoms, the tiny particles of which all

substances are made, Sir Joseph John Thomson had by 1897 discovered that an electric current is produced by a flow of the tiny negatively charged particles which we call electrons. By 1911 Ernest Rutherford's experiments led him to suggest that an atom consists of a central nucleus circled by speeding electrons. By 1920 scientists found that an atomic nucleus contained positively charged heavy particles called protons which balanced the negatively charged lightweight electrons whirling round them. In the early 1930s James Chadwick discovered that atomic nuclei also contain electrically neutral particles called neutrons.

It became clear that each of the 100 odd different elements on earth has atoms with a different combination of sub-atomic particles, and that some kinds of element naturally give off rays of energy and streams of particles, while others can be induced to do so. People often learned of such discoveries through remarkable inventions for communicating knowledge.

DRAWING PICTURES WITH LIGHT

For over 400 years Western civilisation was largely built on the written and the printed word – the two great means of accurately recording, preserving, and transmitting knowledge. But, as we have already seen, by the late 1800s these old-established means of communication were being joined by new ones: the telephone and telegraph which allowed two people far apart to converse instantly with one another; and the gramophone which made sounds imperishable. On the following pages we shall see how people learned to record *images*, and to transmit both sounds and images instantly to an audience of millions to launch a new age in communications.

The first hesitant step towards reproducing images can be seen in the 16th century *camera obscura* – a dark box with a tiny hole in one side which let in light to form an inverted image of the outside scene on the opposite side of the box. Artists traced such images as sketching aids. By the 1660s a lens placed in the hole produced a sharper image. After 1727, when the German physicist Johann Schulze found that light darkens silver salts, men began to see how such devices as the camera obscura might be used to make a lasting image. The first to do so was the French physicist Joseph Niépce.

In 1826 Niépce placed a light-sensitive metal plate inside a camera, exposed it for eight hours, then, using an engraving process, produced the world's first photograph: a blurred image of the scene outside his window. During the 1830s, Niépce's partner

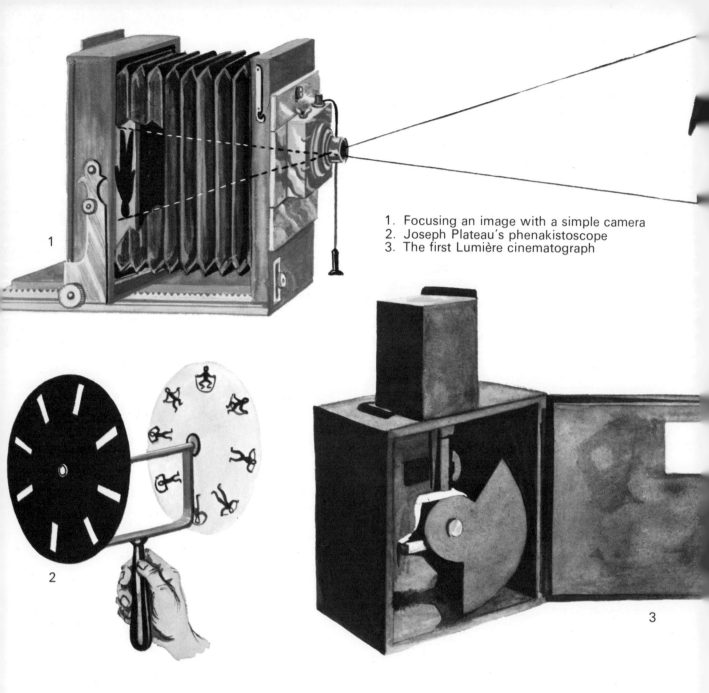

1. Focusing an image with a simple camera
2. Joseph Plateau's phenakistoscope
3. The first Lumière cinematograph

Daguerre perfected the daguerreotype, using mercury vapour to develop the image which he fixed with salt. But copies of photographs could be made only after 1839 when Britain's Fox Talbot invented negatives.

Further advances followed: in 1840 the Hungarian, Josef Petzval, devised improved lenses; in 1871 the dry plate process simplified developing; and by the 1870s a new light-sensitive emulsion reduced the exposure time from the 10 minutes of the daguerreotype to 1/25th of a second. By 1889 America's George Eastman was able to market snapshot cameras using celluloid film, and this made photography cheap and simple. Meanwhile skilled professional photographers had recorded scenes from the Crimean War, the American Civil War, and other historic nineteenth century events.

MAKING IMAGES APPEAR TO MOVE

More than 2,000 years ago the Roman poet Lucretius discovered that the eye sees an object a fraction of a second after it has actually disappeared. In 1832 the Belgian scientist Joseph Plateau used this fact (known as the persistence of vision) to create a toy which gave the illusion of movement — the *phenakistoscope* shown on this page. You will notice that one of its discs has slots, the other shows a sequence of skipping movements. By spinning the discs and looking through the slots, a viewer seemed to see a continuous skipping action.

Many such toys were popular by the 1850s, and people began combining them with an earlier invention, the magic lantern, a device created in 1645 by the German priest Athanasius Kircher. The magic

Black-and-white talking motion pictures dominated the cinema in the 1930s.

lantern involved a powerful light fitted with a re-flector, and a lens which cast the image of a painted glass slide onto a wall. Moving one slide across another created a rather crude illusion of movement. Then, in the 1850s, Austria's Franz von Uchatius improved upon this by projecting a 30-second sequence of moving pictures produced by a method rather like Plateau's.

But the future of moving pictures lay with the newly developed camera. By the late 1800s, camera enthusiasts were seeking ways of capturing a sequence of movements on film, then using the magic lantern technique for reproducing them. In 1878 in California, Eadward Muybridge used a row of cameras to take a series of high-speed photographs of a running horse. These photographs settled an old argument because they showed clearly that there are moments when all four legs of a galloping horse are off the ground. In the 1880s the French physi-

ologist Étienne Marey first produced such photographs with a *single* camera, using first a revolving glass plate, then photographic paper. In so doing he invented the forerunner of the modern cine camera. By the early 1890s, Thomas Edison's development of a perforated film strip made of flexible, transparent celluloid (a substance synthetically created in 1869) allowed a rapid sequence of still photographs to be accurately spun across a camera or projector lens.

But only one person at a time peering through a peephole in a wooden box could see Edison's motion pictures, which were shown lit from behind. In Paris in 1895 it was the French Lumière brothers who held the first film show where a large audience paid to see motion pictures projected on a screen. Later, in the 1920s, sound was synchronised with vision by a sound-track magnetically recorded on film beside the images. With talking pictures the cinema had come of age.

In the 1960s, wide-screen, full-colour stereoscopic films brought added realism to the cinema.

147

SENDING MESSAGES ON WAVES

In 1895, the year in which the Lumière brothers made motion pictures available to audiences of several thousands, the Italian inventor Guglielmo Marconi pioneered wireless telegraphy – forerunner of modern radio which can transmit the human voice to an audience of many millions.

Marconi was building on decades of experimental studies on the mysterious ways in which electricity behaves. As early as 1831 Michael Faraday and (independently) Joseph Henry in America had discovered that electric current in one wire can induce current in another wire (the principle behind the electrical transformer which we have already mentioned). This suggested that electricity can somehow pass through air. In 1864 the British physicist James Clerk Maxwell theorised that electrical energy also travels through space in waves and at the speed of light.

Twenty-four years later, the German physicist Heinrich Hertz proved Maxwell's theory by experiment. He found that when an electric spark leapt across a gap in one electric circuit, radio waves (as we now call them) induced a similar spark in an identical circuit nearby. Scientists quickly accepted that radio waves – like light and heat radiation – were a form of energy capable of travelling across empty space at great speed. Here, it seemed, was a means of long distance signalling without the wires required by telegraphs and telephones.

In 1892 France's Édouard Branly built a wave-receiving device by which radio waves rang a bell. But in 1895 it was Marconi who built the first successful wireless telegraph for sending simple signals across short distances. By 1899 sensitive radio antennae helped wireless telegraphy to span the English Channel, and in December 1901 a radio signal from south-west England was bounced off an outer atmospheric layer to reach Marconi in New-foundland, nearly 2,000 miles away.

Advance was now rapid. Already by 1900 the American physicist Reginald Fessenden had transmitted voice sounds by radio. In 1904 Britain's John Ambrose Fleming pioneered the sensitive radio valve or thermionic tube for detecting signals, and in 1907 Lee de Forest's triode began amplifying weak signals to make long distance radio communication really practical. After World War II such bulky fragile tubes were largely replaced with tiny durable transistors.

Since public broadcasts began in the early 1920s, radio has relayed to countless millions instant news, propaganda, entertainment, and education.

1. Radio device built by Branly
2. Radio receiver equipped with valves
3. Transistorised radio receiver

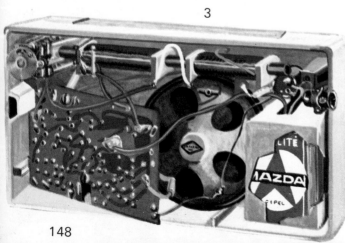

THE STORY OF TELEVISION

By the 1920s inventors were combining sound broadcasting with the broadcasting of images to create a remarkable new means of mass communication: television. Both radio and television work along broadly similar lines. In radio a microphone converts sounds into electrical signals which are broadcast from a transmitter as electromagnetic waves and reconverted into sounds in a radio receiver. In television a camera converts images into electrical signals that are transmitted as electromagnetic waves, and reconverted into images in a television receiver.

Clearly, without the discoveries that created radio, television could not have been invented. But some of the developments that made it possible occurred even before the birth of radio in the 1890s. One of these began in 1817 when the Swedish chemist, Jakob Berzelius, discovered the element selenium; in the 1870s researchers found that selenium exposed to light becomes an excellent conductor of electricity, and that variations in light falling on selenium linked with an electric circuit caused corresponding variations in its electric current.

In 1884 the German inventor, Paul Nipkow, used light-sensitive selenium in a device incorporating several of the basic features of television. He made a disc which he punched with holes in a spiral pattern. On one side of the disc he placed a bright light, on the other the subject to be televised. As the disc spun round, the light shone in turn through each hole in such a way that it scanned the subject from side to side starting at the top and working downwards. Light reflected from the subject struck a surface coated with a selenium compound, causing variations in an electric current which matched the constantly changing patterns of light and dark reflected from the subject. The fluctuating current in turn caused an electric lamp to flicker in step with the variations in light from the subject. This lamp shone on a second disc spinning in time with the first. By looking at this second disc from the far side, a viewer seemed to see a complete image of the subject being scanned.

But Nipkow's scanner – and indeed any such mechanical device – needed extremely bright lights and proved too slow to produce a satisfactory image. The solution proved to be scanning by a fast-moving beam of electrons – the negatively charged particles which are attracted to positively charged atoms and create electric current when they flow towards such atoms in a one-way stream.

The first step towards electron scanning was arguably taken as early as 1740 when the French

television set of around 1950

television camera

priest Jean Antoine Nollet sent a brief electric discharge between wires separated by a glass tube almost emptied of air. Nollet was surprised to notice that the tube glowed steadily. The cause, which he did not grasp, was an electron stream leaping from the cathode (the negative wire) to the anode (the positive wire). Not until 1897 was a specially constructed cathode ray tube patented by the German physicist Karl Braun. Soon the Russian Boris Rosing was experimenting with a television camera based on electronic scanning by a moving cathode ray. But it was only in 1923 that Rosing's former student Vladimir Zworykin patented the iconoscope — the first really successful television camera built along these lines. From this invention sprang the modern telecamera — a tube in which a lens focuses an object's image on a photoelectric plate which emits many electrons from brightly lit parts, few from dark ones. These produce an image on a light-sensitive screen scanned by an electron beam from the far end of the tube, where deflecting plates control its movement. The screen absorbs or reflects these electrons according to variations in its brightness. Resulting variations in the reflected electron beam produce variations in an electric current which can be transmitted in the form of electromagnetic waves to a television receiving antenna which reconverts the wave pattern into electric signals, producing a matching electron beam inside the cathode ray tube of a television receiver. The beam scans the back of a screen which glows brightly where many electrons strike it, dimly where only a few arrive, producing an overall image for the viewer watching from the far side of the screen.

Television has made huge strides since the first short broadcasts began in the 1930s. The year 1953 saw the first broadcast of an hour-long programme in electronic colour, and in 1962 the American earth satellite *Telstar I* provided a sky platform from which, for the first time, television signals could be bounced across the Atlantic Ocean. In 1969 such systems helped a world-wide audience estimated at 600,000,000 to watch man take his first historic step upon the moon.

Above: *the communications satellite Syncom orbiting the earth.*
Middle: *a modern television receiver.*

Below: *areas served by satellites at different altitudes.*

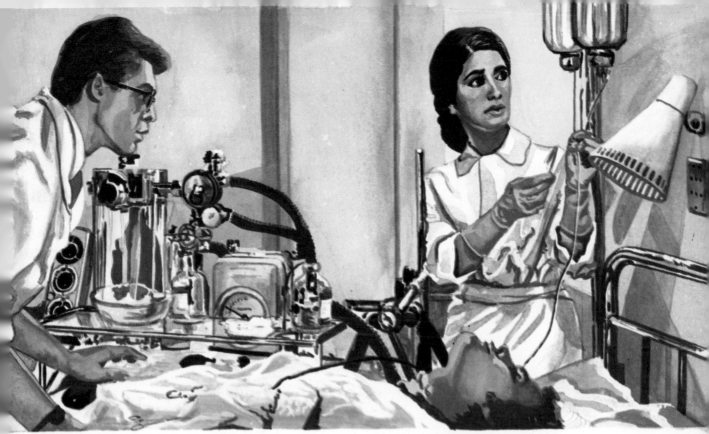

A doctor and nurse cope with an emergency in a modern, well-equipped hospital.

FROM MAGIC TO MEDICINE

Until three centuries ago people in the Western world lived on average only 25 years; little over a century ago life expectation had reached 33 years; today the average westerner can expect to live to 70. Much of this startling improvement comes from a richer, more abundant diet, but it also follows advances in medicine: in our understanding of the causes of killing diseases and injuries, and how these may be detected and cured, or, better still, prevented.

Medicine can be traced back as far as the New Stone Age in archaeologists' finds of broken bones which had knitted together after being deliberately re-set. Archaeologists have also found ancient skulls with holes cut out by stone knives, perhaps in attempts to relieve severe headaches. Regrown bone shows that most patients survived such drastic surgery.

For many centuries, however, doctors were rather like untrained garage mechanics trying to mend broken-down cars with no understanding of how they ought to work. It was true that embalming made the ancient Egyptians familiar with the organs of the human body, but they had no idea of their purpose. When a man fell ill it seemed as though some unseen enemy had struck him down, and the ancient doctors of Egypt and Babylonia blamed diseases upon evil spirits entering the body. Disease, then, was often attributed to witchcraft, and doctors were usually priests whose cures were largely prayers and spells to drive out the disease demons.

Later, the Greeks believed that the god Apollo sent epidemics sweeping through their cities to punish men neglectful of observing proper sacrifices. In medieval Europe, Christians similarly saw the Black Death that carried off perhaps one citizen in three as God's punishment for man's sinfulness. More scientifically minded men for centuries held that disease was caused by an imbalance in the four 'humours' (blood, phlegm, black bile, and yellow bile) which they thought largely made up the body, and could be disturbed by earthquakes, certain winds, and the unhealthy vapours given off by swamps.

While they groped in a fog of ignorance, doctors nonetheless made some progress towards curbing disease. By trial and error, some learned that chewing foxglove leaves might slow down a racing heart, and that bark from certain trees relieved some fevers. In this way the Chinese, Indians, and other peoples built up a whole armoury of herbal medicines as long ago as 2,000 years. At the same time by draining swamps, and building aqueducts and drains to separate drinking water from sewage, the Romans did much to stop some kinds of epidemic scourging their cities.

Several ancient doctors are remembered to this day for their teachings. Perhaps the greatest was the Greek Hippocrates who lived in the 5th century B.C.

By making careful observations of disease symptoms, he learned to diagnose several disease conditions, including pneumonia and pleurisy. He taught his students to follow his example. At Alexandria, Herophilus and other anatomists made strides in studying the structure of the body. But Galen, who studied there and taught in Rome, was much to blame for the misguided belief in 'humours' which persisted through the Middle Ages. In medieval times, the leading doctors were Moslems like Rhazes (born in A.D. 865), the first man to diagnose accurately that smallpox and measles were different diseases.

But modern medicine began only in the Age of Discovery when anatomists began to ignore an old Church ban on dissection and systematically examined the insides of dead bodies to see how they were made. In the 15th century Leonardo da Vinci made fine drawings of muscles, bones, and sinews. In the 16th century the Italian anatomist Vesalius published the first complete description of the human body.

When, in the early 1600s, William Harvey experimentally proved that the heart pumps blood round the body people began to find out not just which organs the body contains, but how they work, and when they may be faulty. To help diagnose organic disease, special tools were invented. For instance, in 1733 England's Stephen Hales invented a device which measured blood pressure, and in 1816 France's René Laënnec devised the stethoscope which magnifies chest and heart sounds. Much later, in 1903, came the electrocardiograph which reveals heart troubles as irregularities in the pattern of electrical impulses produced by heartbeats.

Today, doctors have a complex arsenal of diagnostic devices to detect a huge range of diseases, for instance by studying the chemical make up of blood, urine, and other substances; and by seeing inside the body with the help of X-rays.

This particularly useful diagnostic aid sprang from a chance discovery made in 1895 by the German physicist Wilhelm Röntgen. Röntgen noticed that when he sent current through a cathode ray tube wrapped in cardboard, invisible rays from the tube passed through the cardboard and set a nearby fluorescent screen glowing. When Röntgen put his hand in front of the screen, it showed clearly the bones inside his hand. X-rays, as Röntgen named the mysterious rays, now help doctors to detect broken bones and other damage deep inside the body. Other kinds of radiation can help doctors to treat deep-seated tumours.

In teaching hospitals, students can often watch operations from observation windows.

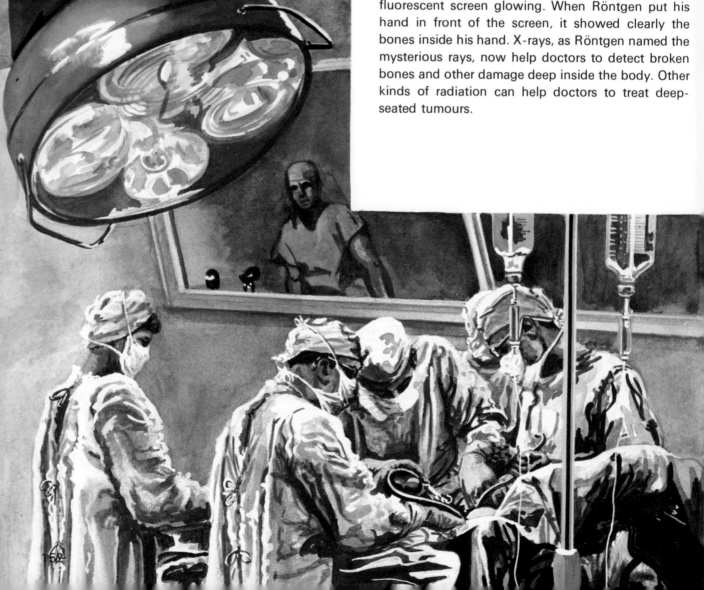

154

But doctors usually treat damage deep inside the body by surgery: cutting through the patient's skin to remove, repair, or replace the damaged part. Army surgeons have been amputating limbs for centuries, but since the middle of the present century, doctors have had the tools and knowledge to undertake far more daring operations on the brain, heart, lungs, and kidneys — vital organs, so called because they are vital to the life of the whole body. Such operations are possible due to the development of blood transfusion which replaces blood lost in surgery. This became successful only after 1900 when Karl Landsteiner showed that there are four main groups of blood, and that blood loss can be made good safely only by transfusing a patient with blood of his own group. Heart operations also owe much to the heart-lung machine, by which surgeons can make blood bypass the patient's heart while they operate upon it.

The results of such advances are dramatic. Where a patient with a faulty heart valve once faced almost certain death, a surgeon can often save him by replacing the valve with an artificial one. In 1967 the South African surgeon Christiaan Barnard completed an even more remarkable operation by replacing Louis Washkansky's diseased heart with a healthy heart taken from someone who had just died. But much as the body rejects blood of a foreign type, it rejects tissues that do not match its own. To prevent transplanted organs from being killed by the very body they are meant to keep alive, doctors treat transplant patients with special drugs and radiations. Unfortunately this treatment tends to lower their resistance to infection, and many heart transplant patients (Washkansky among them) died from tissue rejection or diseases like pneumonia. Nonetheless, spare-part surgery, including several kinds of organ transplant, is now adding years of useful life to patients who were crippled or about to die.

Yet none of these remarkable advances in surgery has preserved a fraction of the millions of lives that were saved by the 19th century British surgeon Joseph Lister. Appalled by the huge numbers of surgical wounds that turned septic and killed hospital patients, Lister pioneered antiseptic surgery in the 1870s, spraying operating theatres with antiseptics, and steeping dressings in antiseptic liquids to kill the germs which Lister believed were killing up to half of all the patients operated on. Deaths slumped to 2 per 100 as a direct result of Lister's pioneering work. Development of Lister's work led to the modern methods of *aseptic* surgery,

Left: *close-up of an operation in progress.*
Below: *two types of artificial organ — (1) an artificial heart; (2) artificial lungs.*

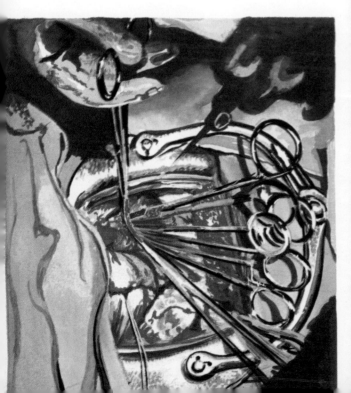

153

which is based, not on killing germs already present in a wound, but on preventing them from entering by having surgeons and nurses use sterilised tools, gauze masks, gloves, and clothing.

Lister's work drew fresh attention to the idea that germs caused many diseases. Back in the early 1600s, the Dutch naturalist Anton van Leeuwenhoek, using one of the first powerful microscopes, became the first man to detect tiny germ-like organisms. But it was the nineteenth century French chemist Louis Pasteur who showed that certain microscopic bacteria made food decay, while other micro-organisms caused the terrible diseases anthrax and rabies. Pasteur's discoveries not only showed Lister a way of making surgery safe, they led to new ways of treating and preventing such killing infectious diseases as cholera, typhoid, diphtheria, and polio-myelitis, caused by disease germs entering the bloodstream and spreading through the body.

In 1935 the German chemist Gerhard Domagk developed the first of the famous sulphonamide drugs, which kill harmful bacteria inside the body by causing them to starve to death. In 1928 Britain's Alexander Fleming noticed that a certain mould which had landed accidentally on some germs he was growing in a dish had killed some of them. Fleming had discovered penicillin, the first of the many anti-biotic drugs which have since saved many million lives.

But in medicine, prevention is even better than cure. As early as 1796 Edward Jenner, an English country doctor, discovered the first safe way of preventing people from succumbing to the killing disease smallpox. He took some matter from a spot on the arm of a girl suffering from *cowpox*, the mild but smallpox-like disease contracted from cows, introduced it into a boy's arm and later added matter from a smallpox spot. The boy remained healthy, and Jenner's preventive method of vaccination made a once-dreaded disease a rarity. A century later, researchers armed with new knowledge of the germs that cause disease, discovered that by injecting weakened germs of a certain type into the body, they could persuade it to produce substances called antibodies which gave future protection against the harmful antigens produced by that particular disease.

Today, vaccination, together with high levels of hygiene, and an understanding of the foods that the body needs are keeping millions free from diseases which once scourged all mankind.

Big challenges still face modern doctors. They have yet to cure most kinds of cancer — types of killing disease caused by body cells which grow and multiply uncontrollably; and they have found no way to halt the ageing process by which the body eventually wears out until a normally mild illness can become serious enough to kill a person. In your lifetime, doctors may make surprising progress in both these fields.

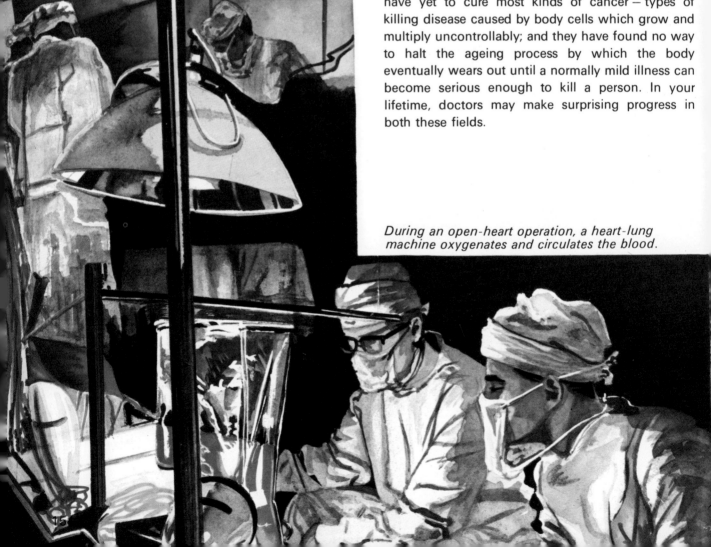

During an open-heart operation, a heart-lung machine oxygenates and circulates the blood.

BUILDING ARTIFICIAL BRAINS

However skilful surgeons have become in making artificial hearts and kidneys, none could make a complete artificial human brain, the most complicated organ known in nature. Yet electronics experts can now make machines which actually perform some of the brain's functions: machines that almost seem to think.

Some such machines can solve mathematical problems and feed the answers to others so as to control complex chains of factory processes far faster and more efficiently than any man. In some steel mills and chemical plants, one or two skilled technicians supervising banks of dials and switches can thus produce far more steel or chemicals than dozens without the help of such automatic controls. These great changes in manufacturing methods have led some scientists to divide the Industrial Revolution into two stages. In the first stage, beginning in the 18th century, man began to make engines which performed much of the heavy work once done by human muscles. In the second stage, beginning in the 1950s, he began to replace the engine operators

Experienced technicians check instrument readings in the control room of a modern automated steel works.

Banks of dials and switches enable men to control the largest of modern cargo vessels

themselves with machines to make production fully automatic.

The age of automation may be young, but the idea of self-regulating devices on which it depends is old. We can see it in the systems of toothed wheels which medieval clockmakers used to regulate the rate at which a weight falls and a spring unwinds. For many years now, people have also been using such devices in their homes. One such device is the thermostat used to control the temperature of an oven. One kind of thermostat consists of two different metals welded together in one strip. The hotter they become the more they expand, but because one metal expands more than the other the bar bends, breaking an electric circuit and cutting off the current which heats the oven.

The thermostat controls the oven by first gathering information about oven temperature, then feeding it back into the electric circuit. All self-regulating

devices work on a similar *feedback* principle. But in a modern automated factory, the feedback process is more complicated. Whole chains of operations are regulated by an army of sensors which feed details of temperatures, pressures, rates of flow and other information into a central electronic brain called a computer. The computer uses the information to calculate the work done by the many separate machines involved in the entire manufacturing process. It then compares their output with the output required, calculates any adjustments necessary, and feeds back this information to mechanisms which automatically regulate the machines.

Computers have their roots in early devices like Blaise Pascal's calculating machine which appeared in 1642 and used geared cog wheels. By the 1830s the English mathematician Charles Babbage had built an analytical engine which was designed to solve problems. A pattern of holes representing

Clinical efficiency is the keynote in this computer section of a modern office.

coded questions, was punched in a tape and this was fed into the engine.

Modern computers are also fed programmes in this way but, unlike the early mechanical models with their slow moving cog-wheels, they use fast-moving streams of electrons. ENIAC, the first all-electronic computer, was invented at the University of Pennsylvania in 1946. Able to make thousands of calculations a second, it was the first of a whole generation of computers built in the 1950s which were controlled by valves (vacuum tubes). In the 1960s came a second generation of computers with tiny transistors in place of valves, which were not only less bulky and less liable to go wrong than the first type, but worked ten times faster. Then, in the middle 1960s a third generation of computers appeared. Instead of transistors, they had electronic circuits small enough to build a radio no larger than a tiny coin. Third generation computers can work one

hundred times faster than second-generation ones, performing up to a million calculations in one second.

All such devices make the greatest mathematical genius seem slow witted. However they work only if they are first given a memory of thousands or millions of facts and the rules for using them. The computer's input system is fed with information broken down into the kind of language it can handle. In most computers this language is built up from only two number symbols to correspond with the flow and interruption of electric current. Thus the computer usually counts in 0 and 1 instead of the ten numbers 0 to 9 in everyday use, so that in computer language 1 may be shown as 1, but 2 as 10, 3 as 11, 4 as 100, 5 as 101, or in other ways, for various computer languages have been devised for handling different kinds of problem.

A key punch operator feeds such information into

the computer on punched cards in which numbers and letters appear as special patterns of holes. Each card holds up to 80 numbers or letters. A card-reading machine electronically scanning over 1,000 such cards a minute translates their information into electric signals which feed into the computer's memory system, often in the form of tiny patterns of magnetic spots on tape, cards, or discs.

Only now is the computer equipped to solve problems. But the computer programmer must phrase his problems in computer language on coding sheets which the key punch operator feeds into the machine. Inside the machine, a control unit selects appropriate instructions from its memory and feeds an arithmetic unit which carries out the actual calculations, first drawing information from the memory, then storing it in so-called registers which link up with special electronic circuits to perform the computations. The answers become data stored in the memory until required. Finally, output equipment translates the answers into numbers, words, or even shapes which it automaticallly types, prints, draws or shows in other ways at tremendous speeds (automatic printers can produce 1,000 lines a minute).

We have already seen that such high-speed electronic brains can switch machines on and off in factories. In offices, computers can also automatically perform book-keeping, accounting and other kinds of work. But besides performing tasks once done by man, computers also carry out operations of which no man was ever capable: without the split second calculations by which computers keep space vehicles on course, space flight would have been impossible. In many ways, then, computers are making life easier and more exciting; but they also create serious problems for the people they replace, robbing them of their jobs.

The maze of wires making up some of the myriad circuits needed for an electronic computer.

LIQUID 'GOLD' FROM UNDERGROUND

The thousands of fine wires in an electronic computer may be sheathed in insulating tubes made from chemicals obtained from petroleum or mineral oil. No other substance has become more precious to us than this greasy liquid found in great lakes trapped deep down in the earth.

At first people simply valued oil as fuel for lamps, and in the early 1850s Rumanians hauled mineral oil by the bucket from shallow wells. Then, in 1859, the American Edwin Drake showed how to obtain oil by drilling deep down through solid rock with the help of a tall derrick which enabled a great length of drilling equipment to be raised. Drake's drilling methods made oil cheaper and more plentiful. But some substances in petroleum proved unsuitable as fuel for lamps. While the paraffin (or kerosene) in oil burnt well, the petrol (or gasoline) tended to explode dangerously. Chemical engineers learned to separate petroleum from kerosene by heating the crude petroleum in stills. As the oil grew hotter, first the petrol was given off as vapour, then the kerosene, leaving heavier substances behind. People threw away the dangerous petrol, used the kerosene for lamp fuel, and sold the rest as lubricating oil to reduce friction between the moving parts of machines, so preventing them from seizing up.

At first, oil producers carted oil from oil fields to oil refineries in barrels, but by the 1870s they were realising that oil could be moved far faster through long pipes. By 1874 the equivalent of 3,500 barrels of oil was flowing daily 100 kilometres (60 miles) in this way from an oil field to Pittsburgh.

By 1900, electric lamps were replacing oil-filled lamps, and the demand for kerosene began to drop. Meanwhile the demand for petrol steadily rose as the first cheap, mass-produced, petrol-driven cars rolled off the assembly lines. Around 1900, oil refineries produced only about 50 litres (11 gallons) of petrol from every 450 litres (100 gallons) of crude oil. But within 20 years this figure had more than doubled, largely because of new methods of distilling petroleum oil under pressure so as to *crack* or break down its heavy ingredients.

Today, many different so-called fractions are extracted from crude oil by heating it, letting the resulting vapour rise up inside a tall fractionating

Drilling an oil well beneath the sea.

tower, and drawing off the different fractions which condense at different levels.

In this way, the oil industry produces huge quantities of asphalt, heavy fuel oil, lubricating oil, heating oil, kerosene for jet aircraft, petrol for road vehicles, and fuel gas.

Since the 1930s, scientists have also discovered how to do the opposite of cracking: to polymerise small fractions in oil to produce larger ones whose chemical make-up can be tailored at will to manufacture many kinds of useful plastics such as polyethylene — the substance used for squeeze bottles, food wrappings, water pipes, and electric insulation. Altogether we now have many thousand different oil-based products.

As the world's appetite for petroleum grew, so prospectors ranged farther afield in search of new supplies. By 1910 Texas and Oklahoma had joined five other oil-producing states in the U.S.A. Meanwhile other countries in the Americas and Europe had begun production. An oil find in Iran in 1908 was followed up by oil strikes in Iraq (1927) and Saudi Arabia (1938), opening up what have since proved to be some of the richest oil fields in the world. Today, forests of drilling rigs appear in the unlikeliest places.

Above: *an oil refinery*

Some tower above the hot desert sands of Arabia and Africa; others jut from the frozen landscape of Alaska. Some stand on massive platforms perched above shallow seas, yet others are buffeted by Caribbean hurricanes and North Sea storms.

To move huge quantities of oil from the often remote and sparsely peopled oil-field areas to the industrial countries which need oil to power their ships, planes, cars, trains, and power stations, shipbuilders have constructed the largest vessels ever built. The first of these so-called supertankers appeared in the 1950s. Since then, sizes have rapidly increased and by the early 1970s ships capable of carrying half a million tonnes of oil were under construction.

Such supertankers create problems. They are too large to use the Suez Canal if it were open, and too deep for most shallow-water ports to handle. Moreover, oil leaking from a damaged supertanker can pollute seas and coasts, and at the same time destroy animal life. But an even greater problem faces our oil-hungry world: its fast dwindling oil reserves may last only a few decades. What will happen to our cars, ships, planes and factories when these have been exhausted?

Below: *a modern oil tanker*

TOWERS THAT SCRAPE THE SKY

Early in the 19th century, railway engineers were daringly spanning rivers with bridges made of factory produced iron girders joined together. But architects still thought in terms of brick and stone and continued to design buildings for erection in the slow old-fashioned way of piling brick on brick, or stone on stone. If they used a skeleton of iron girders, invariably they disguised the metal with stone columns and other decorations borrowed from ancient building styles.

Some designers however were quick to grasp the possibilities of new shapes and a new kind of beauty in the new building materials. One of these was Britain's Joseph Paxton, whose curved exhibition hall of iron and glass, called the Crystal Palace and built in 1851, was the first big building to be made from prefabricated parts.

The Crystal Palace was dismantled and re-erected outside London after the Great Exhibition ended. But as cities grew larger in the later 1800s, and the cost of building land soared in city centres, architects began to seek ways of using new materials to build large permanent buildings so that thousands of people could live or work on a piece of land which before could accommodate only dozens. To do so, architects began to design buildings which developed upwards instead of outwards. In this they were aided by another invention: the lift or elevator, devised in the 1850s by the American inventor Elisha Otis. Instead of plodding exhaustingly up and down hundreds of stairs, people standing inside a lift rode up and down without effort. Without lifts, skyscrapers might never have been built.

The first skyscraper was a 10-floor insurance office built in Chicago in 1884 by William Le Baron Jenney. Soon other architects, including Louis H. Sullivan, were building skyscrapers in which only narrow strips of stone disguised the steel framework; the spaces between were filled with large glass windows.

Designers were moving away from the old idea that to be beautiful a modern bank or insurance office must disguise itself as a Greek temple or a Gothic castle. By the early 1900s the German architect Walter Gropius was teaching that a building is only beautiful when its shape clearly and simply told what it was built of, and for what purpose; and the Swiss-born architect Le Corbusier called a house a machine to live in. As our century advanced, architects stopped adding ornaments and began to make skyscrapers the clean-lined steel-and-glass slabs with which we are familiar today. In the early 1900s many skyscrapers were crowding the long narrow

Left: *the Seagram building, New York (1956–1959), designed by Ludwig Mies van der Rohe.*

Above: *Le Corbusier's chapel at Ronchamp, France, brings a new look to an old type of building.*

island of Manhattan in New York City, where the Empire State Building (completed in 1931) became the tallest inhabited structure in the world: about half a kilometre (one-quarter of a mile) high including its 68-metre (222-feet) television tower. In 1970 this man-made mountain was overshadowed by the nearby World Trade Center, itself soon to be overtopped by Chicago's Sears Tower, soaring 442 metres (1,451 feet) and containing ten times as many floors as the first skyscraper built in 1884.

By the 1970s this style of building which had first been built in Chicago and New York had spread round the world. And as forests of steel and glass sprouted in London, Paris, and Tokyo, cities which had once looked entirely different took on a kind of sameness. But this was not the only way in which they were becoming alike. They were becoming healthier to live in as builders replaced dirty bug- and rat-infested huts with homes of brick and concrete, and engineers replaced polluted wells with special pipes which kept drinking water separate from sewage.

Better hygiene and better medicine halted the waves of killing disease which once swept through the cities, and their citizens began to live longer than ever before. At the same time, as machines replaced workers in the fields outside the cities, thousands of farm labourers and their families migrated to the cities in search of work. For these reasons a city which in the past housed and fed thousands, now counted its citizens in millions. Today, London, New York, and Tokyo each hold more people than the whole world supported 10,000 years ago.

To help house the world's bulging city populations, engineers are now tearing down old rows of houses and replacing them with huge apartment blocks; and to help city workers move between home and factory or office they build big broad highways and huge yet slender and graceful bridges, often made by reinforcing concrete with slim steel rods. But town planners believe that unless populations stop growing no engineer can prevent our cities becoming too overcrowded to live in.

SHIPS BENEATH THE SEA

Although men have been building ships to sail the surface of the oceans for thousands of years, ships that move beneath the waves are relatively new. In 1620, Cornelius van Drebbel built the first submarine which really worked. It had a wooden framework covered with a leather skin greased to keep it waterproof, and men sitting inside the boat rowed it by means of oars jutting out through watertight holes in the sides. Van Drebbel launched his submarine in the River Thames where it moved about 4·5 metres (15 feet) below the surface.

Although such boats might have helped man to explore the vast underwater world, he used the first successful submarines for war. During the American Revolution, the American patriot David Bushnell built the one-man *Turtle*. It was hand-driven by a screw, and it submerged when ballast tanks were filled with water. Bushnell's boat made the first-known submarine attack on a warship when it crept up on the unsuspecting British man-of-war *Eagle* in New York harbour and its operator tried to screw a charge of gunpowder onto the warship's copper-coated hull.

By 1800, the American steamship pioneer Robert Fulton had improved on Bushnell's vessel with the *Nautilus*, a 6·5 metre (21 feet) long oval-shaped submarine sheathed in metal, driven underwater by a hand-operated screw propeller, and travelling along the surface by sail. But no nation felt confident enough to buy her for its navy. Then, in the American Civil War, the Confederate submarine *Hunley* sank the Federal corvette *Housatonic* by ramming her with a torpedo hung from the bow, thereby proving that submerged vessels could be powerful weapons.

The invention of a self-propelling torpedo later in the 1860s encouraged inventors to press ahead

with better ways of powering submarines, for lack of engine power was their main weakness. Ingenious people suggested different devices. In 1884 two Englishmen invented a short range submarine driven by electric motors, while in 1897 America's Simon Lake powered his 11-metre (36 feet) long *Argonaut* with an internal combustion engine. Meanwhile, John P. Holland was perfecting submarines with horizontal rudders to control the angles of climb and descent.

By World War I major navies were armed with submarines combining the best of such inventions. Like many modern submarines they were powered by internal combustion engines on the surface and electric motors when submerged. They dived by flooding ballast tanks with water, and surfaced by blowing out the water with compressed air. Underwater they navigated with the help of periscopes. In both world wars, German submarines firing torpedoes took a heavy toll of British shipping in damaging, though unsuccessful, attempts to cut off the British Isles from overseas supplies.

Since World War II, designers have worked to build submarines which can stay submerged longer, and travel faster and farther without refuelling. America accomplished all these goals with the first atomic-powered warship, *Nautilus*. Launched in 1954 she moved underwater at speeds of over 20 knots, and in 1958, guided by sensitive equipment, she startled the world by sailing under the ice-covered North Pole. Two years later, the nuclear-powered *Triton* travelled round the world completely submerged. Such feats have led scientists to predict that huge submarine supertankers will one day ferry oil under the ice from remote Arctic oil fields.

No such ships have yet been built, but submarines are becoming tools for peaceful underwater exploration as well as deadly weapons.

1. *A conventionally powered submarine*
2. *A British nuclear powered submarine*
3. *A nuclear submarine at the North Pole*

EXPLORING THE OCEAN DEPTHS

By 1900, explorers had combed the earth's land surface, yet almost all that man knew of the great depths of the oceans which cover seven-tenths of our planet came from random soundings and the plants and animals dredged up in nets.

But by 1855 the American naval lieutenant Matthew Maury had compiled charts of ocean currents and winds. In 1872 the British research ship *Challenger* began a 110,000 kilometre (69,000 mile) three-year voyage which added enormously to our knowledge of the world beneath the waves. They dredged up living creatures from thousands of metres below the surface (far deeper than anyone had once thought life existed). They took thousands of soundings which helped cartographers to map the hills and valleys of the ocean bed and they showed that below about 180 metres (600 feet), water temperature is unaffected by the seasons.

Since 1900, men have built ingenious aids to underwater discovery. By the 1950s ships were mapping the sea bed by echo sounding devices. These send sound signals down into the water: the sound waves are reflected by the sea bed, and by measuring the time which the echoes take to return, scientists on board ship can find the contours and depth of the sea bed. Echo-sounding devices can map the sea floor much faster and in more detail than the weighted lines dropped by the *Challenger*. Today, research ships can also study the sea bed by trailing remotely-controlled cameras attached to underwater sleds. And deep-sea drills enable geologists to bring up samples of the rock beneath the sea floor. By 1961 American oceanographers at Guadalupe Island in the Pacific Ocean lowered a drill through 3 kilometres (2 miles) of water, then bored down through 152 metres (500 feet) of soft sediments and 15 metres (50 feet) of solid rock. This was just part of a much more ambitious plan, the Mohole project, in which scientists on a floating platform hoped eventually to bore through 8 kilometres (5 miles) of the earth's crust to explore the mantle, the mysterious layer beneath the crust.

But no remote controlled devices such as cameras, drills, and echo-sounders could give such a full impression of the underwater world as human observations. The problem was to build a craft that could carry an observer safely down into the immense depths of the open ocean — depths at which the intensely high water pressure could crush an ordinary submarine like cardboard. In the 1930s engineers began to devise two kinds of deep sea submarine. One was the bathysphere — a heavy steel ball pierced by tiny windows, equipped with a

Oceanographers lowering a drilling device to take a sample from the sea-bed.

searchlight to penetrate the darkness of the lower depths, and lowered from a ship by cable. Crouching in its cramped interior, and breathing air from special tanks, in the early 1930s William Beebe plunged deeper than 915 metres (3,000 feet) and made remarkable discoveries about mid-depth forms of ocean life.

The tethered bathysphere could not control its

A bathyscaphe. Two men sit in the tiny metal sphere fixed below the main hull.

own movements, but Auguste Piccard's bathyscaphe, or deep boat, proved more manoeuvrable; two men sitting in a tiny metal sphere piloted the craft. Piccard's bathyscaphe sank when petrol was released from a big boat-shaped tank above it, and rose when heavy weights were released. In 1960, Jacques Piccard and Donald Walsh took the bathyscaphe *Trieste* more than 9 kilometres (6 miles) down to the bottom of the Pacific Ocean's Challenger Deep — the deepest known part of any ocean. There the two observers learned that certain shrimps and fishes could and did live under the colossal pressure of more than 1,000 tons per square foot.

The bathyscaphe could move freely only up or down; now there are deep-sea submersibles which can manoeuvre freely in any direction. One such vessel is the American *Aluminaut*, a 15 metre (50 feet) aluminium-built, three-man submarine, able to operate at 4,500 metres (15,000 feet) below the surface.

The men inside such vessels are prisoners cut off from the underwater world around them. This is not true of naked divers who, for centuries, have risked their lives plunging for pearls, clams, and corals in the world's warm seas. But none dare dive below 30 metres (100 feet) without risking crushed lungs; none can hold his breath underwater more than two or three minutes; and anyone who dives in cold water risks paralysis and death.

Today, ingenious equipment is helping divers to overcome these problems. The first effective diving suits, developed in the 1800s, involved wearing heavy helmets and boots, and trailing tiresome air lines. But in the 1940s France's Jacques-Yves Cousteau pioneered aqualung diving, by which divers breathing air from cylinders strapped to their backs are free to swim about like fishes with the help of flippers

Section through a hollow drill about to raise a core sample of sea-bed sediments.

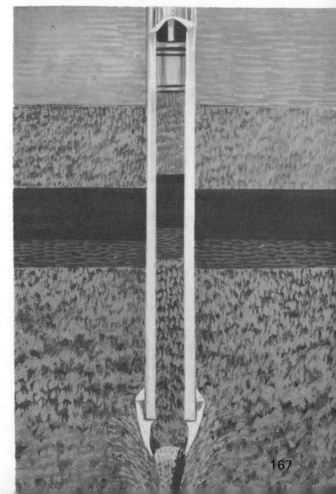

167

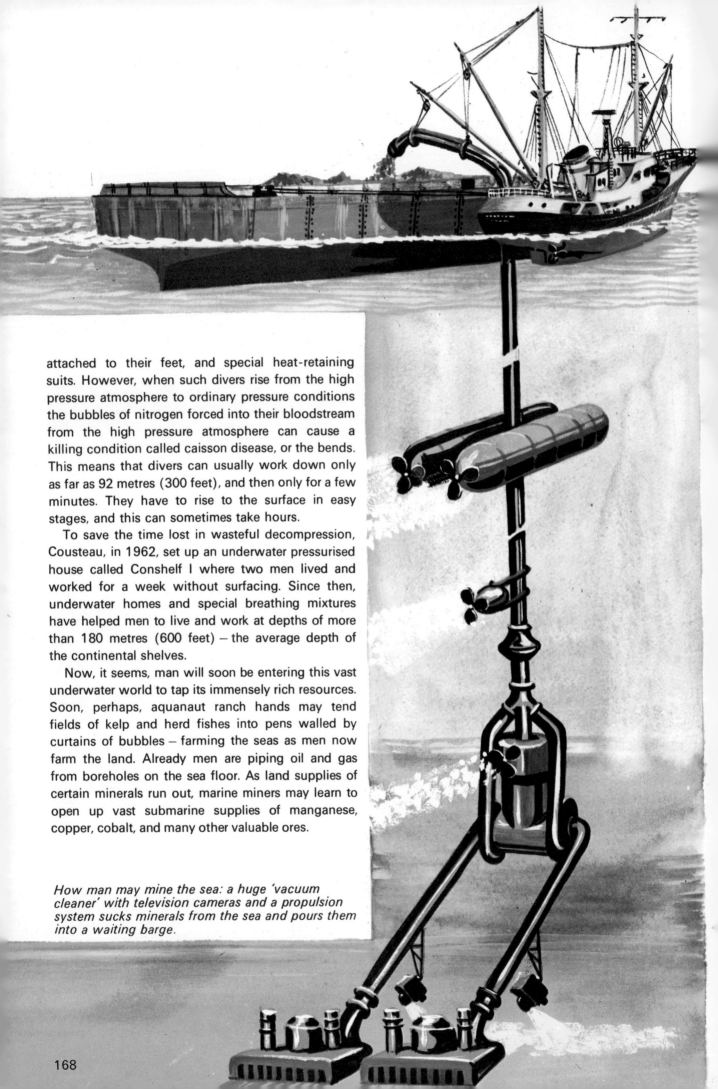

attached to their feet, and special heat-retaining suits. However, when such divers rise from the high pressure atmosphere to ordinary pressure conditions the bubbles of nitrogen forced into their bloodstream from the high pressure atmosphere can cause a killing condition called caisson disease, or the bends. This means that divers can usually work down only as far as 92 metres (300 feet), and then only for a few minutes. They have to rise to the surface in easy stages, and this can sometimes take hours.

To save the time lost in wasteful decompression, Cousteau, in 1962, set up an underwater pressurised house called Conshelf I where two men lived and worked for a week without surfacing. Since then, underwater homes and special breathing mixtures have helped men to live and work at depths of more than 180 metres (600 feet) — the average depth of the continental shelves.

Now, it seems, man will soon be entering this vast underwater world to tap its immensely rich resources. Soon, perhaps, aquanaut ranch hands may tend fields of kelp and herd fishes into pens walled by curtains of bubbles — farming the seas as men now farm the land. Already men are piping oil and gas from boreholes on the sea floor. As land supplies of certain minerals run out, marine miners may learn to open up vast submarine supplies of manganese, copper, cobalt, and many other valuable ores.

How man may mine the sea: a huge 'vacuum cleaner' with television cameras and a propulsion system sucks minerals from the sea and pours them into a waiting barge.

168

The mushroom cloud of an atomic bomb experimentally exploded on a remote Pacific island.

UNLEASHING THE ENERGY IN ATOMS

On 6th August 1945, the citizens of the Japanese city of Hiroshima heard the drone of a high-flying American bomber. During World War II, when thousand-bomber air raids had become common, the sound of one enemy aircraft must have seemed only mildly menacing, and anyone who saw the single bomb falling might have expected it to destroy no more than a few buildings.

What actually happened was far more terrible. A colossal explosion sent a massive blast wave through the air, flattening buildings over an area of $1\frac{1}{2}$ square miles. Where the bomb had exploded a great ball of fire bulged outwards, starting a fire storm which swept the city and killed people for a mile around. At the same time, tiny, invisible, but deadly, particles were flung outwards from the bomb; other particles were whirled aloft in a huge cloud which soared and billowed before flattening out like a colossal mushroom. A slow rain of deadly dust was released over a vast area and a lingering death was the unhappy fate of the many thousand survivors of the blast. Some experts believe that over 90,000 died at Hiroshima while others place the final death roll nearer 250,000.

The single four-ton bomb dropped on Hiroshima had been no ordinary bomb: it had produced an explosive effect equal to 9,140 tonnes (9,000 tons) of the T.N.T. used in conventional bombs, and at the same time it radiated dreadful side effects. For, unlike any bomb previously dropped, it unleashed the colossal energy locked up in atoms, the tiny particles of which all elements are made. This first atomic bomb (to be followed three days later by another which flattened Nagasaki) not only helped to end World War II — the most devastating war in history —

it showed that man was mastering a new and immensely powerful source of energy, so powerful that he could either use it to destroy the world or harness it for peaceful purposes to enrich mankind as never before.

Half a century of research had led up to these remarkable developments. It began in 1895 when Wilhelm Röntgen discovered high energy X-rays. The next year, Antoine Becquerel discovered that uranium naturally gives off penetrating rays, and Marie and Pierre Curie were inspired to find more such radioactive elements, including radium. The Curies and Ernest Rutherford between them found that such radiations came from inside the actual atoms of radioactive substances, and they identified three kinds of rays named *alpha, beta* and *gamma* after the first three letters of the Greek alphabet.

An alpha ray is a heavy positively charged particle consisting of two protons and two neutrons from the atom's nucleus. A beta ray is a lightweight negatively charged particle from the outer part of the atom. By the 1930s, physicists bombarding certain atoms with neutrons found that an atom's nucleus captured a neutron and gave off a beta particle. In 1938 Otto Hahn and Fritz Strassmann actually split a uranium nucleus by bombarding it with neutrons. In 1942 Enrico Fermi bombarded uranium atoms so that they gave off beta particles, also neutrons which struck other uranium atoms, forcing them to yield fresh neutrons. A chain reaction was produced in which a small amount of uranium was changed into a colossal quantity of energy according to Albert Einstein's mathematical formula which he worked out in 1905, long before anyone could demonstrate that mass and energy are interchangeable.

The first atomic bombs gained their immense

Some of the strangely shaped structures to be seen around a modern nuclear power station.

destructive energy from this atom-splitting, or fission. But by 1948 American scientists had also produced the much more devastating weapon of the hydrogen bomb — a bomb in which uranium fission causes hydrogen atoms to fuse together, releasing extra energy to split more uranium atoms, thus producing many hundred times more destructive energy than the first atomic bombs.

By 1956, however, scientists were also using nu-

turbines spun by steam produced in any other way.

As the world's deposits of irreplaceable fossil fuels (coal and oil) are worked out, perhaps in the not too distant future, nuclear energy looks like satisfying a rising proportion of our fuel needs.

In nuclear power plants, a tiny quantity of fuel can unleash a colossal quantity of energy. This is one reason why engineers have also begun to build nuclear powered ships, for such vessels can circle

Nuclear power thrusts the huge American aircraft carrier Enterprise *round the world without refuelling.*

clear fission for peaceful purposes by building nuclear power stations. In these buildings, nuclear fission produces carefully controlled nuclear chain reactions in such a way as to generate huge quantities of heat which can turn vast amounts of water into high pressure steam. The steam can then be used for driving turbines to generate electric current in exactly the same way as electricity is generated by

the world without wasting valuable time refuelling. Moreover, unlike a petrol or diesel engine, a nuclear reactor needs no oxygen to help it burn fuel. This means that nuclear-powered submarines can stay submerged for months at a time. The American submarine *Nautilus*, launched in 1954, ushered in an age of nuclear-powered ships which now include aircraft carriers, icebreakers, and cargo vessels.

A patient receiving deep-ray radiation treatment from a nuclear device popularly called a cobalt bomb.

Today, nuclear energy is being used for peaceful purposes in more ways than as a source of power, especially in the radioactive forms of chemical elements called radioactive isotopes.

For instance, in agriculture, scientists can study how plants use chemicals as foods by feeding soil with radioactive elements, then using special detectors to trace their passage through a plant. By tagging insect pests with radioactive isotopes, scientists have also learned much about their destructive habits. Such studies help farmers to make the best possible use of fertilisers and insecticides. Scientists have, by exposing parent plants to strong doses of radiation, also produced new and useful kinds of wheat and other plants; and in food storage they have helped to stop food from going bad by using radiation to kill the tiny organisms which cause decay.

In industry, radioactive isotopes have many uses. They help experienced workers to measure the amount of metal rubbed off by friction of moving parts. And radiations from a radioactive isotope can be sent through a metal strip to measure its thickness with incredible accuracy, thereby warning a machine operator of any faults in a manufacturing process.

In medicine, radioactive isotopes help doctors to study the ways in which the healthy body uses different chemicals. Doctors can also use such isotopes to detect diseases whereby some organs

have to take up a certain substance more readily than a healthy organ. Radio isotopes can also help doctors to locate the size and position of some forms of tumour. Where deep-seated tumours cannot be removed by surgery, doctors can often treat them by bombardment with powerful and accurately directed radiation from radium or radioactive cobalt: the radiation kills the cancer cells.

Side by side with these developments, powerful nations have gone on stockpiling nuclear bombs, shells, and rockets, until the world's atomic armouries have grown large enough to destroy civilisation on earth. Perhaps the likelihood that neither side could survive an atomic war is our best reason for hoping that no nation will ever be foolish enough to start one.

A British-built hovercraft throws up a snowy cloud of spray as it speeds across the English Channel.

CUSHIONED BY AIR

Since the Wright brothers made the first successful heavier-than-air flight in 1903, engineers have experimented with more than one type of vehicle capable of moving through the air.

While many of them worked to improve upon the aeroplane, some explored the idea of vehicles that would skim just above the surface of the earth, buoyed up not by wheels, but by a cushion of air.

The idea of supporting a ship upon a thin layer of air blown beneath its hull can be traced back to the 1860s, and in 1877 — 26 years before the Wrights' *Flyer* made its first short hop — the British engineer John L. Thorneycroft actually patented a design for an air-cushion vehicle.

By the 1930s American and Finnish designers were developing this hovercraft idea, but the designer of the first successful hovercraft was Britain's Christopher Cockerell. His research led to the Saunders-Roe *SRN-1* which made its first successful trip at the Isle of Wight in 1959, and later that year proved itself by crossing the English Channel.

This first air-cushion vehicle weighed only about 3 tonnes (3 tons), but it inspired engineers to build bigger, more powerful models weighing 27·5 tonnes (27 tons) and capable of carrying 27 passengers at a speed of 70 knots. Today, hovercraft weighing over 152 tonnes (150 tons) can whisk 174 passengers and 34 cars across the Channel at up to 77 knots, and even bigger, faster hovercraft have been predicted for the future: vehicles weighing several thousand tonnes, and carrying many hundred passengers.

Such an air-cushion vehicle hovers by sucking in air through the top by means of fans or propellers, and forcing it out through angled jets beneath the vehicle where skirts hanging down the sides help to trap bubbles of compressed air between the vehicle and the surface beneath it. By adjusting the jets, the pilot can manoeuvre his craft forwards, backwards, or sideways; but he obtains his main propulsive thrust from large aircraft-type propellers.

Hovercraft have advantages over ordinary ships, aircraft, or land vehicles for travel over certain kinds of surface. Because they are buoyed up by air, they can move easily across ground too soft to support the pressure exerted by wheels. And unlike ships they can travel over water without expending energy in thrusting a bow wave aside; one reason why hovercraft can skim across the sea up to twice as rapidly as the fastest ships. Hovercraft combine the advantages of both ships and buses because they are amphibious — moving easily from land to water and back again.

It is true that they have some limitations. Because they need a fairly smooth surface to ride on, hovercraft cannot ride safely through wild seas, or cross rugged or wooded country. But since the 1960s they have opened up a new way of shifting large loads at high speeds.

One of the great advantages of hovercraft is that they can operate over an *unprepared* surface provided it is fairly level. Engineers have also explored the idea of using the hover principle for trains travelling over specially constructed tracks. Unlike the twin metal strips of an ordinary railway line, one such track consists of a low concrete wall flanked by two narrow concrete pavements. This is a development of the monorail or single rail idea. Unlike these earlier systems (in which the train hangs from wheels on a rail or straddles a rail balanced only by guide wheels or a gyroscope), the air-cushion *Aerotrain* developed by France's Jean Bertin in the 1960s rides on cushions of air. The air keeps the train just clear of its T-shaped concrete guide rail and give its passengers a much smoother ride than any vehicle that rests its entire weight on wheels. Moreover, its powerful propeller, powered by jet aeroengines, drives this small, single-carriage train at amazingly high speeds. The Bertin *Aerotrain* can reach speeds of between 400 and 500 kilometres (250 and 300 miles) per hour.

Perhaps one day such hovertrains will enable people living in the country to reach city offices and factories 200 kilometres (over 100 miles) away in only half an hour.

Artist's impression of the French record-breaking aerotrain designed by Jean Bertin to move at over 300 kilometres on compressed air astride a T-shaped concrete rail.

HIGHWAYS IN THE SKY

Remarkable as they are, hovercraft vehicles cannot compete with true aircraft in carrying many passengers across great distances at high speeds. Yet people are alive today who can remember aeroplanes as slow-moving dangerous contraptions incapable of flying more than one man farther than the next field.

In 1903 the world learned that the daring French aviator Louis Blériot had flown his frail glued-wood and sailcloth monoplane the 50 kilometres or so across the English Channel. But it was two world wars which forced the pace in aircraft design. During World War I designers began to invent special types of aeroplane for special purposes. Between 1914 and 1918 new, fast, manoeuvrable fighters raised airspeed limits from 120 to over 240 kilometres an hour and flew up to twice as high as 3,000 metres – the usual prewar limit. At the same time, Germany and Britain built large two-engined planes which were designed to carry bomb loads considerable distances without refuelling.

Flying one such bomber – a converted Vickers Vimy biplane – John Alcock and Arthur Whitten Brown in 1919 completed the first nonstop transatlantic crossing. Ice forming on the aircraft weighed it down, and repeatedly Brown was forced out onto the wings to hack it off. His courage averted near disaster, and after nearly 3,200 kilometres (2,000 miles), Alcock nosed safely down into an Irish bog.

This was just one of many daring record-breaking flights of the early 1900s. In 1924 three American planes circled the world in easy stages. In 1926 Byrd and Floyd Bennett overflew the North Pole. Next year, Charles Lindbergh crossed the Atlantic single-handed in a single-engined monoplane.

The bravery of such pioneers made the way safe for regular travel by air, and as early as 1922 airliners

Struts and wires braced the wings of this Rumpler *biplane, a German spotter aircraft of World War I.*

were plying regularly between cities such as London, Brussels, and Paris.

Meanwhile, designers were replacing the old biplanes with streamlined monoplanes, and increasing the speed of travel. But by 1939 no piston-engined, propeller-driven plane could fly faster than the 750 kilometres (469 miles) an hour achieved that year by a German Messerschmidt fighter.

Then, in World War II, appeared fighter aircraft powered by turbojets; engines with compressor fans which suck in air at high speed and thrust it through combustion chambers where it mixes with fuel vapour. Ignited by a spark, the mixture explodes and expands, thrusting the plane forward. As the exhaust gases escape from the combustion chambers they spin a turbine whose revolving shaft in turn spins the compressor fan to keep the engine working. Soon, turbojet fighters were flying faster than sound.

At first only war aircraft had such engines. But after World War II, turbojet and turboprop airliners began edging from the skies the old, slow, piston-engined aircraft. In 1952 the British *Comet* flying between England and South Africa pioneered intercontinental jet flights. Today, larger, faster aircraft are crossing oceans non-stop, annually carrying millions of passengers across the Atlantic alone at speeds of about 960 kilometres an hour. Thanks largely to such modern navigation aids as radar, automatic pilot systems, and ground-based air-traffic controllers who stack aircraft at different levels in the sky above an airport to prevent collisions, passengers travel in almost total safety.

Now that a single Boeing-747 jumbo jet can ferry hundreds of passengers, airliners have become the true aerial equivalents of the big oceangoing liners which they are replacing. Soon, too, planes like the *Concorde* promise to carry passengers at twice the speed of the jumbo-jets. The main problem will be building airports to handle the huge volume of tomorrow's airborne traffic.

THE CHALLENGE OF SPACE

Before the first powered controlled flight by an aeroplane took place, science-fiction novelists were writing of voyages not just through the air but through the great vacuum of space outside earth's thin atmospheric envelope.

By the early 1900s, scientists were moving beyond fantasy to probe the possibility of actually bridging the great gulfs of nothingness between the earth and the moon and planets. They faced some massive problems. One was the lack of an engine powerful enough to drive a vehicle through empty space; for steam engines, internal combustion engines, even jets, all burn fuels in air drawn from the atmosphere. Moreover most kinds of vehicle move forward by pressing back against land, water, or air. The third problem was the huge speed required to break free from the earth's gravitational attraction. Back in the 17th century, Isaac Newton had worked out that an object must reach 40,000 kilometres (25,000 miles) an hour in order to fly off the surface of the earth.

Curiously enough, children had long been playing with engines of the kind which was to solve all three problems. These engines were simply rockets — devices developed by the Chinese perhaps 1,000 years ago when they packed sulphur, saltpetre, and charcoal inside a tube, tied the tube to an arrow, then lit the back of the tube. As the gunpowder ingredients grew hotter, saltpetre released oxygen which combined with the other substances to burn so forcefully that the combustion gases thrust the rocket forward at tremendous speed without the help of wheels or blades thrusting earth, air, or water backwards. The Chinese let off rockets to celebrate festivals. But they also attacked Mongol invaders with these flying fire arrows.

In 1903 the Russian schoolteacher Konstantin Tsiolkovsky described a rocket large and powerful enough to carry men beyond the earth's atmosphere. Once free from the braking effects of air friction, it was designed to travel at tremendous speeds through empty space. Tsiolkovsky knew that gunpowder burns uncontrollably, so he designed a liquid fuel

Above left: *design improvements eventually produced this streamlined French propeller-driven monoplane.*
Below left: Boeing-747, *first of the jumbo-sized turbojet aircraft to become operational.*
Right: *flames leap from a research rocket at lift off.*

system with controlled combustion produced by storing oxygen and alcohol in separate compartments, then pumping limited supplies of each into a combustion chamber.

Tsiolkovsky's work was largely theoretical. But in 1926 the American inventor Robert Goddard actually launched a liquid-fuelled rocket. And in 1923 the German researcher Hermann Oberth wrote a book on space travel which was to have far-reaching consequences, for Oberth's book helped to found a German society for space travel. During World War II the group's members helped to pioneer the first big rocket missiles which reached speeds far higher than those achieved by any other vehicle.

The first of such devices was the famous *V2* – a complex rocket with over 30,000 parts, capable of soaring nearly 100 kilometres up into the sky before arcing downwards at over 4,800 kilometres (3,000 miles) an hour to land its one-tonne bomb payload on London, over 300 kilometres from the launching site in northern France.

Impressive though they were, the *V2* rockets were incapable of reaching the enormous speed required to break free from the earth's atmosphere and go sailing into space.

But at the end of World War II, captured *V2s* and their chief designer, Wernher von Braun, helped the United States to see how such speeds might be obtained. The answer (which the Russians were also quick to learn) was to launch multi-stage rockets. Once the main rocket had reached its maximum speed, it became a fast-moving launching platform for the second stage, which travelled even faster. Lastly, the second stage released a third which travelled fastest of all. By the late 1950s engineers were building three-stage rockets capable of boosting a small payload to 8 kilometres a second – the speed needed to set it orbiting the earth without being pulled back by gravitational forces. Some rockets were capable even of reaching escape velocity of 11 kilometres a second.

The first artificial earth satellite was the Russian *Sputnik I* (Fellow Traveller I), launched on 4th October 1957 from a secret site north of the Caspian Sea. Less than 60 centimetres across, its tiny ball-shaped payload looped round the earth at over 28,000 kilometres (17,500 miles) an hour in an elliptical orbit, sometimes swinging nearly 960 kilometres (600 miles) out into space, then swooping to within 227 kilometres (142 miles) of the earth's surface. Bleeps carrying coded information about temperature and pressure changes were radioed back to earth.

Only one month later, *Sputnik II* carried a dog aloft. Instruments aboard beamed down messages to

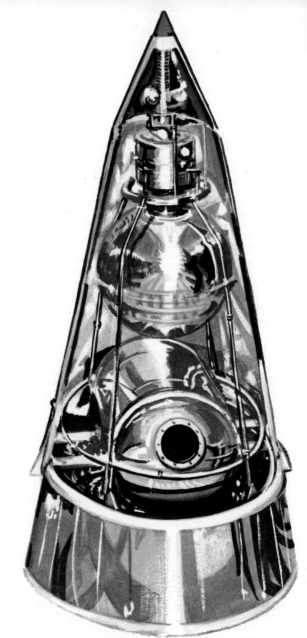

Sputnik II – *the Russian space capsule which, in 1957, proved that an animal could survive a space flight.*

earth which showed that living things could survive a space flight lasting at least several days.

Less than four months after the first Russian man-made moon began circling the globe, America's *Explorer I* went into orbit and helped to detect a huge, hitherto unsuspected, radiation belt girdling the earth.

Soon, Russia and America were pitting their technical resources against each other in peaceful rivalry to build ever bigger and better-equipped

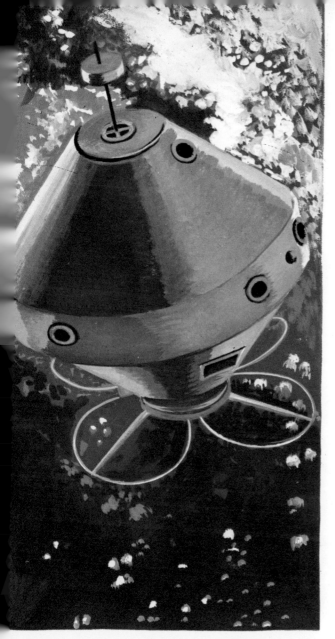

Explorer VIII — *one of a chain of unmanned American satellites which began exploring space.*

and assessing the rain of high-energy cosmic rays which bombard earth from outer space.

Early in 1959 *Vanguard II* transmitted pictures of the earth's cloud cover, and became the first of many satellites to beam down weather information, so giving advance warning of hurricanes.

In 1958 the unmanned United States satellite of *Project Score* broadcast the first spoken message from space, and so foreshadowed the immense usefulness of satellites as relay stations for transmitting radio, telephone, and television messages.

In 1960 yet another use for man-made moons was revealed by the United States satellite *Transit IB* — first of a generation of navigation aids whose radio signals enable ships and planes to fix their positions when the sky is too overcast to take bearings by the sun or stars.

But some of the most exciting space events of the 1950s came in 1959 when both Russia and America launched probes that broke free from earth gravity and headed out into the black emptiness of space towards the moon. In January, Russia's *Luna 1* passed the moon and ended orbiting the sun to become the first man-made planetoid. Two months later, America's *Pioneer IV* followed its example, and on 12th September Russia launched *Luna 2*, the first probe to strike the moon, and in so doing detecting the belt of ionized gas surrounding it. Then, two years to the day after *Sputnik 1* had whirled round the earth, Russia sent a probe which photographed the hidden far side of the moon.

The problems of such launchings were immense. They involved firing probes from our spinning earth moving along one curving path towards a small target many thousand miles away, moving on another course. Electronic computers calculated the different orbits, and took into account the gravitational pulls of earth, moon, and sun, so helping technologists to plot a course accurate enough for *Luna 2* and *Luna 3* to reach their target two days after launching. Boosted off the earth by engines whose power briefly matched that of the world's biggest hydroelectric power station, *Luna 3* sped smoothly on its predetermined path, and its complex instruments automatically photographed the moon and radioed the images to earth.

Meanwhile, space probes had begun relaying their first useful information about the sun and planets. Thus in 1959 *Explorer 7* sent earth new data about solar flares — huge eruptions emitted by the surface of the sun; and in 1960, *Pioneer V* transmitting from as much as 35 million kilometres away, measured the size of the solar system, and recorded details of the so-called solar wind — a stream of high-speed nuclear particles shot off by the sun.

space probes — artificial eyes whose instruments, relaying messages to earth, gave scientists knowledge both of the earth itself and of the distant moon and planets.

Thus the United States satellite *Vanguard I*, launched on 17th March, 1958 revealed that the earth is not round but slightly pear shaped, and *Sputnik III*, launched two months later, became the first complex robot space laboratory, monitoring the composition and pressure of the outer atmosphere,

PUTTING MAN IN SPACE

Whatever automatic space probes discovered, many scientists believed that manned spacecraft would accomplish even more. But sending small lightweight packages of instruments into space was one thing; launching a man into orbit proved much more demanding.

To begin with it called for a far more powerful and far larger rocket than those used in early space exploration. But it meant, too, that its passenger would face hazards unknown on earth, where he was

body weighs many times heavier than it would on earth; but once acceleration stops weight drops to zero. Outside the earth's shielding atmosphere, space travellers also become liable to strikes by meteoroids.

Fortunately unmanned space probes and other automatic detectors revealed many of these hazards before anyone actually faced them. Engineers were therefore able to work out ways of guarding the first space travellers against many dangers. The astronaut's outer defence became the cone-shaped capsule in which he travelled; its outer casing was both strong enough to withstand strikes by tiny meteoroids and the fierce heat produced by air friction as the returning capsule plunged back through the earth's atmosphere. Inside the outer capsule was an air space to insulate the astronaut from outside heat and engine noise. Then came the inner capsule, containing air at the right temperature and pressure for supporting life, and a body-fitting

Yuri Gagarin — first man to orbit earth in space.

A Vostok *rocket of the type that launched Gagarin.*

naturally adapted to breathing the earth's envelope of air, moving under atmospheric pressure, and resisting the force exerted by the pull of earth's gravity. The first astronaut would have to rocket upwards to a region where life as we know it cannot survive. Five kilometres up, air becomes too thin to breathe. Nine kilometres up, gas bubbles form in the blood to cause the fatal bends. Eleven kilometres up the temperature falls below −55° Centigrade. Some 19 kilometres above, atmospheric pressure falls so low that the fluids in an unprotected human body would simply vaporise. Nineteen kilometres higher still comes damaging bombardment by penetrating ultra-violet rays. By the time his rocket has reached escape velocity of 11 kilometres a second, our astronaut's couch to take much of the tremendous strain imposed upon the astronaut by the force of acceleration. His last line of defence was his space suit – a tiny body-encapsulating world in which he could breathe, move and communicate by radio through the silence of space.

Such a space suit includes an outer layer of metallised fabric to reflect the intense solar radiation. The suit is completely pressurised, and has its own air supply, sensors to monitor its wearer's fitness, also earphones, microphones, a radio link, and other equipment.

Even after taking all these precautions, doctors knew that astronauts would undergo severe physical strains, so only the fittest people were chosen for the first space flights. Russia and America both began strict training programmes which included not only complex classroom studies, designed to help space-men master the intricate controls of their vehicles, but stringent physical tests. To accustom them to

extreme forces of acceleration, astronauts were seated in a small cabin attached to a long steel arm which whirled the cabin round until the passenger's body weighed twenty times as much as normal. To simulate weightlessness astronauts became pas-sengers in planes which arced over in steep dives during which the trainees floated briefly as if in space.

In spite of such careful preparations, scientists admitted that space flight might involve unexpected hazards. The whole world was therefore thrilled when on 12th April 1961, the Russian airforce major

Close-up of the capsule in which Glenn travelled.

Blast-off for the Atlas rocket which in 1962 made John Glenn the first American to enter orbit.

Yuri Gagarin, became the first man to orbit earth in space. Travelling in the Russian spacecraft *Vostok 1,* he swept once round the globe at 27,000 kilometres (17,000 miles) an hour – far faster than any man had ever moved before. He landed safely less than two hours after blast off. Less than three weeks later, the American astronaut Alan Shepherd rocketed 187 kilometres (117 miles) up into space on a 480 kilometre (300-mile) flight. But the United States' first manned orbit occurred on 20th February 1962 when an Atlas rocket blasted off from Cape Canaveral (now Cape Kennedy) in Florida, and John H. Glenn hurtled three times round the world in the capsule *Friendship 7* before plummeting down into the Atlantic Ocean to be picked up by a destroyer.

181

A technician makes final adjustments to an American communications satellite which was launched in 1963.

EXPLORING THE SOLAR SYSTEM

Year by year, during the eventful 1960s, courageous astronauts ventured out upon longer, more daring excursions into space. But, until the decade ended, man's most important news gatherers in space were easily his unmanned satellites and probes.

The success of such devices depended upon careful engineering enabling them to work for long periods under extreme conditions. For instance devices like *Sputnik 1* contained a circulating supply of nitrogen which helped to damp down temperature variations inside the vehicle as it passed from the earth's sunlit side into its cold shadow, where a change of 200° Centigrade every 90 minutes took place. Without such internal temperature controls, the sputnik's instruments would almost certainly have failed.

Complex and long-lasting artificial moons like the American *Nimbus* weather satellite tap the energy radiating from the sun to power their mechanisms. They do so with the help of wing-like panels of solar cells; the cells convert solar radiation into electrical energy with the help of a device called a sun sensor which keeps the panels facing the sun as the vehicle revolves round the earth. Solar batteries keep the satellite's mechanisms operating long after any chemical battery would have worn out. This satellite also contains a horizon scanner which keeps

the television cameras facing the earth. The cameras transmit signals to a tape recorder which stores them until scientists on earth send a recall signal to the satellite's command antenna. Then another antenna transmits the signals down to earth. Meanwhile a radio meter, measuring infra-red radiation from the earth, detects warm and cool areas.

Other kinds of satellites and probes carry other kinds of special equipment. Some hold magnetometers to measure the earth's magnetic field, others probe the upper atmosphere with radio transmitters and receivers: beaming radio waves down into the atmosphere to measure their reflections.

During the 1960s, such specialised equipment enabled huge advances in the amount of information relayed by communications, navigation, scientific, and weather satellites.

Among communications satellites, 1960 saw the launching of the great balloon called *Echo 1*. This was merely a passive communications satellite which reflected radio waves like a mirror. But as the 1960s advanced, the United States followed up with active communications satellites (*Telstar*, *Relay*, *Syncom*, *Early Bird*), equipped with receivers and transmitters so that they actually amplified radio or television signals received from earth before transmitting them to earthbound receivers far out of range of the original transmitters.

Advances in navigation satellites were included in devices like *Transit IIIB* which (in 1961) became the first to beam out detailed data on its own position, and (later that year) *Transit IVA* which became the first nuclear-powered satellite.

Scientific space research in the 1960s hinged largely on satellite laboratories, including American devices separately designed to probe earth, sun, and star phenomena. For instance, 1964 saw the launch of the first orbiting geophysical laboratory (*OGO*) which helped to show how the earth's magnetic field affects energy radiated from the sun. Even earlier, in 1962, an orbiting solar laboratory (*OSO*) began studying solar radiations which fail to reach the earth's surface. The United States also developed an orbiting astronomical observatory (*OAO*). The purpose of OAO was to measure radiation, too weak to be detected by earth-bound astronomical observatories, from distant stars and galaxies.

During the 1960s, the *Nimbus* and other weather satellites not only sent back clear cloud photographs, enabling meteorologists to predict the paths of storms; they also laid the basis for photographically mapping the entire earth surface.

Much more spectacular were the probes which roamed through space and sent back information about the moon and planets.

In August 1962 the United States sent *Mariner II* on the immensely long voyage to the planet Venus which had long seemed one of the likeliest planets outside earth itself to be capable of supporting life. Passing within 35,000 kilometres (22,000 miles) of the planet's cloud-shrouded surface, the tiny space probe reported a dry sandy surface with a temperature of 426° Centigrade, far too high to support life as we know it. Later in the 1960s, Russia, too, sent probes to Venus, and in 1965 a Russian space probe actually crashed upon the planet's surface. In 1967 the Russians accomplished the first soft landing on the planet and gathered valuable information about its temperature and atmosphere.

Meanwhile, *Mariner IV* passed within 9,600 kilometres of Mars in 1965 and sent 22 television pictures of this reddish planet over 200 million kilometres back to earth. *Mariner IV* revealed a dry, crater-pitted landscape and a thin atmosphere. It showed, too, that no radiation belt girdles this particular planet, and that Mars lacks a magnetic field like that around the earth.

But it was the moon, the earth's nearest neighbour in space, which went on attracting the most attention during the 1960s.

In 1964 the American space vehicle *Ranger VII* used six television cameras to take over 4,300 close-up pictures of the moon's surface. These pictures revealed craters some as small as a few centimetres in diameter before Ranger VII crashed on the moon. Next year, *Ranger VIII* and *Ranger IX* did even better, before they too were broken up by impact.

The year 1966 saw both Russia and America accomplish the first soft moon landings with robot spacecraft – Russia with *Luna IX* which sent back to earth 9 pictures, and America with *Surveyor I* which transmitted over 11,000 images. Both landed in the relatively level area called the Ocean of Storms, and the firm lava-like surface that they revealed went far to disprove a theory that the moon's so-called seas were covered with layers of dust thousands of feet thick. Landings by more sophisticated devices followed. Later in 1960 Russia's *Luna 13* actually tested the moon's soil density, and the next year *Surveyor 3* scooped up moon rock fragments with a mechanical arm and shovel, placed them on its white foot pad, photographed them, and transmitted the images to earth.

Meanwhile, in 1966, *Luna 10* from Russia and *Lunar Orbiter I* from America became the first man-made objects to orbit the moon. *Lunar Orbiter I* took valuable photographs of the moon's far side before being deliberately crashed to prevent its signals interfering with those from later probes. More

Two American astronauts undergoing ground-based training as part of the Gemini research programme.

Orbiter vehicles followed to take pictures of likely sites for future landings.

As the 1960s drew towards their close, the pace of moon exploration quickened, and devices like America's two-man *Gemini* spacecraft heralded in a new phase in moon exploration – one which promised to set men as well as machines on the soil of an alien world. Early in the 1960s President Kennedy of the United States had boldly promised to land an American upon the moon before the decade ended. But as unmanned Russian probes bombarded the moon it became clear that America had powerful competition: that a moon race was on— a race which promised immense international prestige to the victor.

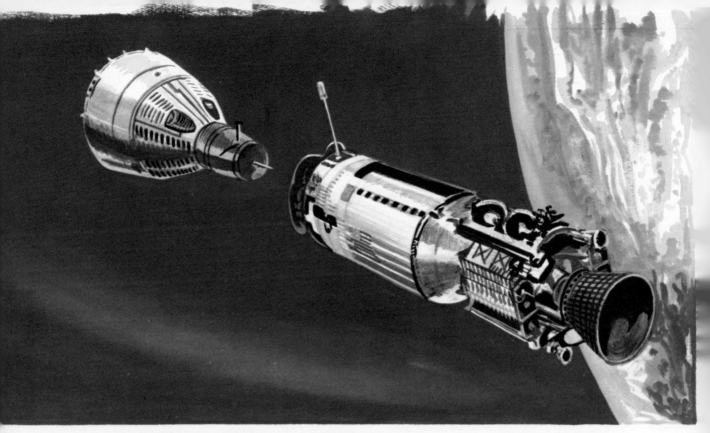

A space rendezvous between a Gemini *capsule (left) and an* Agena *rocket, while both orbit the earth (right).*

LIVING IN SPACE

Before any man could hope to inhabit an earth-orbiting laboratory or land on the moon it was clear that flights such as those by pioneers Glenn and Gagarin must become routinely safe, and that astronauts must learn to accomplish far more complex tasks than either of these space-age trail-blazers had had to perform. Progress in launching more manned spacecraft was therefore slow and cautious.

The first step was to discover whether man could endure safely many hours of weightlessness. Within four months of Gagarin's first single earth orbit, Russia's Gherman Titov safely circled the world 17 times, remaining weightless for more than 24 hours. In 1962 Andrian Nikolayev hurtled 64 times round the world in *Vostok 3* surviving more than 94 hours in space with no serious ill effects. Moreover Nikolayev was closely followed into space by another capsule containing Pavel Popovich. Careful navigation enabled both capsules to orbit in sight of one another – an important first step towards the kind of manoeuvring which proved necessary in space before astronauts could leave earth orbit on a moon voyage.

The first astronauts had been little more than passengers, travelling in craft manipulated entirely by ground-based engineers operating the capsules' instruments by remote control. But in 1963 Gordon Cooper proved that astronauts themselves could carry out critical manoeuvres of their spacecraft. Normally, re-entry into the earth's atmosphere depended on the automatic firing of retro-rocket brakes. However, Cooper's automatic system failed – a fault which could have brought disaster to the astronaut. Acting on the timing given by a ground-based computer, Cooper pressed a manual firing button at the precise second required, and landed safely.

In 1964 the world was impressed to learn that Russia had managed to put into orbit an artificial satellite holding more than one man – a new phase had opened up in manned space travel. Although Russia tended to keep the details of its rocket launch vehicles a secret, experts in other countries calculated that an immensely powerful rocket must have been required to launch *Voskhod I*, the three-man capsule containing a cosmonaut (Vladimir Komarov), a physician (Boris Yegorov), and a scientist (Konstantin Feoktistov).

So far no astronaut had dared to leave the safety of his capsule in space. The man who became the first to step into the void was Russia's Alexei Leonov. On

18th March 1965 Leonov left his companion Pavel Belyayev inside *Voskhod II* and, protected only by his silvery space suit from intense solar radiation and possible bombardment by micrometeorites, he floated into space. A television camera inside the spacecraft showed his 10-minute space walk, in which he remained tethered to the capsule by a 5-metre-long lifeline. If the line had broken, probably nothing could have stopped Leonov from floating helplessly and fatally into space to become a lifeless human satellite circling the earth. But the line held, and Leonov proved that man could move about and perform useful work outside a capsule.

By the time that Leonov made his space walk no known deaths had yet occurred in space travel in spite of its many hazards. But in 1967 two fatal accidents were to underline the risks of space exploration. The first occurred in January, when three United States' astronauts (Chaffee, Grissom, and White) died in an oxygen fire that broke out in their *Apollo* capsule during ground-based training. Then, in April, Russia's Vladimir Komarov died when his returning capsule crashed after its parachutes tangled and failed to open.

Instead of halting manned space voyages, such tragedies only intensified the efforts of technologists to make manned space flight safer. Thus America went ahead determinedly with a programme based on projects Mercury, Gemini, Apollo — each more ambitious and demanding than the one before. Between 1961 and 1963 six astronauts had orbited alone in *Mercury* capsules. The year 1965 saw the start of a series of 12 two-man *Gemini* flights. These lasted up to 14 days, and showed that astronauts were becoming adept at working outside their capsules. Using tiny rocket thrusts to edge them towards unmanned *Agena* rockets, they were joining capsule to rocket by the manoeuvre known as docking. This manoeuvre was to prove vital to the success of the next exercise, Project Apollo, the project aimed at placing a manned capsule on the moon.

Meanwhile back on earth, America and Russia, each with the aim of keeping ahead in the space race, were both harnessing huge resources in men, materials, and money. In both countries, the astronauts themselves represented only the tip of a colossal pyramid of skilled scientists, technologists, and technicians, without whose combined efforts no astronaut could have reached space, survived there, or returned. By the mid 1960s America's aerospace industry alone was employing over 700,000 workers distributed among 10,000 companies. These companies made everything from rocket engines to micro-miniaturised components for spacecraft communications systems.

At a time when millions of people in Africa and Asia still lacked the bare necessities of life, such lavish spending roused harsh comments from critics who complained that the money would be better channelled to ridding our earth of hunger and disease. Aerospace enthusiasts countered by arguing that untold benefits might one day flow from projects for placing men on the moon. The projects went ahead.

In the middle 1960s, scenes of a manned lunar module on the moon were no more than an artist's dream.

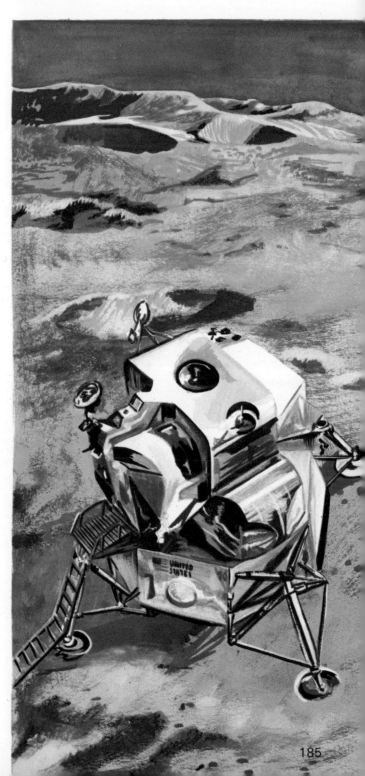

MAN ON THE MOON

No space programme aroused more excitement than the United States Apollo project – particularly after the tragic Apollo capsule fire of 1967 made it seem unlikely that an American astronaut would beat his Russian rivals to the moon, or that, as promised, he would do it before the 1960s ended. Nonetheless, the sheer size and complexity of Project Apollo fascinated millions.

The heart of the project was the colossal rocket, code-named *Saturn V*: a giant three-stage vehicle standing 90 metres (300 feet) high, and supporting a spacecraft complex which added roughly another 12 metres to its huge overall length. The total was seven times the length of a *V2* rocket of World War II. More than 2,032 tonnes of its 2,920-tonne fully-loaded weight consisted of fuel in the form of huge tanks of kerosene, liquid oxygen, and liquid hydrogen, designed to burn up at the almost incredible rate of over 13 tonnes a second for $2\frac{1}{2}$ minutes (consuming over 2,000 tonnes). All told, the three stages generated 175,600,000 horsepower – enough to place a payload of about 120 tonnes in earth orbit or hurl over 40 tonnes to the moon.

To construct this colossal rocket, engineers designed an equally impressive vehicle assembly building at Cape Kennedy in Florida. On completion it became the world's roomiest structure, standing 168 metres high and holding four bays each with 140-metre-high doors. To move the completed rocket and its service tower from this giant hangar to its launching pad, engineers constructed the world's most massive vehicle: an eight-caterpillar crawler which, fully loaded, weighed over 8,000 tonnes.

By contrast with the vast Saturn rocket, its assembly hall, and crawler carrier, its three-part useful load seemed astonishingly small: a tiny cone-shaped command module containing the three astronauts (with little more than enough room to stretch their legs), a service module equipped with a rocket engine, and a two-man lunar excursion module (LEM).

In spite of the delays caused by modifications to avert more fatal fires, the Apollo project gained momentum in 1968 when the towing rocket thrust three astronauts into earth orbit where they parked for 260 hours. After this feat, achieved by *Apollo 7*, the *Apollo 8* mission took Frank Borman, James Lovell, and William Anders out of earth orbit altogether. Following in the wake of earlier unmanned space probes, they reached the moon, circled it ten times, and transmitted close-up views to earth which thrilled millions of television viewers. Their safe return made a manned moon landing in the 1960s suddenly seem much more than a possibility. But two

In 1969 man finally stood upon the moon: a view of Neil Armstrong, his LEM, and the U.S. flag.

more Apollo flights followed before the final critical attempt. In March of 1969 three astronauts sped into space in *Apollo 9*, and on 18th May, *Apollo 10* carried yet another crew to the moon. There they orbited 18 times, releasing their lunar module to circle the moon within a few miles of its glaring desert surface.

But the supreme trial began on 16th July 1969 at Cape Kennedy, when a 3½-million-kilogram rocket thrust blasted Neil Armstrong, Edwin Aldrin, and Michael Collins on the historic mission of *Apollo 11*. The world watched breathlessly as stage one dropped off and stage two fired successfully, hurling *Apollo 11* more than 160 kilometres into the sky. A brief burst from stage three placed the astronauts in earth orbit.

Once it became clear that all was well, stage three fired another burst. This swung *Apollo 11* out of orbit on its preplanned trajectory towards the distant moon. Then there followed a series of critical manoeuvres. First, adapters were jettisoned, freeing the combined service and command modules which the astronauts released and reversed, docking them with the LEM (Lunar excursion module). Next, they jettisoned the spent third stage. By firing the service module's engine they then eased their spacecraft into orbit round the moon, now looming large before them. Aldrin and Armstrong crawled inside the LEM, and came down to within a few miles of the moon, leaving Collins in his lonely parking orbit above. Locating their prearranged landing site, the two astronauts gently descended, braking with the aid of retro-rockets. The LEM landed firmly on its stiltlike legs. Millions of spellbound television viewers next watched Armstrong gingerly descend a small ladder and place his feet upon the moon, taking, as he put it, 'one small step for a man, one giant leap for mankind'.

Under the moon's weak force of gravity, the first men on the moon ambled about easily in their cumbersome space suits, bearing heavy packs of instruments upon their backs — a feat they would have found impossible on earth. They gathered rock samples and made scientific observations before re-entering the LEM to rest. All told, they spent over 21 hours on the lunar surface before using the LEM'S weak rocket engines to hurtle upwards and back into moon orbit. There, they rejoined Collins in his command module. The return to earth in this tiny cone went faultlessly, and the three men triumphantly splashed down in the Pacific Ocean on 3rd August to complete what most people felt to be man's most historic journey since Columbus sailed from Spain to America nearly five centuries before.

More, though, was to follow. On 14th November, *Apollo 12* took Alan Bean, Charles Conrad, and Richard Gordon on a second moon-landing mission, in which Bean and Conrad made more ambitious explorations, collected rock samples, set up robot moon watchers, and recovered equipment from the old moon probe *Surveyor 3*.

But not all the first moon explorers found their tasks so easy. Next April, *Apollo 13* had left earth some 100,000 miles behind when explosions forced its crew to return, fortunately with no loss of life.

The moon's weak force of gravity allowed the first moon men to walk about with ease, although burdened with cumbersome suits and heavy equipment.

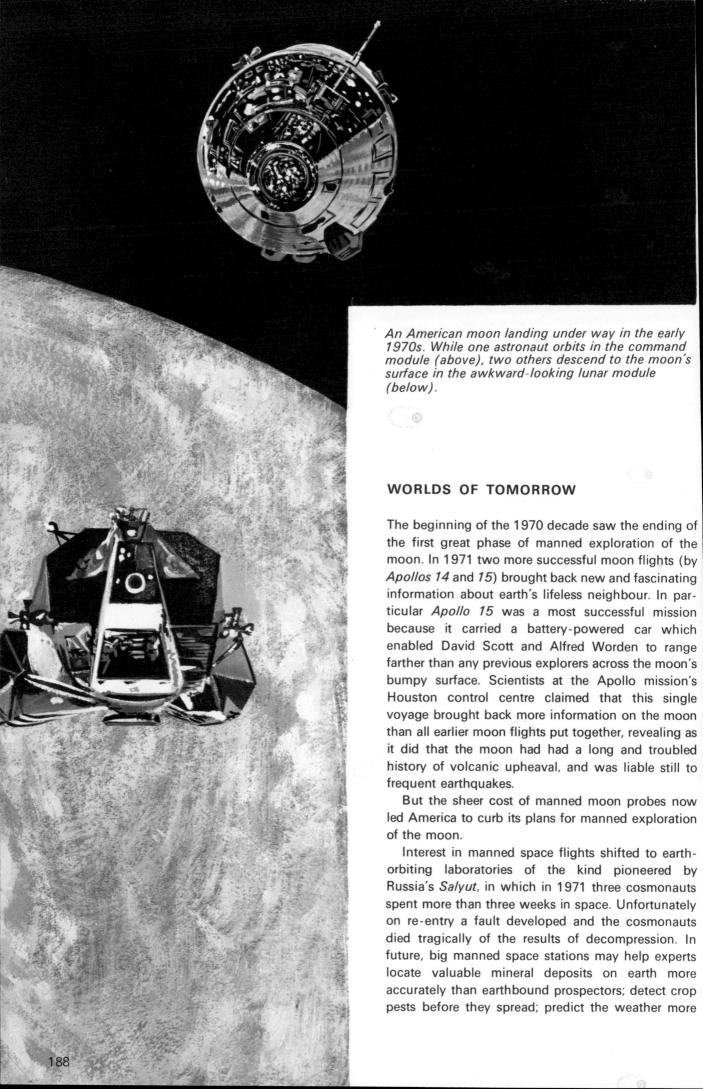

An American moon landing under way in the early 1970s. While one astronaut orbits in the command module (above), two others descend to the moon's surface in the awkward-looking lunar module (below).

WORLDS OF TOMORROW

The beginning of the 1970 decade saw the ending of the first great phase of manned exploration of the moon. In 1971 two more successful moon flights (by *Apollos 14* and *15*) brought back new and fascinating information about earth's lifeless neighbour. In particular *Apollo 15* was a most successful mission because it carried a battery-powered car which enabled David Scott and Alfred Worden to range farther than any previous explorers across the moon's bumpy surface. Scientists at the Apollo mission's Houston control centre claimed that this single voyage brought back more information on the moon than all earlier moon flights put together, revealing as it did that the moon had had a long and troubled history of volcanic upheaval, and was liable still to frequent earthquakes.

But the sheer cost of manned moon probes now led America to curb its plans for manned exploration of the moon.

Interest in manned space flights shifted to earth-orbiting laboratories of the kind pioneered by Russia's *Salyut*, in which in 1971 three cosmonauts spent more than three weeks in space. Unfortunately on re-entry a fault developed and the cosmonauts died tragically of the results of decompression. In future, big manned space stations may help experts locate valuable mineral deposits on earth more accurately than earthbound prospectors; detect crop pests before they spread; predict the weather more accurately than ever before; study stars invisible from earth; and even perform special manufacturing processes requiring a vacuum and conditions of weightlessness.

Meanwhile, unmanned space probes have continued from strength to strength. The early 1970s saw Russia's robot moon rover *Lunakhod I* travel several miles during many months; and America's *Mariner IX* reveal deep canyons on Mars. Soon new information about Venus was being beamed to earth, and probes were reaching out as far as distant Jupiter.

Since space exploration began, man has vastly enriched his meagre store of knowledge about the moon and planets. Who knows where such discoveries may lead? Just as the first scientists slowly and laboriously pieced together the workings of the world about them, so we are still dimly grasping the true nature of the worlds beyond. Early scientists were the trail-blazers for today's technologists, but it will be many years, if ever, before we can put our space discoveries to technological use.

Let us therefore try to keep a balanced view of space exploration — an astonishing accomplishment but not necessarily the most useful of our times. For each man who lands on the moon or some distant planet, hundreds of millions will never leave the planet earth. For these earthbound masses what matters more than the most remarkable discovery in outer space is finding new and better ways of using our own earth's rich yet limited resources. For only by so doing can we hope to rid mankind of hunger, disease, and war.

Lockheed project for a big manned space station. In such stations, rotation creates artificial gravity.

INDEX

A

Aardvark, 81
Aardwolf, 70
Aborigine, 44, 45, 86, 92, 93
Ader, Clement, 140, 141
Aeroplane, 140, 173, 175–6, 177
Afghanistan, peoples of, 89
Africa, 19, 45, 46; East, 27, 30, 32,
   33; fossil bones, 34; North, 45, 102;
   peoples of, 88, 90–2; South, 20, 30
Age, Bronze, 96, 97, 98, 99, 100,
   101, 125; Dark, 110; Iron, 101, 106,
   137; Middle, 110, 114, 116, 125
Air, craft. See Aeroplane; cushion
   vehicle. See Hovercraft; raids, 169;
   ships, 140, 141
Alexander the Great, 104, 106
Alpaca, 79
Aluminium, 136, 137, 144
America, discovery of, 114; mines,
   132; North, 19, 22, 23, 32, 45, 94,
   179; oil industry, 159–60; South,
   19, 32, 93, 94; transatlantic cable, 135
Amerindians, 94, 120–1
Amphibians, 17, 20, 22, 23, 58–9, 60
Annelids, 54
Antarctic, 95; circumpolar current, 50
Anteaters, 68–9, 80–1
Antelopes, 75, 76
Apes, 27, 29, 30, 84, 85
Arabia, 161; peoples of, 88; Saudi, 160
Archimedes, 104–5, 127
Architecture, 102–3, 107–8, 112, 163
Arctic, 28, 45
Aristotle, 102, 111, 118
Arthropods, 18, 19, 54, 66
Asia, peoples of, 88, 89; Central, 100;
   fossil bones, 34; Minor, 103, 109;
   South-east, 46, 93, 109;
   South-west, 46
Ass, 79
Astronauts, 180, 181, 182, 183, 184–9
Astronomy, 7–10, 12, 104, 119, 145
Atomic bomb, 169, 170–1
Atoms, 145, 149, 169, 170
Auroch, 33, 41, 43
Australia, 19, 26, 45, 93; Aborigines,
   44, 86, 92, 93; mammals of, 26, 68
Australopithecines, 27, 29, 30, 31
Austria, Stone-age hunting in, 40;
   Venus of Willendorf, 42

B

Baboon, 30, 84
Babylonia, 99–101; medicine in, 151
Badger, 70
Ballooning, 127, 140
Bathyscaphe, 166–7
Bathysphere, 166
Bats, 27, 81; flying fox, 81; vampire, 81
Bear, 33, 36, 41, 43, 70; Alaskan
   brown, 70; cave, 33, 35, 42;
   Himalayan, 71; sun, 70
Beaver, 81
Becquerel, Antoine, 170
Bee-eater, Southern carmine, 63
Bell, Alexander Graham, 136

Benthos, 49
Benz, Karl Friedrich, 139
Bessemer, Henry, 136, 137
Birds, 25, 27, 42, 43, 62–5
Bison, 33, 40, 41, 42, 43, 44, 45, 77
Blériot, Louis, 175
Blood, circulation of, 119, 153
Boars, 43, 78–9
Bongo, 74–5
Boyle, Robert, 128
Brachiopods, 54
Branly, Édouard, 148
Britain, 45, 100;
   Industrial Revolution, 122
Brunel, Isambard Kingdom, 133
Buffalo, 76–7
Bushmen, 90; Kalahari, 45
Butterflies, 66

C

Caesar, Gaius Julius, 106
Cambrian period, 18, 19; pre-, 15, 16,
   17, 19
Camels, 27, 79
Camera, 146–7; obscura, 145
Canada, 122, 144; Ice Age in, 28
Canal, Panama, 133; Suez, 133, 161
Capybara, 81
Car, 139, 159; steam, 131
Carboniferous times, 22
Carnivores, 27, 30, 32, 56, 70, 73
Cats, 27, 70
Cattle, 75, 76, 79
Cave paintings, 44–5
Cavendish, Henry, 128
Cayley, Sir George, 140
Cenozoic era, 15, 17, 26, 27
Cephalopods, 19, 24
Cetaceans, 56
Chadwick, James, 145
Chameleon, 60, 61
Chamois, 43
Chappé, Claude, 135
Chemistry, 128; organic, 129
Chimpanzee, 26, 27, 30, 82–4
China, 33, 97, 109; great wall of, 100
Chondrichthyes, 55
Chordata, 52, 55
Clocks, 117
Coal, 22, 123, 171; gas, 130
Cobego. See lemur
Cobra, 60, 61
Coelenterates, 53, 54
Coleoptera, 66
Columbus, Christopher, 114, 119,
   120–1
Computer, 155–8, 159, 179
Copernicus, 119
Coral, 16, 22, 53
Cortes, Hernando, 120
Cotton, 122
Cousteau, Jacques Yves, 167–8
Crane, 64; crowned, 64, 65
Cretaceous times, 24, 25
Crete, 100
Crocodiles, 22, 24, 26, 60, 61
Cuckoo, 63; emerald, 62

Cugnot, Nicolas, 131
Curie, Pierre and Marie, 170
Curtis, Charles, 143
Cuvier, Léopold Baron, 15
Cyclostomata, 55
Czechoslovakia, Stone-age hunting,
   40; Venus of Vestonice, 42

D

Daguerre, Louis, 145, 146
Daimler, Gottlieb, 139
Dalton, John, 128
Darwin, Charles Robert, 15
Dasyure, 68–9
Deer, 75–7; red, 76–7
Democritus, 102
Devonian period, 20, 22
Diatoms, 49
Diaz, Bartholomew, 120–1
Diesel, Rudolf, 139
Dinosaurs, 24, 25; horned, 25
Dogs, 27, 45, 70
Dolphin. See whale
Domagk, Gerhard, 154
Dubois, Marie Eugene, 31
Dugong, 56

E

Eagle, 64; white-tailed, 65
Earth, 7, 9, 10, 11, 12, 13, 14, 51;
   cloud cover, 179; crust, 13, 14, 48,
   166; gravity, 13, 179, 180; mantle, 13,
   166; rotation, 50; space probes, 178
Earthquakes, 51, 151
Echidna, 26, 68
Echinoderms, 54
Edison, Thomas, 136, 143, 147
Egypt, 96; peoples of, 88; civilisation,
   104; pyramids, 98, 99, 100
Eland, 74–5
Electricity, 135, 136, 137, 140, 142–3,
   144, 148, 149, 159, 171; hydro-, 144
Electron, beam, 150; scanning, 149
Elephant, 27, 33, 78–9
Elk, Irish, 33
Empire, British, 122; Carthaginian, 106;
   Hittite, 101; Roman, 106–9, 110
Emu, 64
Engine, 125, 133; internal
   combustion, 138–9, 140, 142, 165,
   177; jet, 177; multiple-cylinder, 139;
   steam, 124, 125, 131, 136, 177
Eskimos, 38, 94
Euclid, 104, 119
Europe, 19, 22, 32, 33, 37, 40, 45,
   46; art in, 42; peoples of, 87; Ice
   age in, 28; medieval, 151
Evolution, 15, 16, 26; man, 27, 29;
   tree of life, 17

F

Faraday, Michael, 142, 143, 148
Farming, 46, 122, 129
Finland, peoples of, 87
Fishes, 17, 18, 21, 24, 43, 45, 49, 55,
   59, 167; Age of, 20; bony, 20, 55, 59;

cartilaginous, 55; jawless, 19, 55
Fleming, Sir Alexander, 154
Fleming, Sir John Ambrose, 148
Ford, Henry, 139
Fox, 43, 70; flying. *See* Bats
France, 24, 37, 38, 120, 132; Alpine peoples of, 87; art, 42; fossil bones, 34, 36; Lady of Lespugue, 42; Roman civilisation, 106; Solutrean hunters, 40
Francolin, 62, 64
Franklin Benjamin, 142
Frogs, 58, 59
Fulton, Robert, 132, 164

G

Galago, 82
Galaxies, 8, 9
Galilei, Galileo, 118, 125
Gecko, 60
Gemsbok, 74–5
Generator, electric, 142, 143, 144
Geology, 15, 166
Gerenuk, 74–5
Germany, peoples of, 87; fossil bones in, 34; Hanseatic League, 111
Gibbon, 82–4
Giraffe, 75
Goats, 46, 75–6, 79
Goddard, Robert, 178
Gondwanaland, 19, 23, 24
Goodyear, Charles, 130
Gorilla, 26, 82, 84
Gramophone, 145; recording, 136
Greece, 101–3, 107, 109
Guanaco, 79
Gutenberg, Johannes, 116–17, 138

H

Hales, Stephen, 153
Hamster, 81
Hares, 43, 81
Harvey, William, 119, 153
Hawfinch, 64
Hedgehog, 81
Hemispheres, 13, 19, 23, 45
Henry, Joseph, 148
Herbivores, 73, 79
Hero of Alexandria, 105, 125, 143
Hertz, Heinrich, 148
Hippocrates, 102, 151
Hippopotamus, 28, 73, 79
Hominidae, 29, 30, 52, 84
Homoptera, 67
Horse, 27, 33, 40, 41, 42, 43, 45, 79, 110, 113, 125
Hovercraft, 173–4, 175
Hyaenas, 30, 70
Hydrogen bomb, 171
Hymenoptera, 67
Hyrax, 79

I

Ibex, 30, 36, 43, 76
Ice ages, 28, 33, 34, 35, 38, 45, 93, 95; sheets, 29, 40, 45
Ichthyosaurs, 23, 24

India, 46, 97, 119, 120, 122; peoples of, 91
Indonesia, 33, 92, 93, 120; Krakatoa, 51
Industrial Revolution, 122, 136
Insects, 17, 20, 22, 54, 63, 66–7
Invertebrates, 16, 18, 19, 22, 54
Iran, peoples of, 89
Iraq, 96, 99; oil, 160
Iron, 136, 137; age, 101, 106; in industry, 123–4, 138; ore, 123
Italy, Alpine peoples of, 87

J

Jackal, 70
Jaguar, 70
Japan, 59; Ainus of, 92
Java, 38
Jenner, Edward, 154
Jouffroy d'Abbans, Claud, 132
Jupiter, 9, 11, 189
Jurassic times, 24, 25

K

Kangaroo, 27, 68; grey, 69
Kinkajou, 70
Kiwi, 64, 65
Koala, 68–9
Koenig, Friedrich, 138
Komodo monitor, 60

L

Laënnec, René, 153
Lagomorphs, 81
Landsteiner, Karl, 153
Lavoisier, Antoine, 128, 130
Lebanon, 96
Leblanc, Nicolas, 129
Lebon, Philippe, 130
Leeuwenhoek, Anton van, 154
Lemur, 26, 27, 29, 81, 82; flying, 81
Lenoir, Jean Joseph Étienne, 139
Leonardo da Vinci, 118, 152
Leopard, snow, 70
Lepidoptera, 66
Lesseps, Ferdinand, Vicomte de, 133
Liebig, Justus von, 129, 130
Lilienthal, Otto, 140, 141
Lion, 28, 42, 70
Lister, Joseph, Lord, 153–4
Lizard, 26, 60
Llama, 78–9
Loris, 82
Lumière, Auguste Marie and Louis Jean, 146, 147, 148

M

Macadam, John Loudon, 131
Macaw, 64, 65
Magdalenian period, 44
Magellan, Ferdinand, 120–1
Magpie, 65
Mammals, 17, 25, 26, 27, 28, 33, 42, 52, 68–81; sea, 56, 59
Mammoth, 28, 35, 40, 41, 42, 43, 45
Man, 17, 27, 28, 32, 33, 43, 52, 84, 85, 95; ape-, 30; burials, 36, 45; Cro-Magnon, 29, 38, 40, 41; Handy, 30; Heidelberg, 33; *Homo erectus*, 31, 32, 33; *Homo sapiens*, 33, 34, 52, 85; Java, 29, 31, 32, 33;

Neanderthal, 29, 34, 35, 36, 37, 38, 40; Palaeolithic, 33; Peking, 29, 33, 35, 36; Pygmy, 85, 90, 91, 92; Swanscombe, 33, 38
Manatee, 56
Mandrill, 82, 84
Marconi, Guglielmo, 148
Marggraf, Andreas, 129
Mars, 9, 11, 183, 188
Marsupials, 68–9
Mathematics, 99, 102, 104, 119
Maxwell, James Clerk, 148
Medicine, 102, 151–4, 163, 172
Mège-Mouries, Hippolyte, 129
Mendel, Gregor Johann, 145
Mercury, 9, 10, 11
Mergenthaler, Otto, 138
Mesolithic, 45
Mesozoic era, 15, 17, 23
Metazoa, 52, 53
Mexico, 120–1
Mining, 108, 125–6, 132, 134
Mole, 81
Molluscs, 17, 19, 22, 24, 54
Mongoose, 70
Monkeys, 27, 29, 84
Monotremes, 68
Montgolfier, Joseph Michel and Jacques Étienne, 127, 140
Moon, 7, 9, 13, 14, 51, 179, 183; exploration, 183, 185, 187, 188, 189; man on, 150, 186–9
Moose, 77
Morse, Samuel, 135; code, 135
Mountains, Andes, 94, 120; building, 26; Everest, 48; Jura, 24; Rocky, 94
Mouse, harvest, 81
Murdock, William, 131

N

Narwhal. *See* whale
Nebuchadnezzar II, 99
Nekton, 49
Neptune, 11
New Guinea, 93; mammals of, 68
Newcomen, Thomas, 125–6, 131
Newton, Sir Isaac, 119, 177
Newts, 23, 58, 59
Niépce, Joseph, 145
Nipkow, Paul, 149
Nollet, Jean Antoine, 150
Norway, 144; peoples of, 87
Nuclear energy, 171, 172; power, 170–1

O

Ocean, 13, 47–51; Arctic, 47; Atlantic, 47, 50, 133; currents, 50, 166; exploration of depths, 166–8; Indian, 47; Pacific, 47, 48, 93, 166–7; tides, 51; waves, 51
Oersted, Hans Christian, 142
Oil, 159–61, 171; drilling, 159
Okapi, 74–5
Opossum, 68
Orang-utan, 82–3, 84
Ordovician period, 19
Osteichthyes, 55
Ostracoderms, 19, 20
Ostrich, 62, 64
Otter, 43, 70

Otto, Nicolas August, 139
Owl, 63, 64; Snowy, 42
Ox, 33, 113, 125

P

Palaeozoic era, 15–18, 20–3
Palestine, 34, 96; peoples of, 89
Panda, giant, 70, 71
Pangolin, 80–1
Papin, Denis, 125, 132
Parsons, Sir Charles Algernon, 143
Passeriformes, 63
Pasteur, Louis, 154
Paxton, Sir Joseph, 162
Peccary, 79
Pelican, 64–5
Penguin, 64
Permian period, 23
Petroleum, 159
Pheasant, Swinhoe's, 65
Photography, 145–7
Photosynthesis, 16
Piccard, Auguste, 167; Jacques, 167
Pigeons, 62, 63, 65
Pika, 81
Pinnipedia, 56
Pizarro, Francisco, 120
Placoderms, 19, 20, 21
Plankton, 48, 49
Plants, 15, 19, 22, 23, 25, 45, 49,
  52, 145
Plateau, Joseph, 146, 147
Platypus, 26, 68
Pleistocene epoch, 28
Plesiosaurs, 25
Pluto, 10, 11
Poland, peoples of, 87
Pole, North, 13, 50, 165; South, 13, 50
Polynesia, 93
Pongid, 84
Portugal, 119–20
Pottery, 98, 103
Prairie dog, 81
Priestley, Joseph, 127, 128, 130
Primates, 26, 27, 29, 30, 52, 82–4
Printing, 116–17, 118, 138
Proteus, or Olm, 58, 59
Protozoa, 52, 53
Pterygota, 66
Pudu, 77
Pyramids, 100
Pythagoras, 102

Q

Quaternary period, 17, 27, 28

R

Rabbit, 81
Raccoon, 70
Radiation belt, 179, 183
Radio, 148, 149; isotopes, 172;
  receivers, 148, 182; telescope, 7;
  transmitters, 182; waves, 148
Railway, 134–5
Rat, 81
Reindeer, 39, 40, 41, 42, 43, 45
Renard, Charles, 140
Reptiles, 17, 23, 24, 25, 26, 43, 60–1
Rhazes, 152

Rhinoceros, 27–8, 33, 35, 43, 72–3, 79
Rhynchocephalia, 60
Rochas, Beau de, 139
Rockets, 177–9, 180, 181, 184, 186
Roman empire, 106–9, 110
Röntgen, Wilhelm, 153, 170
Ruminants, 75, 76
Russia, 23, 40, 45, 179; art, 42;
  peoples of, 87; hunting in, 40
Rutherford, Ernest, 145, 170

S

Salamander, 23, 58, 59
Salientia, 59
Salmon, 40
Santos-Dumont, Alberto, 140
Satellites, 150, 178–9, 182
Saturn, 9, 11
Sea, Aegean, 102; Aral, 47; bed,
  166–7; Bering, 94; Black, 102, 103;
  Caspian, 47, 178; currents, 50–1;
  Dead, 47; Ionian, 102
Sea-lion, 56
Seal, 56, 68, 70; elephant, 56
Shag, 62, 64
Sharks, 20, 55
Sheep, 46, 75, 76, 79; bighorn, 76–7
Shellfish, 18, 45
Shipbuilding, 103, 114, 124, 133,
  164–5
Ships, caravel, 115, 118; clipper,
  132–3; nuclear-powered, 171;
  steam, 132–3, 134; supertanker, 161
Shrews, 26, 27, 81
Siemens, Ernest Werner von and
  Sir William, 137, 142
Silurian times, 19
Skunk, 70
Smith, William, 15
Snakes, 26, 60; cobra, 61
Solar, flares, 179; laboratory, 182;
  radiation, 181, 182, 185; system, 7,
  8, 10, 11, 12, 182–3; wind, 179
Space, 177–89; craft, 180; distances in,
  7; exploration, 178, 180–9; laboratory,
  179; probes, 179, 180, 182, 183;
  stations, 188; suit, 181; walk, 184–5
Spain, 45, 102, 110, 119, 120;
  Roman civilisation, 106–7
Sponges, 18, 53, 54
Squamata, 60
Squirrel, 80–1; red, 81
Stahl, George, 128
Stars, 7–11, 145
Steam, aircraft, 141; hammer, 136;
  locomotive, 131, 134, 138; power,
  125, 143; pump, 125; transport,
  131; turbine, 143
Steel, 101, 136, 137
Stephenson, George, 134
Stephenson, Robert, 137
Stone Age, 46, 95, 100, 120; art, 41;
  burials, 45; Early Old, 32, 37; Late
  Old, 37, 39, 40, 41, 43, 45; mammals
  of, 33; Middle Old, 37, 45; Neolithic,
  46, 96, 97, 99, 151; Old, 32, 33, 36, 37,
  38, 41, 43, 45, 98
Stork, 64
Submarine, 164–5, 166, 167, 171
Sumeria, 100
Sun, 7, 10, 11, 12, 13, 16, 51, 145

Swan, Joseph, 143
Sweden, peoples of, 87
Switzerland, 24, 144; peoples of, 87
Symington, William, 132
Syria, 96, 111; peoples of, 89

T

Talbot, William Henry Fox, 146
Tapir, 73, 79
Tarsier, 27, 29, 82
Tasmania, mammals of, 68
Telegraph, 135, 136, 142, 145, 148
Telephone, 136, 145, 148
Television, 149–50, 186, 187
Tenrec, 81
Tertiary times, 26, 27, 30
Thales of Miletus, 102
Thecodonts, 23
Thomson, Sir Joseph John, 145
Tiger, 70–1; sabre-toothed, 32, 33
Toad, 58, 59
Tortoises, 60–1
Tree-creeper, 64
Tree-shrew, 27, 82
Trevithick, Richard, 131, 134, 138
Triassic period, 23
Trilobite, 16, 18, 19
Tuatara, 60, 61
Turkey, 46; Hittite empire, 101;
  peoples of, 89
Turtle, 26, 60; prehistoric, 23

U

Ungulates, 73
Uranus, 11

V

Vasco da Gama, 119, 120–1
Venus, 9, 10, 11, 183, 188
Vertebrates, 19, 20, 52, 55, 60
Vesalius, Andreas, 152–3
Volta, Alessandro, 142, 143
Vulture, 64

W

Walrus, 56, 70
War, 114–15; American Civil, 164;
  Napoleonic, 134; photography in,
  146; World I, 165, 175; World II,
  148, 165, 169, 176, 178, 186
Warthog, 79
Waterhen, 63, 64
Watt, James, 126
Whale, 27, 49, 56, 68
Wildfowl, 45
Wolves, 43, 70
Wright, Orville and Wilbur, 140, 173

X

X-ray, 152, 170

Y

Yak, 77
Yugoslavia, peoples of, 87

Z

Zebra, 78–9
Zeppelin, Count Ferdinand von, 140